EATING DISORDERS
DON'T DISCRIMINATE

of related interest

Eating Disorder Recovery Handbook
A Practical Guide to Long-Term Recovery
Dr Nicola Davies and Emma Bacon
ISBN 978 1 78592 133 9
eISBN 978 1 78450 398 7

What Does Eating Disorder Recovery Look Like?
Answers to Your Questions about Therapy and Recovery
Lucia Giombini and Sophie Nesbitt
ISBN 978 1 83997 220 1
eISBN 978 1 83997 219 5

The Eating Disorder Recovery Journal
Cara Lisette
Illustrated by Victoria Barron
Foreword by Dr Emily David
ISBN 978 1 83997 085 6
eISBN 978 1 83997 086 3

Weight Expectations
One Man's Recovery from Anorexia
Dave Chawner
ISBN 978 1 78592 358 6
eISBN 978 1 78450 699 5

EATING DISORDERS DON'T DISCRIMINATE

Stories of Illness, Hope and Recovery from Diverse Voices

Edited by
Dr Chukwuemeka Nwuba & Bailey Spinn

Foreword by Professor Janet Treasure OBE

Jessica Kingsley Publishers
London and Philadelphia

First published in Great Britain in 2024 by Jessica Kingsley Publishers

An imprint of John Murray Press

1

A CIP catalogue record for this title is available from the British Library and the Library of Congress

ISBN 978 1 83997 699 5
eISBN 978 1 83997 700 8

Printed and bound in Great Britain by TJ Books Ltd

Jessica Kingsley Publishers' policy is to use papers that are natural, renewable and recyclable products and made from wood grown in sustainable forests. The logging and manufacturing processes are expected to conform to the environmental regulations of the country of origin.

Jessica Kingsley Publishers
Carmelite House
50 Victoria Embankment
London EC4Y 0DZ

www.jkp.com

John Murray Press
Part of Hodder & Stoughton Ltd
An Hachette Company

MIX
Paper from responsible sources
FSC® C013056

To the heroism of eating disorder sufferers and their families

Contents

About the Editors

Chukwuemeka 'Chuks' Nwuba is a London-based mental health doctor with a particular interest in eating disorders. He was voted on the list of Powerful Media's Top 10 Black Future Leaders 2017–18. He is the Clinical Lead for the charity Mind of the Student. He is the Co-founder of ed/md, the UK's first eating disorders conference for medical students. He is a member of the Association of Black Psychiatrists. His prize-winning essay on eating disorders and race-related issues, 'Leanne', was published by the Royal College of Psychiatrists in 2021. His words have been featured in *The Lancet Child and Adolescent Health*, NHS Race and Health Observatory and the BBC. @drchuks_

Bailey Spinn is a musician and social media influencer. Ever since her move to Los Angeles, from Virginia, she has been focusing on her point of view videos, which have gained her over 14.9 million followers on TikTok, along with more than 4.45 million on YouTube. Bailey has also started exploring her interest in being a rock musician. Throughout her influencing career, she has been featured on *Allure* magazine's YouTube, *New York Post*, *USA Today* and ET Canada. Her first single was released in 2023. She has eating disorder lived experience and uses her platform to raise awareness and collaborate with organizations such as the National Eating Disorder Association (NEDA). @baileyspinn

Editors' Note

Just to be clear: disordered eating is not the same thing as an eating disorder. There are arguments to suggest that most of us, at some point, have had disordered eating. But an eating disorder is different. It's a mental health condition which can have life-threatening implications. And if you're someone who's either personally experienced, or knows of someone who has suffered from, or currently suffers from an eating disorder, then you probably know just how serious it can get.

Long before Dr Chuks' work as a London-based doctor, caring for some of the UK's most unwell eating disorder inpatients, he used to know Juliet and Jasmine. Two young, White, English, middle-class women – both with eating disorders. Unbeknown to him at the time, this was both helpful and unhelpful. Helpful because they highlighted a demographic that eating disorders greatly affect in the UK – young, White, middle-class women. But unhelpful because he quickly became deluded, thinking that eating disorders didn't wander beyond those demographics. That was until many years later, in an inpatient job, when he and his team admitted Musa onto the ward. His encounter with Musa – a young, British, Pakistani male – was a turning point. It was the point at which he realized that this plight extended beyond the four walls of his misconceptions and biases, and that others were involved too. He eventually came to realize that it was because of such widespread misconceptions and biases that, in many circumstances, we were failing to recognize serious illness.

With the explosion of social media, the narrative of achieving a 'perfect' body has grown with it. Many promote unhealthy eating habits and an unrealistic expectation of what we all should look like. Fad diets, which have been around for a long time, are now being shown to us every day when we switch on our phones. During Bailey's time as a content creator, she has fallen victim to these herself. She has also experienced how cruel people can be online, shaming others for their appearance and weight. Being honest online about such difficulties can be overwhelmingly tough when anyone can bully you at the touch of a button. But it's vital to raise awareness about the effects that having an eating disorder can have – both physically and mentally. Bailey has personally experienced the pain of having an eating disorder. Unfortunately, there is still a serious lack of information about eating disorders on the web. You, or people around you, could be struggling and you may never know. Everyone struggling should know that they aren't alone, and Bailey believes that proper education can help everyone better understand the vast effects of disordered eating.

So, this book was born out of necessity, really. Born out of a need to educate, and to highlight the indiscriminate nature of an eating disorder; that it knows no boundaries and exists across intersectional lines of gender, race and class. To do this, we set out to gather some influential and inspirational individuals, with remarkable stories. And they're all remarkable because they're all different. Each story, unique. *Eating Disorders Don't Discriminate* brings together 31 of them. These powerful stories span the spectrum of eating disorders, along the way challenging widely held beliefs, giving fresh perspectives on what life with an eating disorder looks like and the hope that lies beyond. The stories are thought-provoking, emotional, sensory, at times hilarious, but most importantly, they leverage the power of a recovery story – which, in the moment, felt far-fetched to both the writer and those in the vicinity – to educate and inspire. Helped by multidisciplinary team expert insights as well as perspectives from friends and family, this book hopes to provide a holistic view of the most common eating disorders.

Our hope is that this book will use lived experience to shed some much-needed light on the shadowy culture of misinformation around eating disorders. That misplaced attitudes, much like our own from times past, will be challenged. That the power of knowledge will be realized. But most importantly, that the stories of those suffering in silence will be validated. Our hope is that this book will act as an avenue via which their recovery can be encouraged and sought.

To be honest, our former misinformed selves could have done with this book, because we believe that the humanness and transparency with which these stories are shared have the ability to pierce a hole through even the thickest veneers of ignorance and cynicism. This journey for us was, and still is, one of learning as much as it is evangelism. We hope you discover as much, from each of the authors, as we did.

Foreword

Having worked with eating disorder patients for nearly four decades, it gives me great joy to connect with those at the early stages of their journey in this field. I had such a pleasure when I spoke to Chuks for the first time. Chuks and I discussed what we thought the future of eating disorders may look like. We briefly spoke about how, in recent years, there have been increasing numbers of people that fall under binge spectrum disorders (Smink, van Hoeken and Hoek 2012), and that this may continue to climb. We also discussed how, on a clinical level, anorexia nervosa has not changed much over the years but that there is still much more to learn.

In general, there are much wider eating disorder diagnoses now than when I first started. Fortunately, there is now exciting biology showing us just how different all these respective diagnoses are. However, within these eating disorders, research into the diversity of those with lived experience is only just hitting conferences, textbooks and libraries. Until recently, there has been very little on minority groups. This has resulted in clinical assumptions being made and missed opportunities to deliver timely care. This book, by Chuks and Bailey, will help with the efforts to redress this balance.

When I heard Chuks was collaborating with Bailey, I could not think of a couple that more aptly represent the future. Chuks' growing presence in the arena of mental health is clear, and his passion to tell the stories of those from underrepresented groups is palpable.

Bailey's positive influence on her generation is vast, sparked by deeply profound personal experiences of mental illness of her own. Together, they form an exciting duo and have curated a truly original book.

This book is a collection of wide-ranging personal experiences from terrific contributors, but more than that, it covers important topics, taps into sources of expert knowledge throughout, and discusses the future of eating disorder care. So, whether you just want to learn more about eating disorders, whether you are in – or know someone who is in – the midst of a battle with an eating disorder, or whether you are an avid reader of medical non-fiction and popular medicine, this book is for you.

Eating Disorders Don't Discriminate is an extraordinary insight into the many ways eating disorders can present. It will hopefully act as a balm to those suffering in silence, and to those who feel unseen and unsupported. This book will undoubtedly be a shining light in a society which often disregards the existence of eating disorders, and I highly recommend it. The more books of this nature, the better.

Professor Janet Treasure OBE

Acknowledgements

Dr Chuks: Thank you to Bailey for being a brilliant co-pilot, and to everyone at Jessica Kingsley Publishers, especially Jane, Maudisa, Gracie and Vicki, for supporting and championing this mammoth project, and all the contributors. Temima and Rebeca at Next Step Talent for enabling this collaboration. Dr Susmit Roy, Dr Nilama-dhab Kar, Dr Jayashree Viswanathan and Dr Nabil Anees for igniting an enthusiasm for psychiatry. Dr Amit Mistry for wise counsel and inspiration. My two eating disorders 'mothers': Dr Sara McCluskey and Dr Sarah Cassar. Natalia-Nana Lester-Bush for encouraging me to write, Dr Agnes Ayton and the Royal College of Psychiatrists for ongoing support and for publishing *Leanne*, everyone at the Association of Black Psychiatrists, and everyone at Cygnet Hospital Ealing (you rock!). Segun Apampa, Natalia Masternak, Seun Keshiro, Daniel Mansaray and Elena Pop for constant encouragement. Ana Goncalves and Dr Paul McLaren for taking a leap of faith with me, and everyone at Priory Hospital Hayes Grove. Mark Hanna for being the best photographer I know. The Manchester Lot. Olivia Russo and Andrew Wilson for being brilliant agents, and Chimene Suleyman for timely advice.

Extra special thanks to my heavenly Father, my beautiful wife Hannah and daughter Kairaluchukwu, Bryn Jones for all the book chat, and the rest of my family for advice and support. Also to Farah

Cheded, Nancy Adimora, Simi Dhami, Felicity Bown and Stephanie Barrett for being unbelievably reliable and backing this project.

Bailey: Thank you to Dr Chuks for allowing me to be part of such a phenomenal project. I am appreciative of the chance to share part of my personal journey and to be a voice for others struggling. To the team at Next Step Talent for bringing this connection together, and encouraging me to vocalize my health battle. To everyone who supports me as a content creator, for making all of this possible. Much thanks to my family in Virginia for loving me through my time of need, pushing me forward. Love to all who are struggling with an eating disorder themselves – you are heard and understood.

Preface

Dr Chuks

Outside was England. And at home was Nigeria. Outside was jacket potato and baked beans. And at home, amala and egusi soup. Outside, Oasis. At home, Fela. Outside, cups of tea. At home, actually, well... were also cups of tea. Dang, I was on a roll there (but, seriously, who doesn't like tea?!).

Growing up, my life was very much dualistic (apart from the tea). Born and brought up in one of the Whitest boroughs of London, England, yet much of the way I lived – but, more importantly, felt – outside of public spaces, was Igbo (one of the most populous Nigerian tribes). And, in fact, despite living in London my whole life, I could probably count on two sets of hands the number of non-Black people who had entered the front door of my family home. (It really is amazing the extent to which we can live in our communities and not extend into the next.)

I think my entire upbringing was why my secondary-school biology lessons had such a profound impact on me. Besides being a subject that I found, on the whole, painstakingly boring (I know, a doctor, how?!), I used to sit next to Juliet (name changed).

As well as being the brightest in the whole class (she used to put me to shame in tests), Juliet was the nicest girl you'd ever meet, and extremely shy. Now, this is probably a weird thing to say, but when I think of Juliet, I think of her hands first (in fact, yes, that was a weird thing to say, but stick with me, I'm going somewhere). I think of her hands – the pink, flaky skin enveloping slender, bony fingers – before I think of her face. She had what looked like such incredibly dry skin. Not the eczema type, but a harsher, more anaemic kind. I used to regularly offer her some of the moisturizer I kept in my bag (my mum was firmly on #TeamAntiAshySkin and insisted I had some permanently on my person). Juliet would always accept.

I massively cringe when I think back at the things I used to say to her; things like 'Juliet, you need to look after yourself more – look at your hands!' Because it wasn't until many years later – coincidentally, after I had completed my psychiatry placement at medical school – that someone told me that Juliet was in the throes of a serious mental illness throughout her time at school. Anorexia nervosa. At the time, I had heard the term only a few times before. I thought of it as no more than a colloquial description of someone who was incredibly skinny. I also thought that one week spent with my grandmother, and her cooking, would cure anyone's anorexia right out. I had never knowingly met anyone with it. And I definitely didn't know that it could affect the quality of one's skin.

On reflection, lots of clues were hidden in plain sight. First, apart from her poor-quality skin, she was noticeably very thin (don't forget the bony fingers). Second, I distinctly remember that she used to eat the same scanty lunch every day, in her well-ordered packed lunch box, and never seemed to enjoy the process. She ate it with an intense, laser-eyed focus – almost as if it was something she had to endure. And, third, she was always, always cold. I used to say to her things like 'Of course you're cold, Juliet, look at you!' (again, awful, I know). My biology lessons had inadvertently provided me with an education about the human body in a way I hadn't anticipated. The subtle, but present, dermatological (hands), nutritional (eating) and thermoregulatory (cold intolerance) clues. Juliet's serious mental health challenges were camouflaged by her academic excellence (which I now know is not uncommon with anorexia nervosa).

At the time, for the life of me, I couldn't fathom what was going on. Why was she so skinny? Why did she not eat much? I remember thinking that she probably suffered from anxiety, which shut off her appetite – an autonomic response that I was, and still am, all too familiar with. It *had* to be this because why would someone *choose* not to eat enough? The brain of this naïve 16-year-old boy was battling hard to make sense of her.

I used to always wonder what my parents would think if I ever decided to bring her to the house. Apart from her being White, which I imagined would stun my family into silence (much like it did later when I brought my wife home for the first time), I envisaged the car-crash scenario of my mum welcoming her at the front door with a platter of Nigerian meat pies. (Juliet was vegetarian and my mum was, at the time, still grappling with the concept of vegetarianism – and probably still is, to be honest. Sorry, Mum.)

But seriously, though, the thought of finding myself in a position similar to Juliet – where I wasn't eating enough despite there being enough – seemed impossible. Especially given what I knew of my parents and their underprivileged upbringings. I remember thinking that it would have felt like simultaneous slaps to both of their faces for all their hard efforts; first immigrating to the UK, and then battling away to carve out a better future for my siblings and me. Eating was the least I could do to show gratitude. And I couldn't imagine anyone else in my position thinking any differently.

But I've since come to realize that, in the case of Juliet, I had naïvely been attempting to understand her through the lens of *my* upbringing and context, and had made a fundamental error in doing so. My experience, and the experiences of those immediately around me at the time, shaped my thought processes which I guess, to a large degree, is inevitable. So, I've since been forced to re-evaluate. What were the causes of Juliet's illness? Maybe her decision not to eat more was more nuanced. Maybe it wasn't a choice at all?

Over the years, many of my steadfastly held eating disorder-related assumptions have changed; I needed a significant amount of evidence to bring me to this point. Since the 'Juliet days', I've met many people, some with upbringings similar to mine, with eating disorders. I've learnt that eating disorders are not always predictable, that they can emerge stealthily, and that demographics have only a partial role to play. Whether it's a traumatic experience layered on top of years of low self-esteem or a new, unrealistic expectation placed onto an already overwhelming heap of anxiety and control, there are an infinite number of possibilities. It's the right (or, I guess you could say, wrong) combination of such events that can then go on to coalesce, resulting in illness.

But, unfortunately, societal depictions of eating disorders are often too simplistic and reductive. Eating disorder portrayals are often limited 'to self-inflicted behavioral and physical symptoms – habit-forming lifestyle choices brought on by the sufferers themselves' (Michel 2015). Such depictions fail to mention that eating disorders often have genetic origins; they are often used as refuge and solace; they can be avenues via which an uncontrollable and chaotic world can become more manageable; they are mechanisms with which self-destruction can be sought.

Since school, I have scrolled back through old pictures of Juliet – her standing alongside various members of our year group – and thought, 'How could I have missed it?!' And as life would have it, being able to recognize symptoms of, and being involved in the diagnosis of, eating disorders became something that was required of me every day. Typical.

Introduction

Dr Chuks

There is (conservatively) estimated to be 16 per cent of the UK population that screen positive for an eating disorder, and 4 per cent that are severely affected by one (NHS Digital 2020). In America, nearly 30 million people are estimated to have an eating disorder over the course of their lifetime. And, as it stands, eating disorders are estimated to affect at least 9 per cent of the global population (Deloitte Access Economics 2020). Despite all this, there is a surprising lack of eating disorder awareness worldwide. In a 2018 poll, 39 per cent of people thought that when someone has an eating disorder, they are just 'going through a phase', and 13 per cent didn't believe eating disorders were serious at all (Hunnicutt 2018). Unfortunately, this level of ignorance appears to be endemic, with very few signs of things changing despite several eating disorder campaigns highlighting how serious eating disorders are. This is an observation Bailey and I have made based on statistics like the ones above, media reports, talking to colleagues and those with lived experience, our charity work, and through ad hoc observations in our day jobs.

So, what is an eating disorder? Well, the term 'eating disorders' is a bit misleading to be honest. Because, whilst there are often challenges with the consumption of food, the actual 'eating' aspect of it (the act of putting food to the mouth, chewing and swallowing it) is often *not* disordered and doesn't present a problem. Rather, in such people, the feelings and actions *around* eating can be harder to navigate (I guess they could always rename it 'around-eating disorders', but that's far less catchy and a bit of a mouthful). For example, take the relatively unknown rumination-regurgitation disorder described in the International Classification of Diseases 11th Revision (ICD-11; WHO 2023e). With this type of eating disorder, food is intentionally and repeatedly brought up after it has been swallowed, and is then re-chewed and re-swallowed, or deliberately spat out. However, there are examples where the eating *is* disordered. For example, with pica (another less well-known eating disorder) non-nutritive substances – such as clay, soil and plastic – are consumed by those old enough to know the difference between edible and non-edible substances. With pica, the *content* of what is eaten is 'disordered' (or abnormal). With other eating disorders, the content may be normal, but the *volume* of what is eaten may be abnormal, either too little or too much. At other times, the content and volume may be normal, but the *way* food is consumed may not be. For example, eating food may cause a state of distress.

The five most common eating disorder categories – which this book will focus on – are binge eating disorder, bulimia nervosa, anorexia nervosa, avoidant/restrictive food intake disorder (ARFID) and other specified feeding and eating disorder (OSFED). Together, they have been rising continuously for more than 50 years (Treasure, Duarte and Schmidt 2020). In particular, in the UK, hospital admissions for people with eating disorders have risen by 84 per cent in the last five years (NHS Digital 2021).

Binge Eating Disorder

Binge eating disorder is rarely discussed despite being one of the most common eating disorders, accounting for 22 per cent of all eating disorders in the UK (Beat 2023). It is massively underdiagnosed (Kornstein *et al.* 2016).

According to the ICD-11 – the World Health Organization's

standard when it comes to diagnoses – binge eating disorder is characterized by 'frequent, recurrent episodes [at least once a week or more over a period of three months] of binge eating'. The ICD-11 defines binge eating as 'a distinct period of time during which the individual experiences a subjective loss of control over eating, eating notably more or differently than usual, and feels unable to stop eating or limit the type or amount of food eaten'. Binge eating, in this context, is distressing, can negatively affect day-to-day functioning and is 'often accompanied by negative emotions such as guilt or disgust' (WHO 2023a). This is probably why, in my experience, binge eating disorder insights are less frequently shared.

It's not uncommon for people to joke to me that they have binge eating disorder when they don't. Oftentimes, they describe having a 'see-food diet' – a diet where you eat everything in sight – making reference to having large appetites, and typically throw in inane, self-deprecating comments about their bodies. From my experience, binge eating disorder is probably the most trivialized eating disorder. Perhaps this has to do with the word itself: binge.

Binge, much like the word *depressed*, is an ordinary word. It's commonly used in everyday speech. Regarding being depressed, we may say that we're depressed about a situation regarding work, or the outcome of a sporting event, or maybe after an uneventful weekend. But being depressed (unhappy and without hope) is not the same as a diagnosis of clinical depression – the latter being much more severe and warranting more rigorous intervention. A similar narrative can be seen with the word *binge*. If I didn't work in eating disorders, I would probably say that I hear the word *binge* more in relation to newly released TV series than anything else. The point is that people use the term casually. So, when it's used to convey more serious matters, such as binge eating disorder, it often lacks potency. This is especially problematic as I've spoken to many who would argue that binge eating disorder is one of the hardest eating disorders, if not the hardest, to recover from.

Binge eating disorder is serious and can have devastating whole-body ramifications. It can lead to musculoskeletal, cardiovascular and gastrointestinal complications, even infertility and pregnancy issues in women (Sbaragli *et al.* 2018; Sebastiani *et al.* 2020). Those with binge eating disorder can also suffer with body esteem issues – typically becoming preoccupied by them – as well as experience anxiety and depression.

There is still so much for us to learn about binge eating disorder. We know that risk factors include perfectionism, substance abuse, parental mental illness, and physical and sexual abuse, among others (Hilbert 2019). Latest research suggests that those with binge eating disorder appear to have abnormally low activity in areas of the brain that are responsible for impulse control (Balodis *et al.* 2013). Also, in these people, seeing, smelling and tasting a food (but not necessarily eating it) significantly increases dopamine to greater levels than in those without a diagnosis (dopamine is a chemical linked to the motivation to eat and is associated with habit learning). Dopamine levels are linked to the severity of binge eating disorder – not weight, as was previously thought (Wang *et al.* 2011).

Bulimia Nervosa

Bulimia nervosa, more commonly known as bulimia, is often portrayed uncharitably in mainstream media. The attributes of 'weakness, greed, and impulsivity' are commonly associated with it (Michel 2015). As a result, bulimia nervosa is probably the most secretive of all eating disorders and its prevalence is notoriously hard to ascertain. Estimates have predicted it affects as many as half a million people aged 16 and over currently living in the UK (CPD Online College 2023) and a total of 7.2 million in America at any point in their lifetime (Hudson *et al.* 2007). In total, bulimia nervosa makes up 19 per cent of all eating disorders in the UK (Beat 2023).

According to the ICD-11, bulimia nervosa is characterized by recurrent episodes of binge eating. However, unlike binge eating disorder, binge eating episodes are regularly followed by inappropriate compensatory behaviours with the aim of preventing weight gain. These could include reducing energy intake (restrictive eating) or purging behaviours. Purging, in the context of eating disorders, doesn't just include self-induced vomiting, which is often the assumption, even amongst clinicians. It can also include the misuse of laxatives, excessive exercise or any other behaviour which is intended to counteract nutritional intake. People with bulimia nervosa are 'preoccupied with body shape or weight, which strongly influences self-evaluation'. There's also 'marked distress about the pattern of binge eating and inappropriate compensatory behaviour or significant impairment in personal, family, social, educational, occupational or other important areas of functioning' (WHO 2023b).

Bulimia nervosa can be deadly. The most common cause of death, in people with bulimia nervosa, is heart disease secondary to an imbalance in essential electrolytes, such as potassium, calcium, magnesium and phosphate (Jáuregui-Garrido and Jáuregui-Lobera 2012). Another life-threatening eating disorder, without its own diagnostic code, is diabulimia. Diabulimia, as its name suggests, lies at the intersection of diabetes and bulimia nervosa. It is a condition in which insulin-dependent diabetics fail to administer their insulin in an attempt to lose weight. This can lead to the early onset of serious diabetic complications such as blindness and limb amputations. It can also lead to an untimely death.

Neurodevelopmental disorders, such as attention deficit hyperactivity disorder (ADHD), are significant risk factors for bulimia nervosa and binge eating disorder. In one study, females with ADHD were 5.6 times more likely to present with bulimia nervosa (Biederman *et al.* 2007). Other risk factors for developing bulimia nervosa include posttraumatic stress disorder (PTSD), low self-esteem and body dysmorphia. Bulimia nervosa has the highest rates of comorbid depression of all eating disorders, with more than 70 per cent of individuals with bulimia nervosa being diagnosed with depression at some point (NIMH 2021).

Anorexia Nervosa

Most people I speak to about eating disorders tend to think of anorexia nervosa – more commonly known as anorexia. They tend to think of stories like that of Juliet. If I had a pound coin for every time someone (for some reason, it always seems to be some uncle at some wedding) said something like, 'Ooh, well look at me, I'm definitely not anorexic!', I would probably be on a beach somewhere, retired. Yes, it's normally said in jest. But far from being something to joke about, anorexia nervosa infamously has the highest mortality rate amongst all mental health conditions in the UK (Morris and Twaddle 2007) and the second highest in the USA (Guinhut *et al.* 2021). Nearly one-quarter of those with anorexia nervosa attempt suicide (Udo, Bitley and Grilo 2019).

Anorexia nervosa is often referred to in popular culture and frequently gets glamorized. In particular, the 'heroin chic' style, popularized in early-1990s fashion and characterized by pale skin and emaciated features (also traits associated with the abuse of heroin), led to a sharp increase in cases of anorexia nervosa between 1990 and 1998 (Our World in Data 2022).

In the world of academia (a far less glamorous sector), anorexia nervosa assumes a disproportionately large amount of eating disorder research funding. In a 2011 UK inquiry into eating disorder research funding, Dr Dasha Nicholls, Strategic Director for National Audits and Research at the Royal College of Psychiatrists, reported that out of 190 studies of eating disorders, 72 (38%) were for anorexia nervosa (APPG 2021). This is despite anorexia nervosa making up only 8 per cent of all eating disorders (Beat 2023).

The ICD-11 lists three main defining features of anorexia nervosa: significantly low body weight for the individual's height, age and developmental stage (that is not due to another health condition or to the unavailability of food), low body weight or shape central to the person's self-evaluation, and a persistent pattern of behaviours to prevent restoration of normal weight (similar to the compensatory behaviours described for bulimia nervosa) (WHO 2023c).

Anorexia nervosa is the only eating disorder that uses a weight measure in its diagnostic profile. Here, low body weight is a body mass index (BMI) less than 18.5 kg/m² in adults. In children and adolescents, a BMI-for-age under the 5th percentile, or failure to gain weight as expected – based on the individual's developmental trajectory – are used. Rapid weight loss (more than 20% of total body weight within 6 months) may be used to replace the low body weight guideline, as long as other diagnostic requirements for anorexia nervosa are met. The use of rapid weight loss is particularly important for capturing those experiencing symptoms of anorexia nervosa whose weights may not be low enough to reach the threshold for diagnosis (defined in the DSM-5 as atypical anorexia nervosa).

Negative, obsessive thoughts about body weight and shape can occur very early in the development of anorexia nervosa. Such thoughts being central to the person's self-evaluation are an important differentiator of anorexia nervosa from its variants: anorexia mirabilis ('holy anorexia') and anorexia athletica ('sports anorexia'). Neither anorexia mirabilis (restrictive eating to engage in religious piety) nor anorexia athletica (over-exercise and/or restrictive eating to optimize athletic performance) are to do with body image.

A pathway pioneered at King's College London, aimed at improving clinical outcomes for those with a dual diagnosis of autism spectrum condition (ASC; also known as autism spectrum disorder (ASD)) and anorexia nervosa, found that approximately 35 per cent of patients with anorexia nervosa also have ASC or 'high autistic features' (PEACE 2023). Other research suggests that there is a strong link between anorexia nervosa and obsessive compulsive disorder (OCD) (Swinbourne and Touyz 2007). And, just as with OCD, anorexia nervosa can present with inflexibility and perfectionism. The neuro-degenerative changes seen in the brain in anorexia nervosa are partly culpable (Scharner and Stengel 2019).

Avoidant/Restrictive Food Intake Disorder

Avoidant/restrictive food intake disorder, more commonly known as ARFID, is a frequently misunderstood eating disorder and, even among clinicians, little is known about it. Some statistics have ARFID as affecting 1–5 per cent of all people (Schmidt *et al.* 2018; Dinkler *et al.* 2022). However, in general, its prevalence is inconclusive. We know that, of children and adolescents either presenting for eating disorder evaluation or currently in treatment for eating/feeding behaviour problems, up to 22 per cent meet the diagnostic criteria for ARFID (Nicely *et al.* 2014).

ARFID is often confused with simple food selectivity (eating from a small range of foods) and food neophobia (refusing to try new foods). A clinician once said to me that ARFID is 'just picky eating' and jibed that it ought to stand for 'A Really Fussy Intake Disorder'. The thing is, nearly half of young children struggle with 'picky eating' (Cardona Cano *et al.* 2015). ARFID – which can occur at any age – is more complex than that.

In the ICD-11, ARFID is characterized as:

Avoidance or restriction of food intake that results in: 1) the intake of an insufficient quantity or variety of food to meet adequate energy or nutritional requirements that has resulted in significant weight loss, clinically significant nutritional deficiencies [which can lead to compromised growth and development], dependence on oral nutritional supplements or tube feeding, or has otherwise negatively affected the physical health of the individual; or 2) significant impairment in personal, family, social, educational, occupational or other important areas of functioning (e.g. due to avoidance or distress related to participating in social experiences involving eating). (WHO 2023d)

Notably, in ARFID, food restriction is not driven by body dissatisfaction, a desire to lose weight or a preoccupation with body weight or shape.[1] Instead, it is due to sensory aversion (e.g. smell, taste, appearance, texture, colour and temperature of food), low appetite (or lack of interest in food and eating) and fear of negative consequences of eating (such as choking, vomiting or ill health[2]). And, in many cases, no cause is elicited.

ARFID is believed to be the most heritable eating disorder, and amongst the most heritable of all psychiatric disorders. New research led by Lisa Dinkler (Dinkler *et al.* 2023), postdoctoral researcher at the Karolinska Institutet Centre for Eating Disorders Innovation in Sweden, suggested that ARFID's heritability is as high as 79 per cent. We also know that ARFID has high rates of comorbidity with ASC, as well as ADHD and anxiety disorders (Thomas *et al.* 2017; Zimmerman and Fisher 2017).

ARFID involves a range of biological, psychological and sociocultural factors, and these factors interact differently in different people, leading to diverse perspectives, experiences and symptoms. For example, because those with ARFID tend not to find much challenge in eating their preferred foods, they often present with a variety of body types. Treatment of ARFID can be complex and wide-ranging, and much like other eating disorders, a broad range of treatment options, settings and healthcare professionals is often required.

---

1   The restricted food intake and its effects on weight, other aspects of health or functioning is not due to unavailability of food, nor a manifestation of another medical condition (e.g. food allergies, hyperthyroidism) or mental disorder, nor due to the effect of a substance or medication on the central nervous system including withdrawal effects.

2   Often related to a history of aversive food-related experience.

Other Specified Feeding and Eating Disorder

Although probably the least known eating disorder category, other specified feeding and eating disorder (OSFED, previously EDNOS, or eating disorder not otherwise specified) is actually the most common (Mitchison *et al.* 2020; Santomauro *et al.* 2021). Around 30 per cent of people who seek treatment for an eating disorder have OSFED (Jenkins *et al.* 2021). It is estimated to affect up to 6 per cent of the US population (Eating Recovery Center 2023). A diagnosis of OSFED is given when symptoms similar to those of one or more eating disorders are present, but not all the criteria are met. And when one's thoughts and behaviours don't align with those of another disorder, or when there is insufficient information to determine a more specific diagnosis, the label 'unspecified feeding and eating disorder' (UFED) can be given. UFED falls under the OSFED spectrum of conditions. A 2016 study found that, of those that fell into the OSFED category, one-third met OSFED criteria while two-thirds met the criteria for UFED (Keski-Rahkonen and Mustelin 2016). The latest definition of OSFED is described in the *Diagnostic and Statistical Manual of Mental Disorders, Fifth Edition* (DSM-5) – the American equivalent of the ICD-11.

The five examples that the DSM-5 covers as meeting the diagnosis of OSFED are atypical anorexia nervosa, binge eating disorder (of low frequency and/or limited duration), bulimia nervosa (of low frequency and/or limited duration), purging disorder and night eating syndrome:

- Atypical anorexia nervosa is a condition where one has all the symptoms of anorexia nervosa apart from being underweight. Approximately 2.8 per cent of females will experience this eating disorder by 20 years of age (Stice, Marti and Rohde 2013). A survey led by Dr Erin Harrop, an assistant professor in social work at the University of Denver, showed that sufferers waited an average of 11.6 years before seeking help (Siber 2022). This is partly due to a lack of awareness of what constitutes an eating disorder, with the common assumption being that they primarily exist in smaller bodies.

- Binge eating disorder (of low frequency and/or limited duration) is a condition where all symptoms of binge eating disorder are present, but the symptoms occur less frequently, or have been ongoing for less than three months.
- Bulimia nervosa (of low frequency and/or limited duration) is a condition where all symptoms of bulimia nervosa are present, but the symptoms occur less frequently, or have been ongoing for less than three months.
- Purging disorder is a condition where there is recurrent purging in an attempt to influence weight or shape. However, there is no persistent binge eating.
- Night eating syndrome is a condition which, as the name suggests, involves regular episodes of eating during night-time hours. It typically causes distress and functional impairment. It is important to take into consideration the potential for a different diagnosis (e.g. binge eating disorder), environmental influences and social norms before diagnosing this.

The reasons for developing OSFED differ from person to person, and the known causes include genetic predisposition as well as a combination of environmental, social and cultural factors. Nearly half of OSFED patients have a comorbid mood disorder, and one in ten have a comorbid substance abuse disorder – usually alcohol misuse (Ulfvebrand *et al.* 2015).

✳ ✳ ✳

As with all eating disorders, it takes good judgement, and the assessment of a multitude of factors, before a diagnosis can be reached. Diagnoses, which can be extremely validating, can also signal huge life changes for the patient, and therefore should be thoroughly considered. Minimizing the amount of subjectivity is important, as it is on this very diagnostic foundation that a patient will work towards recovery.

The R Word

When talking about eating disorder recovery, so many questions arise. What even is it? (Recovery means different things to different people.) When does it officially start? (If the target was to get sober, we'd have a sobriety date; not with eating disorders, though – far too ambiguous.) Also, when does the process of recovery end? How do you know when you are 'fully recovered', if ever?

In October 2021, Dr Jessica Schleider, director of the Lab for Scalable Mental Health in Stony Brook, New York – who herself has eating disorder lived experience – tweeted:

> Framing mental health problems as chronic illnesses that have flare-ups (as all chronic illnesses do) would save so many patients from self-criticism over lapses. The idea/goal of 'full recovery' is still common in treatment settings, and it puts so much undue pressure on people. (Schleider 2021a)

This tweet has been liked over 25,000 times, with someone replying, 'This is by far the best description of an eating disorder – or any mental health problem – that I have ever heard' (Barrett 2022a). I remember having visceral excitement upon reading Schleider's tweet, probably born from my own personal experience of looking after patients with eating disorders. Recovery is hard. Some patients have described it to me as them having to learn about themselves all over again – as though they were someone new. Exchanging a toxic identity for something sustainable. And, over the years, many patients have expressed to me their frustrations with the arduous process. The physical process of recovery itself – from hormonal changes to other bodily changes – often results in high levels of stress and anxiety. But what can feel even weightier are the intangibles. These include the expectations of others, as well as the expectations patients have of themselves.

The notion of being 'fully' or 'completely' recovered has a feeling of finality about it, as though it were a peak to reach. It comes with expectations. Expectations to reach a certain pinnacle. The problem with such a narrative is that failing to do so often results in feelings of shame, failure and weakness, with core beliefs such as low self-worth – common in those with eating disorders – bubbling up to the top. The idea of potentially relapsing, or having a slight setback, can feel overwhelming, often preventing patients from seeking the support they need to begin with. In an online discussion with Madi, a patient with lived experience, she told me:

> Recovery isn't black and white, yet the way it is presented gives yet another – often unattainable – perfectionistic 'ideal' and can deter sufferers from trying to recover, for fear they will 'fail' if they don't reach a point where they are 100% free from their eating disorder. (Barrett 2022b)

The idea of 'full recovery' can heap pressure on the individual to fall within a binary: all or none. Either complete recovery or complete failure. As a society, we often impose this outlook on mental health treatment, as though it were a broken leg that can be 'fixed' in a single operation. With mental health, treatments are often lengthier and improvements more subtle. Those that work in eating disorders regularly talk of recovery as not being linear. And it's true. Recovery is like a game of rugby: full of forwards and backs. In rugby, you're expected to move forwards whilst only passing the ball backwards (which I've always found quite impressive). This is what recovery can feel like: as though you're not getting anywhere, but in fact you are. I remember having to make this clear to one of my patients who expressed to me that she felt 'like a failure' after she had just been admitted as an inpatient to a specialist eating disorder unit for the third time. The COVID-19 pandemic saw the re-emergence of eating disorder behaviours from many who thought they had 'recovered' (Baird 2022).

Which is partly why I liked Schleider's tweet so much; it's affirming. She later explains that thinking of recovery as more of an active, ongoing, iterative process has helped her for all the times she's felt 'not recovered enough' (Schleider 2022). Along the way, lessons about oneself are learnt and knowledge of potential pitfalls discovered. This, in turn, often (but not always) leads to regressions being less severe and there generally being less turmoil when life decides to cough up repeated challenges. Schleider elaborates: '"chronic" doesn't mean you'll always be ill, that meds are needed, or that problems are uncontrollable...just that recurrences may happen, they aren't your fault, and you can always manage them' (Schleider 2021b).

However, some prefer the idea of a 'full' recovery, to squeeze the illness into a corner, not allowing it any room, or excuses, to remain. Some don't like the idea of normalizing relapses as part of recovery. And while there isn't necessarily a right or wrong answer, it's important to understand the risks associated with both viewpoints.

Personally, instead of 'full recovery', I like the word 'freedom' (as corny as that may sound). It gives the feeling of emancipation. Room to breathe and space to think. The feeling of liberation from something that once had power over you. *You* are now in control, not the eating disorder dominating and dictating every life decision. Actually *living*. Reaching a point where you're able to try new meals in social settings, such as restaurants, without worrying about the number of calories listed on the menu; being able to negotiate comments on your body which would have previously been triggering, including positive comments; no longer having rules around food; being able to eat intuitively; being able to tolerate fluctuations in weight;

no longer engaging in destructive eating behaviours such as over-exercise (often very challenging to resolve), but instead partaking in socialized sporting events; finally finding a bin for the scales, tape measure and mirrors. Freedom will look different depending on the eating disorder and depending on the person.

Despite most scoring methods, including the ICD-11, defining eating disorder recovery as being one year symptom-free (WHO 2023c), a study concluded that 'a single definition of recovery does not seem to fit individuals' lived eating disorder experience' (Kenny, Trottier and Lewis 2022).

A Tough, Long Road

When I worked in general medicine, occasionally we used to administer a drug called adenosine. It's used to treat an abnormal heart rhythm called paroxysmal supraventricular tachycardia. The side-effects of adenosine are deeply unpleasant, a typical one being the sense of impending doom. So, prior to giving it, we typically warned patients that they would literally feel like they're about to die. Fortunately, these side-effects were short-lived. But we forewarned them so that they could immediately adjust their expectations for what was to come. Because with a properly adjusted expectation level, issues often become more manageable and less destabilizing when they occur. Making those with eating disorders aware of the notoriously challenging road ahead of them may give them the warning shock needed to set their expectations right, enabling them to buffer any forces against them as they recover.

Research suggests that the process of recovery can be harder the longer the person has an untreated eating disorder, as the illness becomes more entrenched and the cognitions more concrete. According to the First Episode and Rapid Early Intervention for Eating Disorders (FREED) team – a South London and Maudsley service model and care package, led by Professor Ulrike Schmidt, for 16–25-year-olds who have had an eating disorder for three years or less – over time, eating disorder symptoms 'can still be changed, but it gets harder to make changes and there may be long-lasting consequences' (FREED 2023). Such consequences may be physical (such as irreversible damage to the bones in anorexia nervosa, or osteoarthritis in the knees in binge eating disorder) or social (such as loss of certain friends due to social isolation in ARFID), among others.

In 2022, the term 'terminal anorexia' was coined by Jennifer Gaudiani, eating disorders expert physician and founder and medical director of the Gaudiani Clinic, and her colleagues (Gaudiani, Bogetz and Yager 2022). In essence, 'terminal anorexia' permits patients with anorexia nervosa to withdraw consent to all treatment. Healthcare professionals were also encouraged to consider the role of palliative care in their management, in countries where the law allows this. This term has generated a lot of clamour. Many in the field dismissed the term as disturbingly unambitious and described it as a fatal submission to resource limitations. Since then, new American Psychiatric Association (APA) guidelines for eating disorder treatment have been praised for their opting instead to avoid mentioning end-of-the-road eating disorder care and avoid descriptions of arbitrary intervention windows (RCPsych Eating Disorder Faculty 2023). Because, whilst the focus on early intervention is important in order to minimize the aforementioned long-lasting consequences, recent evidence suggests a limited association between the duration of different eating disorder diagnoses and recovery outcomes (Downs *et al.* 2023). This is great news, because many who have lived with an eating disorder for a very long time, often referred to as a 'severe and enduring eating disorder', often cannot imagine ever overcoming their eating disorder 'voice'. There is the tendency to feel as if all hope is lost.

But recovery, whatever that may look like, is never completely out of reach. A life of stability, free of hospital environments and flourishing in the community, is possible even in the most hopeless cases. In a discussion with E. K. J. Wright, author of *How Do You Stop a Magpie Mobbing Your Mind?*, she told me:

It took me 20 years to stop the relentless yo-yo of recovery and re-lapse. But glad and proud to say that with a lot of determination I eventually got there. And it was worth every difficult step for the life, freedom and beautiful children I can now enjoy! Never, ever give up! (Wright 2021)

And this is one of many such discussions that I've had whilst work-ing in eating disorders. Yes, for some, the journey is longer. Indeed, recovery can be lifelong. But as I like to say, everyone's recovery GPS is different. Because it can take time.

Acceleration and Deceleration

As much as one could engage in individual acts (such as mindfulness, journalling, relaxation and music, to name a few), the recovery pro-cess often needs the help of others – family and friends, the support of healthcare professionals, or a community of other people in recovery.

Family and friends often know the individual best and may be available to provide the emotional and practical support needed in the moment. Patients' family and friends can also be integral to the process of recovery.

Healthcare professionals can provide a variety of support includ-ing outpatient care, one-to-one or group therapy (there are countless therapy options), intensive home treatment, day hospital or inpatient care. They can also provide education. From my experience, those with eating disorders appreciate having a better understanding of the consequences of malnutrition, whether they take it in or just decide to intellectualize it. I remember one case where a patient of mine desperately wanted 'abs'. Despite being undernourished, she engaged in an excessive amount of physical activity to try to achieve this. Upon explaining to her that her muscles store energy, and that if she wasn't getting enough energy from food, then her body would break down her muscles to get its energy from there – essentially limiting her chances of achieving the very abs that she was after – she consequently improved her detrimental behaviour with exercise. And whilst education alone doesn't necessarily result in behaviour change (and in this case there were reasons behind her thought processes in the first place that needed deep and thorough exploration), the process of learning through education was empowering and proved helpful.

Friendly support shouldn't be underestimated in recovery. Recently, I was thrilled to come across the hashtags #recovtwt and #recoverytwt online. These take you to a world of fellow runners in the recovery race, of all ages. Many of my patients have found spending time with others – often in a completely different age bracket to themselves – very motivational. There are also books (such as *Elegy for an Appetite* by Shaina Loew-Banayan – a particular favourite of mine), podcasts (such as *The Recovery Warrior Shows* with Jessica Flint and *Real Pod* with Victoria Garrick) and television shows (such as Netflix's *Everything Now*) that can add value. These are examples of where insights from lived experience are offered up.

But eating disorder recovery is odd, because the very things that can enhance and aid recovery are often the things that can set it back.

Family and friends can inadvertently make comments which are received negatively. This may even include well-intentioned positive comments. The environment in the family home, or amongst friends, may not be conducive to eating disorder recovery.

Interactions with medical professionals can both accelerate and decelerate the process of recovery. Patients have described to me moving deeper into their eating disorder due to a lack of validation from healthcare professionals. Patients with binge eating disorder or atypical anorexia nervosa – those more likely to present in larger bodies – often describe weight stigma from healthcare professionals. In a recent large-scale study, half of the participants had experienced weight stigma, with more than two-thirds of those being from doctors (Puhl *et al.* 2021). In a *New York Times* article, Virginia Sole-Smith, journalist and author of *Fat Talk* and *The Eating Instinct*, highlighted her research which suggested that 'doctors rushed conversations, grabbed bellies and made jokes about kids' bodies' (Sole-Smith 2023).

As life-saving as specialist inpatient eating disorder units can be, being in a setting surrounded by others with a similar diagnosis can carry its own challenges. In such settings, many patients with bulimia nervosa and anorexia nervosa, for example, find it hard to untangle themselves from thinking about weight and numbers when they are incessantly tracked by their eating disorder teams, including out-patient teams. A patient described to me the staff's preoccupation with weight as 'dizzying'. Regular weighing and target weight brackets can make it hard to not hyper-focus on numbers. In this context, there is often a huge focus on body mass index (BMI).

Body Mass Index

A colleague I used to work with asked me, 'Doc, what's the best way to lose weight that you would recommend?' I think she was shocked when I asked her, 'Why do you want to lose weight?' She assumed that, given her larger body, I would have rolled with her question. But I didn't. Turns out what she *really* wanted was improved cardio-vascular fitness. But she didn't see it as this. She saw it as weight (and yes, she may have ended up losing some weight in the process, but that's not where her focus should have been). This is not uncommon: for people to conflate weight with health. In fact, some of the fittest people I know would flag as a concern on the BMI.

BMI, measured by dividing someone's weight in kilograms (kg) by their height in metres squared (m²), was first calculated in the 1800s by Belgian mathematician Lambert Quetelet. The way in which it is used in healthcare today is controversial. Using BMI categories as the main indicator of health is misguided and simplistic, and misclassifies overall health. This is partly because the BMI fails to account for sex (women carry more fat than men), age (BMI measurement has limitations when used on children as they grow tall during puberty at rates that may not directly match their weight), ethnicity (for example, many Asian races, particularly those from the Indian subcontinent, tend to carry a proportionately higher fat mass for a given BMI than White people, and the reverse is true for most Black people and for Polynesians) (Prentice and Jebb 2001) and muscle mass (for example, an athlete who has a very high percentage of muscle will often have a high BMI, as muscle weighs slightly more than fat). In a study by the Centers for Disease Control and Prevention (CDC), nearly 50 per cent of 'overweight' individuals and 29 per cent of 'obese' individuals were cardio-metabolically healthy (Tomiyama *et al.* 2016).

If BMI is being used in the context of eating disorder care – and many would argue that it shouldn't be used at all – then it should be used alongside many different pieces of information to draw a conclusion about a person's health. Unfortunately, governmental interventions aimed at 'tackling obesity' (GOV.UK 2020) often focus on BMI, and many of them fail to appreciate the eating disorder community. Recovery is a combination of physical, behavioural and psychological indicators, and this is why other pieces of information are needed besides just someone's weight. Ostensibly, one may appear 'free' of an eating disorder (based on weight), but the eating disorder may be livelier than ever. It's not uncommon to mask behaviours with other disordered eating or behavioural patterns (such as becoming hyper-focused on fitness or being preoccupied with 'clean' eating). A team at Lee Kong Chian School of Medicine found a high prevalence of ongoing eating disorder behaviours in those who identified with eating disorder recovery on social media (Goh *et al.* 2022).

Other Challenges
There are other challenges that can make recovery tricky.

Recovery can be financially costly. First, therapy can be prohibitively expensive (this includes the travel costs to and from in-person sessions). In the UK, funding eating disorder treatment (such as private day care or private therapists or dietitians) is becoming more and more common as people go private due to inundated NHS services (Gregory 2022). Unfortunately, this means that the wealthy often have better access to care.

Second, soaring food and energy prices affect outcomes. Financial stresses and strains may mean that nourishing one's body properly is relegated in importance. For example, adhering to dietitian-approved recovery meal plans may be more difficult (as part of the cost-of-living crisis in the UK, food and non-alcoholic drink inflation rose by 16.5 per cent in the 12 months to November 2022, the highest increase since 1977) (Butler 2022). Unfortunately, rising food costs may have further knock-on effects as patients may avoid restaurants – ordinarily environments where patients with OSFED, for example, may challenge themselves. Undernourished patients, often cold, also have higher energy bills, which further creates financial pressure.

Remember the game Whac-a-Mole? Adrenaline pumping, stick in hand, as you look to bash the furry mammals which pop up indiscriminately (although you soon come to your senses and realize they're actually just plastic and unnaturally fast which confirms their inanimateness). Well, unfortunately, eating disorder recovery can feel like a game of Whac-a-Mole. Upon dealing with certain issues relating to an eating disorder, other things may rise up in its place. This is natural and often part of the recovery process. For example, there may be increased issues with substance abuse, self-harm and other mental health challenges. One study found that a group considered 'fully recovered' had elevated rates of anxiety disorders (Harney *et al.* 2014).

The Book

There are many things that this book is and also quite a few things that it isn't. It's a selection of stories of different people. It's the perspective of a few brilliant people – contributors from different countries across different continents of different body size, gender, race and socioeconomic status – who have journeyed with an eating disorder and experienced the power of hope in their recovery. To properly communicate the breadth of eating disorders, and the different contexts from which they can arise, we need many different perspectives and stories. We get that here. Whether it's Dianne talking about dance, Lee talking about race, or Hope shedding some light on motherhood, this book will highlight the complex relationship many of us have with our bodies. This book also seeks to give airtime to much lesser-known eating disorders such as OSFED and ARFID – which Bailey and I think is important.

Interspersed are 'Interlude' sections which cover important topics that often closely interact with eating disorders yet are frequently overlooked when discussing them, such as neurodiversity and trauma.

At the start of each section, there will be introductory insights from world-leading eating disorder healthcare professionals. Bailey and I felt it was important to incorporate the viewpoints of the multidisciplinary team, as treatment is collaborative. When looking after patients with eating disorders, each member of the team has a different area of expertise as well as a different viewpoint of the patient. Please note that the specialty of the individual who writes the chapter introductions doesn't reflect how important that specialty is in the treatment of the particular eating disorder. For example, the introduction to the first section – binge eating disorder – is written by Jessica Wilson, a registered dietitian. Whilst dietitians are a key part of the multidisciplinary team and absolutely crucial in recovery, this isn't to say that dietitians are the most important team member in the treatment of binge eating disorder. We also include insights from family and friends, as these people are often integral to the patients' stories.

We hope that this book will entertain, educate and stimulate thought. It's meant to be comforting as well as challenging, informative as well as eye-opening. People may even see a part of their story in some of those told. A key aim of this book is to dismantle the many stereotypes that state that there are limited ways to experience an eating disorder. This is, we hope, the start of more discussions. Our wish is that this book is used in future years, even in university settings. Currently, there is very little education about eating disorders at medical school, which is why I co-founded the ed/md conference, the UK's first eating disorder conference for medical students.

Then there are the things that this book *isn't*. It's not a definitive collection of eating disorder experiences. There are so many other perspectives, and hundreds of books wouldn't be enough to encapsulate the breadth of this topic.

Nor is this book a treatment manual. Despite mentions of various treatments throughout, and contributors including different aspects of what helped them on their respective journeys, this isn't a textbook, a do-as-I-do guide or a replacement for in-person or online support. In fact, a deliberate attempt has been made to avoid treatment recommendations because, as much as there are commonalities in eating disorders, treatment isn't formulaic; rather, it is individual.

Familiar Faces

In the aftermath of George Floyd's brutal murder in 2020, American basketball supremo LeBron James and Swedish footballing legend Zlatan Ibrahimovic clashed. Ibrahimovic claimed that sportspeople should not involve themselves in political issues. But James disagreed. In an interview, James said:

> At the end of the day, I will never shut up about things that are wrong... I preach about my people and I preach about equality, social justice, racism, voter suppression, things that go on in our community because I was a part of my community at one point and saw the things that were going on, and I know what's still going on because I have a group of 300-plus kids at my school that are going through the same thing and they need a voice. I'm their voice and I use my platform to continue to shed light on everything that might be going on, not only in my community but in this country and around the world... there's

no way I would ever just stick to sports, because I understand this platform and how powerful my voice is. (ESPN 2021)

It was pretty spectacular to watch these two heavyweights of the sporting world have such a public feud, playing out for all to see. James was highlighting that familiar faces such as himself – especially in basketball, the second most-watched sport in America (Statista 2022) – are often uniquely placed for major impact. And that he would try and make this count.

In the hospitals that I have worked at, the patients have expressed delight at familiar faces being invited to share their lived experience stories – those who have been through the fiery trials of an eating disorder. The benefits this brings our patients cannot be overstated. Paula Saukko, senior lecturer in sociology at Loughborough University, said that familiar faces were 'an important conduit through which stories on eating disorders [are] conveyed, because they offer points of emotional identification' and raise public awareness of the illnesses (Saukko 2006). Each of the contributors in this book has been in the public eye, in one way or the other, and each one was eager to share parts of their story in whichever way they knew best. This is not to say that any recovery story is more important or valuable than the next.

Depth, Not Detail

Writing about eating disorders in an autobiographical way can be notoriously difficult. One of the biggest challenges is communicating the depth of illness without highlighting the detail within it. This is important for three main reasons. First, and very importantly, so the content is not triggering to those in a more vulnerable position. We have tried to make sure you always feel safe reading these accounts, whilst still including the cold, hard truths, and the many nuances, that exist within an eating disorder story. This is why we have done our best to remove triggering material. This is also why, in this book, we don't talk about specific BMIS.

Second, so the writings do not inadvertently become a manual for tips and tricks for an eating disorder to leech on to. We've consistently asked ourselves: how much detail about the eating disorder is enough to make the story real to you, but not so much that it may teach someone with an eating disorder how to harm themselves?

And third, so that the focus is in the right place – on the way *out* of the eating disorder, not the way *through* it. Real situations where people emerge victorious. So, to avoid misery porn, hope is a theme that runs throughout.

Point to Note

Bailey and I think it's important to mention that there are noticeably more essays for anorexia nervosa. This is not to say that it's more important, or indeed, more common. As already mentioned, it isn't. Far from it. This is intentional, and due to the large amount of attention it receives, there are equally many misconceptions about it, and as a result a lot of dismantling via these stories that we felt needed to happen.

Binge Eating Disorder

Diagnostic Criteria

1. Frequent, recurrent episodes of binge eating[3]
2. No regularly accompanying behaviours aimed at preventing weight gain
3. Distress about the pattern of binge eating, or impairment in functioning

(Based on ICD-11)

" Watching my brother suffer from binge eating disorder was heartbreaking. He went from being so sporty, confident and outgoing to becoming a shell of his former self; so introverted and full of self-hatred. I didn't know what was going on as he was so ashamed and embarrassed that he didn't tell anyone. It was his own secret which was gnawing away at him. I only found out what the problem was when I went into his room and found sweets stashed under the mattress, in his shoes and in his pencil case, and masses of wrappers in his overflowing bin. He thought people would hate him if they found out, but I wish he didn't believe that the amount he ate decided his worth as a person.

Petra Lancaster, a sister

---

[3] Not due to a medical condition, mental disorder or effects of a substance or medication.

Introduction

Jessica Wilson

Jessica Wilson, MS, RDN is a clinical dietitian, consultant and author. She is the co-creator of the Amplify Melanated Voices challenge that went viral in 2020. Her experiences navigating the dietetic fields as a Black, queer dietitian have been featured on public radio shows and in print media, including the *New York Times*, *Bustle* and *Cronkite News*. @jessicawilson.msrd

'It's like a warm hug,' Destiny (name changed) told me. She was a graduate student during the COVID-19 pandemic; stress and isolation in lockdown were high and joy was at an all-time low. After a long day of research, grading papers and writing her dissertation – and having only eaten a few snacks instead of meals – she would often binge during dinner. Eating until she was overly full was a sensation that she could count on; it was something reliable during a chaotic time in her life. Bingeing was one way of organizing her days and enjoying her evenings.

Western societal norms pathologize Destiny for her eating patterns. Anglo-Saxon values have continued to influence society and cloud how we view those who eat for reasons other than biological need. Our eating is supposed to be restrained and contained; the sin of gluttony is a lens through which we view others' eating habits and our own. After eating for something other than biological need, we are conditioned to feel shame and guilt. Compensatory actions like restriction and excessive exercise are normalized, and often encouraged, because of our association of bingeing with weight gain. Fatness in society has been constructed as a moral failing of the individual, and we are to prevent weight gain by all means possible.

After binge eating disorder became a diagnosable eating disorder in the *Diagnostic and Statistical Manual of Mental Disorders, Fifth Edition*, I toured eating disorder treatment centres that had built binge eating disorder recovery programmes and purchased wider, size-inclusive chairs. For many years, the field was aware – though unwilling to accept – that fat people could have anorexia nervosa. Clinicians had advocated for size-inclusive environments for all patients, but it was not until binge eating disorder was recognized that treatment centres provided inclusive seating. The eating disorder field is subject to society's perception that bingeing is linked to fatness, and prioritizes thin people in the treatment of other eating disorders.

Binge eating disorder is a diagnosis that relies heavily on the experience and lens of clinicians to assess compensatory actions. Restriction can be unintentional; it may be that someone simply cannot make time to eat during the day. Some medications inhibit appetite. Some people experience periods of time when they have access to food and a safe environment in which to eat, and times when they do not. Many people have a history of restricting food categories. Each of these scenarios creates an environment in which bingeing makes sense and is often protective. Even if bingeing serves a function of survival, it is still often distressing to clients because we live in a society that views eating large quantities of food to be the wrong way to eat. Skilled clinicians are also able to identify ways that clients are restrained and contained in other areas of their lives and how this shows up in the ways that they eat.

Destiny was able to put her experiences into context. She recognized that her eating patterns were one way to organize her days when each day blended into the next. Food was one way that she was able to experience joy. We did not pathologize her patterns so she did not hold onto shame and guilt. She felt like she had agency in her choices to eat food and knew that when it was time for her to eat in a different way, she would. And she did.

Reflections

Afftene Ceri Taylor

Afftene Ceri Taylor is an actress, speaker and writer in Atlanta, GA. Originally from Bessemer, AL, she graduated from Duke University in 2012 with a bachelor's degree in public policy studies. In her other time, she works as a UI (user interface) developer. In 2021, she gave a TEDX talk on the lack of diversity in the coverage of eating disorders which drew widespread attention. She is currently working on a book of poems, a reflection on her insights from her first year in therapy, and a horror screenplay about the generational ghosts of disordered eating. @madebyafftene

The body. Our chief identifier. A multitasking flesh machine. Our soul's home while earthside. Carrier of the mind and the heart. Bearer of pain. Feeler of pleasure. Scorekeeper of the past. An ever-present entity. Receiver of judgement. Determiner of worthiness. Ingester of that which God made. The body is both personal and political.

Let's not mince words: when a person's body is Black and female, it is born with a particular kind of history and will have a myriad of experiences that will inform the inhabitant's mind on how to respond. I came 'out' almost a year ago as a recovering binge eater on the TEDxDuke stage. It was a thoughtful discussion about the lack of diversity in the understanding of eating disorders and whom they affect. Since then, I've had time to reflect more deeply on the topic regarding what I discovered on the road to that speech, the complexities of it surrounding Black women particularly, and how it connects with my own journey.

I possess a curiosity about how the body and eating disorders interact. It can go from a tightly choreographed dance to an out-of-control boxing match in a blink. According to Maslow's hierarchy of needs, food is at the base level of a human being's needs. We literally can't do without it. So why would a person's mind choose the manipulation of food as its coping mechanism for the stressors of life? This is a question I've been wrestling with since my talk.

The truth of the matter is, I didn't get access (nor was I really open) to language regarding disordered eating until my late 20s. Just as I was coming into my own awareness, a dear friend and fellow Duke alumna reached out to me to collaborate on a potential talk regarding the subject. What culminated was a near two-year research explanation of not just eating disorders but the intersectionality of them with race and gender. As a Black woman, not only was this intellectually enlightening, it was spiritually healing as well.

I always felt I wasn't alone, but now I had evidence that I wasn't:

- research
- data
- personal testimonies
- memoirs.

They did more than pique my curiosity. They filled in the gaps. Learning that Black women, out of all the eating disorders, experience binge eating the most and that we come into an awareness of our behaviour later on in life made me feel like, 'Girl, it ain't JUST YOU!'

No shade to White girls; we hold a prayer circle for you, too. But to finally read about Black women at the centre of this topic was a healing balm. While there are many similarities between all groups of people when it comes to this disorder, Black women are unique in how they get there and how they experience treatment from society and the mental healthcare field. It gave me vocabulary and validation. I wasn't just someone who lacked willpower. I was someone who possessed a brain that had experienced trauma and was doing its best to respond to it.

In my healing journey, I've had to ask myself some pretty deep questions: Where do I go when I binge? What am I looking for? What do I want to get?

My discovery so far? The sensation of feeling full.

There is a sense of safety. It is brief, but it *is* present when I have a really full stomach. I imagine normal eaters consume until they are satisfied and drink until they get that 'Okay, I'm *done* done' feeling. But when I binge, there is a desire to compel that feeling. I don't want to wait a reasonable amount of time for 'full'. I want to force its hand to deliver that intra-abdominal pressure that I crave.

I command my body to tell me I am okay and I am without scarcity!

It's hard to admit that binge eating carries some psychological value for me, and I imagine for many other Black women.

But like many coping mechanisms, there is the slamming back to reality.

The nearly devoured bag of potato chips.

The half-eaten loaf of bread.

The empty pizza carton...next to the graveyard of chicken wing bones.

It's a sobering sight with reverberating consequences.

Because binge eating leads to excess fuel, therein comes the additional weight. And when you've been binge eating and dieting for as long as I have, there is difficulty in seeing whether you are stopping the cycle 'for real this time' or setting yourself up for the next go round.

It's a carousel in hell.

The binge eating that brought you safety and then shame in its aftermath now ushers you into the cold brutal world of fatphobia, where you will be informed in explicit and implicit ways of how your Black, female and now FAT body needs to 'go somewhere and lose some fuckin' weight'. And when life really begins to 'life', in comes the sort of bingeing that hits even harder, and out goes any semblance of a normal, balanced life.

Binge eating and all its little cousins (body image problems, social anxiety, depression, etc.) form a very complex mountain to climb. A climb that is made even tougher for Black women.

So let's tell the truth and shame the devil... If it wasn't for the fact that I was in a high-paying field, I wouldn't have the necessary (and yes, I say necessary because I don't think you can fight this battle by yourself) equipment like therapy to do the emotional and mental excavating to get to the root of my issues, and have someone lovingly hold me accountable about some of my deepest scars.

Black women and binge eating disorder – and disordered eating as a whole – represent the continuing onion-esque consequences of racism and sexism. It is the convergence of experiencing life with fewer resources and more opportunities to be harmed (both within and outside of our communities of origin). So, when Black women show up to the table, we're coming with a tanker truck full of trauma to unpack. There is the daily racial discrimination, acculturative stress, plus the epigenetic trauma of our foremothers, who often endured their own version of the same intersectional system of oppression (see trans-Atlantic slave trade, Reconstruction, Jim Crow, the crack epidemic and/or mass incarceration).

And when we show up, guess where we have to show up to? The American healthcare system which, for generations, has routinely shown its ass to how little it cares for, and about, Black women. We all know somebody who knows somebody who went in for care and felt dismissed, demeaned and disrespected by someone who was tasked to help us.

Black women remember, and do so deeply. And we pass that word to our sisters, daughters and nieces so they, too, may have a better opportunity to avoid the snares of an uncaring system.

So the idea of having a shrink poke around in our heads is new and not appetizing to most of us either. Add to that the high expense and scarcity of mental healthcare professionals that look like us. I count myself as lucky to find someone who is Black and female, but she ain't cheap. She costs me US$155 a session and isn't covered by my insurance. When a Black woman finally musters the strength (and the coin) to get the help, she will be looking for assistance among a workforce where only 5 per cent identify as Black, according to the American Psychological Association (American Psychological Association 2019).

Listen, having mental healthcare professionals of colour matters. Life is hard enough as it is without having to play professor to some well-meaning but still culturally inept clinician. Again, no shade to them. They do important work, but as for me and my vulnerability, I need someone who understands that being in this body and at this day and hour means I am contending with more than just 'beauty image issues'. I am battling internalized fatphobia, colourism, featurism and texturism plus all the 'normal' childhood trauma shit.

And if you are brave enough to engage in treatment with a non-Black clinician, will they be able to detect what the issues are? Why is it so hard for people to see the problems with Black women? The education they receive lacks diversity and nuance. Whether it's intentional or unintentional, what can be expected from a non-Black clinician when they learned everything they know from a typically non-Black professor who taught from textbooks filled with research that didn't centre Black people? That is what racism does in every sector of society. Whiteness is centred as default, and it penalizes those who can't subscribe to it with often uninformed culturally incompetent providers who possess little to no research on how mental illness presents in their specific community.

I know I am blessed to have reached the point in my recovery where I have access to a new set of coping tools and have begun to heal some deep wounds. It's been a long while since I last binged, and I don't take that for granted. But now that I know more, I am saddened that I never took into context the social, political and structural ways in which my mind was performing. I was so hard on myself. Needlessly so. And I now know that many other Black women are in that very same place. The question now is 'What are we going to do about it?'

The Evil Circle and Toxicgram

Selina Tossut

Selina Tossut is a content creator and certified nutritionist. She is currently completing her BSc in business psychology and economics. Her work of raising awareness of dangerous eating habits and sharing personal recovery tips has led to a combined Instagram and TikTok community of over 1.5 million people. @tastyselly

I told myself that 'I'll start on Monday!' literally every week. I had always wanted to live a 'perfect healthy lifestyle' with a 'perfect body' (back then, this was how I defined success. I wanted to be *that girl* so bad). And I thought a 'perfect clean diet' would help me get there. So, I told myself that this diet would start on Monday. That, on this Monday, I'd finally eat better; how I had wanted to eat for years – cutting out 'bad' food completely and only leaving room for 'good'. But Monday never seemed to arrive.

The problem: the weekend. It always happened at the weekend. The weekend was when I would lose control. As soon as the week-days were through, I binged. I used to stuff my mouth with as many 'bad' foods as I could find. All the foods that I had vowed would no longer touch my lips, I binged on at the weekend. And I'm not talking about letting down your hair after an intense week. These episodes were different. Long, uncontrolled, emotion-filled, hazy, trance-like bingeing fests. From the moment I allowed myself to eat something 'bad', it would snowball, and I wouldn't be able to stop. Even though my stomach fired off pain signals, my brain didn't compute, and I continued to eat and eat and eat. Sometimes, if I was in the company of others, the urges meant finishing everything that was on the table, and most of the time this meant mopping up my friends' and family's leftovers. It got to a point where I started to be scared of Saturday nights out and my vacations (I would binge on holiday too) because I knew that it was in these moments that I would totally lose control.

For my *grand plan* – you know, the one that always threatened to start on a Monday but never did – I had spent a lot of time researching the 'best' and 'healthiest' ways of eating. This became a priority for me. It became a thing of me scouring the Internet for the most 'weird and wonderful' diets that I could find. Every month, I'd look up some more. At the time, I thought it was just a hobby – 'you know, I just find nutrition interesting' – but, on reflection, it was definitely more than that and became a bit of an obsession if I'm being completely honest. I was stuck in a bingeing cycle, and was dreaming of the day that I would be able to get out of it. Food was on my mind 24 hours a day, seven days a week. I had such an unhealthy relationship with food, but nobody knew. Probably because I was your average weight.

Back then, school and society gave us a clear picture of what someone with an eating disorder looked like: someone skinny or someone fat. Those were the options. That's what I got taught. Skinny or fat. No average. No shades of grey. No in-betweens. No outrageous ideas that eating disorders are mental health conditions that reflect differently on different bodies depending on the person and their background. It was nice and straightforward: skinny or fat, without there being much attention to the reasons for it, apart from the fact that you apparently either ate too little or ate too much.

It's only now that I recognize how dangerous this sort of 'education' is, and how this sort of narrative may (in part) be responsible for some people living with eating disorders – often, for their whole life – without even realizing. I never looked classically 'sick' or 'unhealthy'. Not once. My external body fell within socially acceptable limits, in spite of my bingeing. But an intense sickness was going on in my head. And, till today, I'm extra cautious to take care of it.

But, like I said, growing up, I had always wanted to live a 'perfect healthy lifestyle' with a 'perfect body'. As part of all of this, I thought about my weight constantly. It meant everything. That's why I weighed myself every day. The dream of being a skinny teenager played on repeat. I was so preoccupied with my weight and thought that I would be happier, and feel much prettier, after losing a few pounds. These thoughts intensified when the bingeing intensified. I got to the point where I struggled to distinguish between fact and fiction. Everyone saw one thing, and my mind told me that I looked entirely different.

Every time I looked in the mirror, I absolutely hated what I saw and I blamed myself week after week after week. 'Stop bingeing!' I told myself. 'Stick to a normal eating plan!' and 'Hurry up and start your diet already!' Looking back, the obsession with my body – and dislike of it – took away from my teenage years. My efforts to always try to look 'my best' cost me time and happiness.

And I'm really annoyed about it.

I resent the fact that I caved to the culture of dieting and the pressure from society when it came to beauty standards; things that I absolutely despise now. And I get so sad thinking that even today there are so many teens, and young adults, blaming and hating themselves for not reaching these artificial beauty standards; many pressured into Photoshop and plastic surgery. But diet culture does this, right? It takes advantage and makes a lot of money off people being dissatisfied with how they are – much like I was.

I remember social media, back then, taking the societal pressure – which had been around for decades – and amplifying it to a whole new level. Pressure which was, and still is, pretty hard to escape. In my case, Instagram caused the most damage. If it wasn't Instagram though, I'm sure it would've been something else. I virtually grew up on this platform. I spent hours a day on it as a teen. Remember the whole influencer era that began around 2014/2015? Remember when every girl wanted to look oh-so 'perfect' and thin? Yeah, I was one of those girls. A non-stop diet of comparison with people apparently without any insecurities or blemishes. Crazy thing is that even when I grew up, had taken off the rose-coloured glasses and came to know that these pictures were often heavily photoshopped, taken using flattering camera angles and bathed in synthetic lighting, I still compared my real, living and in-person body with pixels on a screen. I cried *so* often. It really caused my eating disorder to escalate.

I opened up to my boyfriend, friends and family, about how I was starting to see my body. I avoided looking in mirrors or looking at pictures. I hated if someone took candid photos of me, always worrying if it was taken from a 'bad' angle. I photoshopped most of my photos. No picture of me was ever good enough not to get edited because I *needed* to look a certain way on my Instagram feed. I had body dysmorphia: a mental health condition where you spend a lot of time worrying about perceived flaws. In my case, this meant seeing my body as bigger than it actually was. I don't think people talk about body dysmorphia enough and how it can trigger maladaptive coping mechanisms such as binge eating. When I'm thinking about my recovery, I definitely think of *this* as being the most difficult part to overcome. It took me a very long time to realize that I'm beautiful no matter what the number on the scale says; that my weight doesn't define me; that I have so much more to give than just my body.

Nobody should experience what I went through, and especially not in those innocent young years of a human life. This was one of the reasons why I started sharing my experiences online. Recovering from binge eating disorder, or any other eating disorder, can be really hard, and it really does take some time to break certain rules you've created for yourself in your head. Some things that helped me included:

- taking some time off from social media and unfollowing all the people who made me feel bad about myself
- not categorizing food into 'good' or 'bad' and allowing myself access to all food groups
- educating myself in nutrition
- discussing my feelings and emotions by journalling
- finding ways to reduce my stress levels such as meditation, yoga, going for a walk, reading a good book, and taking a bath.

Of course, every person is different and what helped me might not necessarily help someone else. But the first step is being *conscious* of something. Then, the next step is the *willingness* to change that something. I also highly recommend reaching out to a professional, because nobody should be ashamed to ask for help.

Getting back to 'normal' eating habits with a healthy relationship with food is a process and different for everyone, but it's totally worth it. We only have this life, and life is definitely too short to worry about food!

Never Heard of That

Ryan Sheldon

Ryan Sheldon is a speaker, Brawn model, eating disorder activist and self-love advocate. He has been featured on NBC's *Today*, *Huffington Post* and *Teen Vogue*. He regularly speaks to young adults about masculinity, identity and body confidence. @realryansheldon

'You look too fat.'

'You're a growing boy.'

'You're not good enough.'

'You look ugly today.'

'If you don't eat that, maybe you'll be more popular 'cause you'll look thinner.'

These were things that the little, yet loud, voices in my head were telling me for the majority of my life, only to be reaffirmed by other people's comments.

To paint the picture for you: I'm a 34-year-old White, gay, cis man, and it took me 32 years to finally start allowing myself to love me for me. To love myself for who I truly am. Now, the question is, why did it take so long?

Growing up, I had a pretty 'typical' household arrangement. I was raised by a single mum, and I had one sister. We all got along fine – minus my dad. But I always felt like I was different. When I was eight, I vividly remember going to my neighbourhood swimming pool wearing a t-shirt because I was too ashamed of my body. An anxious feeling overwhelmed me. I thought that I would be shunned from the vicinity if people knew what I looked like underneath the thin fabric. I thought, 'Yes, then they'll certainly kick me out.' I often look back and think how, by the age of eight, had I already reached the point of hating my body? So much so that the thought of having it on show terrified me. And, by the way, I'm not just being melodramatic by using the word 'hate'. That's exactly how I felt. I truly hated my body and wanted to do whatever I could to get out of it.

Was it the media's fault? Did the bodies portrayed define a 'masculinity' which I thought I could never achieve (even at that early age)? Were they highlighting certain men as the definition of attractive? Yes, maybe that was triggering these thoughts. Or yet still, maybe it was being told repeatedly at a young age, 'You don't want to get fat, so don't eat that'? I'm not sure. It probably had a bit to do with all of these things.

❊ ❊ ❊

I was put on my first diet at the age of 12. I was taken to Weight Watchers and was rewarded with 'prizes' every week that I lost weight. Being fat was a bad thing. And that warped thinking was ingrained in me from a young age. Like a lot of people who struggle with an eating disorder, my weight fluctuated. In high school, I was tortured for the size I was, for the acne on my skin and for my perceived sexuality (wow, it makes me cringe just thinking about it). One time, some kid poured superglue in my hair while I was giving a presentation in class. This asshole poured *superglue* in my hair. Needless to say, I had to get my head shaved.

I hit my first rock bottom in high school. I don't often share this with people because it's not something I like to think about, but I started having suicidal thoughts. To me, my life was *that* bad. And I didn't know how to get out of it. I was bullied by people at school. I reached the point where I felt I would be happier if I just wasn't around any more.

Eventually, I decided to confide in my mum. She felt awful, and the next day she marched into my school and pulled me out. From that moment on, I got homeschooled. To be honest, this was probably one of the best things that ever happened to me.

※ ※ ※

I never thought I'd be 'popular'. But that's exactly what I was at college. It was weird. I couldn't tell you how it got to that point to be honest, but it did. Despite this, the negative thoughts I had about my body grew louder and louder. I went years without thinking about my body and then, seemingly out of nowhere, it was all I could think about. I lost weight whilst at college and was feeling on top of the world. I was the thinnest I'd ever been, and for me, that was all that mattered. Not good enough for my eventual partner, though. I got into a relationship with someone who had a diagnosed eating disorder (bear in mind I wasn't diagnosed at this point). Throughout the entire relationship, I was body shamed.

'Ryan, why don't you have abs?'

'Ryan, if you really want to be my partner, then you must look your best because you're representing me. Please lose weight.'

The digs cut deeper and deeper as time went on. Eventually, that relationship ended, and I was a shell of the man I once was – literally. I didn't know what my purpose was, and I felt like absolute shit. I found myself reverting back to my old ways of bingeing. I was spiralling and unsure of what to do.

❖ ❖ ❖

'Ryan, are you OK?' I remember feeling pretty confused as to why my friend, who had accompanied me to a drive-thru that day, was asking me that. 'Yeah...why?' I retorted.

'Oh, nothing'. She paused, but I waited, anticipating more to come by her body language. 'Ryan, you realize you just spent 70 dollars at a fast-food restaurant?'

This was totally normal for me, so I wasn't bothered by it. But it was at this point that my friend continued, opening up about how she thought I'd had abnormal thoughts about food, calories and my body for a while (clearly, I had been talking about these things more than I had even realized). She then asked if I had ever heard of binge eating disorder. No, I hadn't. But I immediately looked it up.

In an instant, everything made sense. I'd been going to therapy for about six years by this point, and never once did my eating habits, or my feelings about my body, ever get brought up by my therapist. Despite him knowing that I had issues with my eating, nothing was mentioned. Because there was nothing normal about it. And there was definitely nothing normal about finding myself in stacks of financial debt because of it.

I did my research and then, in our next session, told my therapist squarely that I thought I had binge eating disorder. His initial response was 'I've never heard of that.' But then he did a bit of research himself and went on to diagnose me. It was such a relief. There was now a name, a framework, for what I had been experiencing. It's fair to say that I thought the diagnosis was the cure. No one told me what to do *after* the diagnosis. So I went on, living my 'normal' life.

I often think back and question why my therapist – who I really liked actually and got on with a great deal – never talked about my thoughts on food, or my body, *especially* given that I brought it up so often. Was it because I'm a guy? I don't know – maybe he thought that guys aren't supposed to have problems with eating? Hmm...or maybe it was because doctors already have so much to screen for – for insurance reasons – and this just wasn't high enough up on his list of priorities?

❆ ❆ ❆

My second rock bottom was when a guy I was dating dumped me. He left me for a guy who had that cultural 'ideal' body. You know, the one with the six-pack. I'm not going to lie; this rocked my world. I immediately went to that place of 'I'm not good enough' and 'maybe if I had a six-pack, then I wouldn't have been left for someone who did'. Needless to say, my eating disorder took a turn for the worse and I started taking on characteristics of another one entirely. I was crushed and felt lost. Worthless. I'll never forget sitting on my cold bathroom floor, staring at the toilet. Never in my life had I looked at a toilet in this way. I resisted the urge to empty out what lay in my stomach, and immediately called my therapist.

❆ ❆ ❆

I've been in recovery from my eating disorder for a few years now. And I sometimes have doubts as to whether I'll ever be fully recovered. In fact, to be totally honest with you, the thought of being 100 per cent free from it scares me a bit. My eating disorder is a huge part of my identity, and I don't know who I'll be without it. But I'm intrigued to find out. I'm pretty darn proud of everything that I've accomplished so far (not forgetting that along the way, I've had the help of some extraordinary people, including my therapist). This has led to me being able to do things I never thought in a million years that I'd have been able to. I've shared my story on national radio, television, on podcasts, at live events and in articles. Recently, I signed a modelling contract for a 'plus size male model'. It blows my mind. To be making money off of something that I hated for such a long time – my body – seriously blows my mind.

Modelling's an interesting one, though. I think it's fair to say that I initially got into it for the validation. But it didn't take me long to realize that being a model probably isn't the right choice for that. I'll never forget getting flown overseas to do a shoot – one of my biggest ones to date. And, of course, I was the only guy on the set with no abs (I've since gotten used to this). I left the set and called my mum, crying, 'Why am I here? Why do they want me? Am I the token fat guy?' My negative associations with the word 'fat' resurfaced. I struggled with this for a long time, re-evaluating my career choice on several occasions. 'Seriously, is this something I want to do?' I thought. By choosing modelling, I thought I was celebrating my body, but it turned out I was shining the world's brightest light on my biggest insecurities.

When COVID-19 happened, and all shoots were put off for about 18 months, this was such a relief for me. It gave me the time I didn't know I needed to start working on the feelings I had about my body, on a much deeper level. Time out to think, reflect. The sort of time that is precious nowadays, and we barely get any of it. Then the wildest thing happened. When things started opening back up, I booked a huge campaign. I was going to be on all the packaging of Hanes underwear worldwide! *What?!* I remember thinking that they had made a mistake. Me? It couldn't be. Me? The big guy. The thought of me standing around in nothing more than briefs was absolutely terrifying. The reality of the shoot, though, in the end, was so much better. It felt liberating.

Sharing my story has been so incredibly healing for me. I realized that, for such a long time, I put all my worth in my appearance. No matter how much success I had. Any success, in whatever it was that I was doing, would *always* be overshadowed by the way I felt about my body. I also share my story because when I was struggling, there wasn't really anyone out there who was sharing theirs – especially not any men that I could think of. Men need to know that they're not alone. There are millions of men out there, literally, who are grappling with an eating disorder. They also need to know that recovery is possible. Now, I'm not sure what that'll look like for them, but it's there. And it's important to trust the journey. Sometimes, a one-step-forward-and-two-steps-back situation doesn't mean that you're wrong or broken. There's no right way. There's just *your* way. Let's break down mental health stigma by sharing our stories.

Healing Wish

Bobby Kasmire

Bobby Kasmire is a college student and content creator. He shares his past and ongoing experiences of eating disorder recovery on social media to help break the stigma amongst males and eating disorders. He shares his most helpful ideas, tactics and thoughts on finding a better relationship with food with a community of over 280,000 followers across TikTok and Instagram. @bobbykazz

I wouldn't wish it on anyone. Everything about it. It starts with the urge that arises when you least expect it, like an itch that just can't go unscratched. The pacing back and forth across the kitchen, opening and closing the pantry and fridge every other minute, debating if you should follow through with the pounding impulse to eat everything in sight. Giving in to that pressure you've been feeling and trying to fight off for several minutes, you tell yourself that this WILL be the last time. This helps you justify eating peanut butter by the spoonful, directly from the tub, with no idea how to stop. Ten more minutes go by. On coming to your senses, you look around, gazing at your surroundings. Wrappers upon wrappers all over the place – the table, the floor – along with a gallon of ice cream, loaf of bread, sleeve of cookies and a jar of Nutella. All gone. The guilt and shame immediately set in, and you begin to ask yourself why you, of all people, are going through this. You feel as though you don't have an ounce of discipline. Repeatedly telling yourself that 'this is the last time' and that 'the diet starts tomorrow' is the only way to make yourself feel better in the moment, even though deep down you know this probably wasn't going to be the last time and that in not too long you'll find yourself taking out several trash bags in order to hide the evidence of what you just did, again.

For a long time, this was me. I felt as though this vicious entrapment of bingeing was going to be my lifelong reality. That cleaning out the fridge in a matter of minutes would never stop. And that the monumental shame, embarrassment and guilt I felt during these binges would continue indefinitely. I legitimately thought that there was no way out, and assumed that, for the rest of my life, I was going to be either thinking about binge eating, bingeing or feeling agitated about a binge I just had.

The idea that you simply *can't* stop eating is ludicrous to many. And to be honest, there have been plenty of instances where I've thought the same. Even *I* couldn't believe that I was going through it sometimes. I still remember my last binge. I remember exactly what I ate. Basically, because, at the time, I was so taken aback by everything I had just consumed that I wrote it all down on the notes app on my phone. I titled it 'Rock Fucking Bottom'. That binge was absolutely the lowest point of my life. But looking back now, I'm glad that day, and that binge, happened. Because I *finally* recognized how low I felt and knew that this couldn't go on any longer. It ended up being the day I chose recovery, again. It wasn't the first time I had chosen recovery. My prior attempts of 'recovery' included me restricting my binge foods, exercising until I physically couldn't any more, blowing off social events with friends and falling behind in my classes. So, not real recovery *really*. That was me lying to myself because I was too scared to *actually* recover. Bingeing was a coping mechanism, and I was too afraid to give it up. So masking recovery, with more unhealthy habits, felt easier – which only made my bingeing worse. When I hit 'Rock Fucking Bottom', though, I felt in my soul this time that things were going to be different. I felt that it was time to put binge eating in my past, and thought that 'this WILL be the last time'.

It's been months since I last binged, and I say that not to boast or brag, but to show that recovery and healing are fully and completely possible. But although they're absolutely possible, and I'm living proof of this, for most people (including myself) the process is extremely difficult and time-consuming, whether you decide to go into treatment or not. Everyone's recovery process looks different. For me, a few things got me to the point I am now, where I can wake up, go about my day, and the thought of binge eating doesn't even cross my mind for a single second.

I think that coming to terms with the fact that you're not alone is the first step. You really aren't. There are literally millions of others in a similar position, many of whom are undiagnosed. For a while, I felt like I was alone. Feeling like you're the only one in the world, whilst going through anything in life, can feel crippling – let alone having binge eating disorder. It felt so isolating. The number of special occasions and social events that I intentionally skipped just because I was afraid of how I would react to certain foods being on show – only to end up bingeing on them by myself later alone anyway – are countless. In the moment, you feel too anxious and scared to tell anyone because you're unsure how they'll take it. Then, the thought of their *actual* reaction – after the news has properly sunk in – is a thing of nightmares. But it's never as bad as we think it's going to be, is it? As daunting as it may seem, telling just one person eases some tension. In my case, a heck of a lot of tension. This was a huge step in my recovery, and I'm beyond thankful that I had someone who I knew I could tell anything to without feeling judged. I think we all need someone like that in our lives. If you already do, take advantage of it. If you don't, I would say find someone, but I know it's not that easy. A bit of a privilege, really. Telling someone about my binge eating struggles felt like a giant weight was lifted off my shoulders. It felt uneasy yet amazing to let another human being into this closed-off section of my life. Because nothing happened. I had built in my mind all the bad stuff that would happen – after I had told someone my deepest, darkest secret – but it never did. Nothing bad happened. Not just that, but it ended up being a bit like the wardrobe in Narnia: it opened the door to the rest of my recovery. It was almost as if telling someone was a kick-start for the remaining process of healing. I don't think I would be where I am today if I didn't tell a loved one of my struggles. It's a blessing to have someone whom you can trust with your life. Someone who won't judge you on the words that come out of your mouth. When you come to the realization that you truly aren't alone after all, that's special.

When I became serious about recovery, I recognized my past flawed attempts at healing. I figured the next step towards recovery was eliminating all moral value on food and granting myself unlimited access to any food, at any time. This logic may sound crazy. Why would you allow yourself to eat any food you want at any time? Wouldn't that just lead to a binge? Well, it turns out, when you let your brain know that it doesn't have to avoid or restrict certain foods because they're too 'bad' for you, the craving for those foods can eventually tone down. When you view food as simply *food*, it can become neutral. You view an apple as just an apple, and a slice of cake as just a slice of cake. That's it. That's all they are. Nothing more and nothing less. This really helped me overcome.

But dealing with the *urge* to binge was easily my biggest challenge. It's a pretty crazy concept when you think about it. Just going about your day and all of a sudden you receive this signal to go raid. First stop, fridge. Second, pantry. For the longest of times, I would almost instantaneously concede defeat. No second thoughts given. Never once stopped to break down and analyse *why* I felt this way. So, pretty early on, I recognized that somehow, in order to stop binge eating, I was going to have to quiet this urge. Choosing to recover was good, but the urges weren't going to just magically go away because I chose to recover. I like to think I'm an optimist, but that's wishful thinking. I was going to have to figure out a way to stop, by fighting this urge.

So I got creative using technology. Every time I felt the earliest sensations of an urge, I pulled out my phone, opened the camera app and hit record. You can probably tell: I like my apps. I propped my phone up, recorded myself going through the urge and told myself that I wouldn't hit the stop button until I figured out why I was having this urge, and until the urge had passed. At first, it was hard. And the recordings were long. Very long. I was so used to bingeing the second I felt the urge, and the camera would still be rolling. But over time it got easier, and I began to understand what was causing these urges. Was I stressed? Having a bad day? Did something happen at school or work? Personal life? The more I began to *think* about the root cause of the urges, the more time went on, the urges dulled. I continued with this tactic until I felt I didn't need to any more.

Binge eating disorder is something I truly wouldn't wish on anyone. But the amount of personal growth I've encountered along the way has been transformative. I feel a better person, and a better human, because of it. So, in a weird way, I'm not too unhappy I went through it. Hitting the lowest of lows and feeling like there was no way out, to now being in a place where I can comfortably and openly discuss my history and journey just further proves the feasibility of healing.

Now, to those of you on the rocky road (pun intended):

1. Recovery is a day-by-day process.
   Chances are it won't happen overnight – it's a long and gruelling process, but it's so worth it.

2. Always make sure to celebrate the little victories along the way.
   If you made it just one day without binge eating, that's incredible, and you should be proud of that. Then, one day turns into two, two days turn into a week, a week into a month, then a year, and so on.

3. Celebrate each day in recovery – the good *and* the bad.

Yes, there WILL be bad days, and potentially whole relapse PERIODS. But it's so important not to dwell on those. You're getting somewhere.

4. Have compassion on yourself when you notice a slip-up, or even a relapse.

It's okay and you'll be okay. As long as you're striving to improve, on your healing journey, you're doing everything you need to be doing.

Healing is possible.

Dismantling Stereotypes

Dr Chuks

When I was applying for university accommodation, I had one non-negotiable: to have my own bathroom. I know, I know, I didn't *need* it. But I had heard enough nightmare stories from my older sister from her time at university that I knew to play it safe. In the end, it was relatively easy for me to get – thankfully. I had to compromise a bit on location, though, away from the buzz and much-desired areas of hectic student energy, but not having to contend with others' shower grime, to me, felt well worth it. Also, it turns out that being able to go straight to sleep at night without having to worry about sirens ringing at 3 a.m. because someone in a drunken state pulled the fire alarm as a joke (which was apparently a regular occurrence at some other people's accommodation) was an additional, unexpected gain.

I had another non-negotiable when I was looking for a house in third year: to always live with one girl. The stereotype of girls being cleaner than boys was sensationally upheld during my first and second years, and from that point on, I told myself that I would always live with one girl. Never just a house with 'the lads'. And this would work in two ways: first, the girl would generally not make much mess. This was assuming we picked the right girl; I knew girls at the time who definitely didn't fit the clean stereotype. And second, the boys would make less mess. Because the girl would be there, and they wouldn't want to look like slobs or annoy her (more so the latter).

Anyway, at least that was my thought process at the time – as warped as I now realize, in retrospect, it may have been.

Two other guys and I found an absolute bargain of a five-bed in Withington, South Manchester. My good friend Yvonne had already said yes too, which was great. But my at-least-one-girl theory wasn't fully thought through, as I didn't consider that Yvonne might not want to live in a house with just boys – which she didn't. So the last spot had to be filled by another girl. And it was a painstaking process finding someone, in all honesty. So when Jasmine said 'yes', which finally completed the numbers, I was ecstatic.

'Oh my goodness, you're thinking of living with her?! Do. Not. Live with her.' Someone I knew was talking about Jasmine. He went on to say that Jasmine 'would be a nightmare to live with' because she had an eating disorder. It was something about the speed and frantic tone with which he said it that made me put my antennae up, and, naturally, my brain catastrophized. He seemed well informed on eating disorders. But then I remembered someone jokingly telling me that adolescents have a brain defect which renders them completely incapable of thinking of anyone apart from themselves, and I briefly thought that maybe my friend who was telling me this was suffering from this affliction. Thoughts crossed my mind that Jasmine may be perfectly pleasant to live with. But those thoughts didn't last very long, and I ended up turning down her offer. I decided against living with her despite her being eager to live with us, and we ended up having to find a different girl to live with. (Funnily enough, my at-least-one-girl theory actually worked out really well in the end, though. But not for the reasons I had presumed; it turns out that one of the *boys* in our house was incredibly clean and whipped us all into shape. I've since learnt that gender stereotypes are garbage. Well, you do go to university to learn, right?!)

But, all jokes aside, Jasmine was on the receiving end of some serious stigma because of her eating disorder. And I still feel bad about it. Unfortunately, stigma when it comes to mental illness is endemic.

This is made worse by misinformation fed by stereotypes; simply put, stereotypes are a fuel for stigma.

I remember my first few weeks working as an inpatient doctor in eating disorders largely involving me undoing inaccurate information I had accumulated over the years. Social media, TV and film were just some of the reasons I had formed so many misplaced stereotypes about eating disorders. Eating disorders are not restricted to any demographic – age, gender, size, race or wealth.

Age

The first time I came across the term SEED (severe and enduring eating disorder) was when we admitted a 64-year-old female to our inpatient unit (the term SEED is given to those who have had an eating disorder for a long time and have had many unsuccessful treatment attempts). In an instant, all my preconceived notions of how old a patient with an eating disorder should be were shattered.

The most common age of onset of an eating disorder is between the ages of 12 and 25 (Johns Hopkins Medicine 2023). In particular, the median age of onset for other specified feeding or eating disorder (OSFED), bulimia nervosa and anorexia nervosa is 18 years old, the median age of onset for binge eating disorder is 21 years old, whilst children as young as two years old may be diagnosed with avoidant/restrictive food intake disorder (ARFID) (ARFID Awareness UK 2023). As a result, eating disorders are typically seen as afflicting only the young. But they can occur at any age. Anyone, of any age, can develop an eating disorder. Some develop an eating disorder for the first time when young, and of these, many recover. But some remain chronically unwell for years. Others develop an eating disorder for the first time when middle-aged or much older. Recent studies showed that up to 3.8 per cent of women over the age of 60 had signs of an eating disorder (Mangweth-Matzek et al. 2006; Gadalla 2008).

A recent article highlighted the steady increase in eating disorders in over-50s, stating that a rise in pressure to look younger and social media-induced expectations to emulate 'glamorous' older stars are partly to blame (Cassidy 2008). There are, of course, other reasons for the rise in illness. To allay the natural biological changes that the body goes through with age (especially in mid-adulthood), and as a way to regain control, it is not uncommon for older individuals to put their bodies through extreme dieting, which can place one at an increased risk of an eating disorder. Also, with the process of ageing, there is often an expectation that people eventually give up control over very basic aspects of their lives, such as driving, or living independently where food choices are often their own. Such losses may result in eating disorder behaviours as a way of coping.

The narrative that eating disorders only exist in younger people is dangerous, because often eating disorder symptoms in older people are assumed to be due to other causes and eating disorders can be missed as a result. For example, malnutrition, diarrhoea, vomiting, painful joints and hair loss may be interpreted as just part of the normal ageing process when, in reality, they could very well be the side-effects of an eating disorder. Unfortunately, older adults are often very skilled at masking their illness when compared to younger people.

Gender

In 1911, legendary American writer and poet Ambrose Bierce observed the discrepancy in societal expectations of gender, remarking, 'A man is but a mind. Who cares what face he carries or what he wears? But woman's body is the woman' (Bierce 1911). Depressingly, more than a century later, Bierce's statement about women doesn't sound too misplaced when considering today's sociocultural demands which still seem to place the external appearance of a woman as the cornerstone of her individuality. Anita Johnston, founder of Hawaii's premier eating disorder treatment centre, argued that it's impossible to understand eating disorders without 'questioning the experience of being female in our society today' (Johnston 2013).

But Bierce's statement also fails to acknowledge the relationship *men* have with their bodies. It reinforces the stereotype that such issues don't exist. But we know that they do. One in four people struggling with an eating disorder is male (Sweeting *et al.* 2015). This may, of course, be a huge underestimation because men are often ignorant of the extent of their problems, or choose not to come forward despite having identified that they have a problem.

In February 2021, American clothing brand Tommy Hilfiger and British body activist Jameela Jamil launched an Exploring Body Neutrality and Body Image online course, with both women *and* men signing up. Body dissatisfaction amongst men has been increasing over the years, which has led to a variety of outcomes, including heightened body image concerns, compulsive exercise and increased rates of eating disorders (Talbot, Smith and Cass 2019). Unfortunately, men are typically underdiagnosed and undertreated (Strother *et al.* 2012).

The underdetection of eating disorders in men could be due to the fact that the context of the male presentation is often different. For example, men frequently have a history of being larger-bodied before developing an eating disorder, whereas this isn't the case with most women with eating disorders (Andersen 1999). Males with anorexia nervosa, for example, are 'more likely to be preoccupied with being insufficiently muscular or lean and, in response, may exhibit unusual eating behaviors (e.g. excessive protein consumption along with caloric restriction)' as opposed to striving for thinness, which is often the case in females (Blouin and Goldfield 1994). Males with binge eating disorder are more likely to struggle with substance abuse when compared to females, and oftentimes substance abuse masks the eating disorder issues. We also know that men are less likely to report sexual abuse, childhood bullying, depression and shame, which can be drivers for eating disorder activity (Costin 2007). Eric Strother,

Arizona-based eating disorder programme coordinator, said that 'eating disorders are significantly different in men and women, providing evidence that there is a need to develop a valid and reliable eating disorder assessment tool specifically for men' (Stanford and Lemberg 2012).

Then there's a gap between the men identified as having an eating disorder and those seeking treatment. We know that at least half of men with eating disorders don't seek treatment for it (Salmon 2023). David Wheeler, football player for Wycombe Wanderers FC, revealed to BBC Sport that he has seen 'numerous' team-mates suffering from eating disorders and described a 'culture of silence' which prevented them from seeking help (Nassoori 2022).

There is much to be learnt about men and the drivers behind poor uptake in treatment. Unfortunately, at present, very little research centred around eating disorders studies men. It's important that men aren't left in the cold and without care. It's also important that when they *do* arrive at services, they aren't mismanaged or confronted by an ill-prepared, gender-biased service. It's important that the stigma and stereotypes, which we know form part of the reasons why men don't seek care, are minimized.

Such stigma and stereotyping are also experienced by the lesbian, gay, bisexual, transgender, queer or questioning, intersex and asexual (LGBTQIA+) community, a community disproportionately affected by eating disorders. Research suggests that gay men are seven times more likely to report binge eating and twelve times more likely to report purging than heterosexual men (NEDA 2018). This is whilst 32 per cent of transgender people report having used their eating disorder to modify their body without hormones (Duffy, Henkel and Earnshaw 2016).

Size

In 2018, Australian model Robyn Lawley launched a boycott against

Victoria's Secret. The American beauty retailer, famous for its annual fashion show with supermodels, was called out for its lack of body diversity. Lawley said, 'Victoria's Secret has dominated the space for almost 30 years by telling women there is only one kind of body beautiful' (Lawley 2018). In 2023, Victoria's Secret announced that its fashion show – which had been on a hiatus since 2019 – was finally back, but this time with a mix of body types. This was seen as a welcome, albeit overdue change by those in larger bodies.

We often forget that the vast majority of people with eating disorders are larger-bodied. Indeed, a larger body size is a risk factor for developing an eating disorder (Barakat *et al.* 2023). It's also a common outcome for those with bulimia nervosa and binge eating disorder. Less than 6 per cent of people with eating disorders are medically diagnosed as being underweight (Flament *et al.* 2015). But, for some reason, people in larger bodies are half as likely as those with a 'normal' weight or who are 'underweight' to be diagnosed with an eating disorder (Nagata *et al.* 2018). American writer Roxane Gay stated that 'the bigger you are, the less you are seen', and explores this in her best-selling book, *Hunger* (London Review Bookshop 2018).

Many larger-bodied people have internalized the narrative that an eating disorder is a 'skinny illness' and thus do not seek help soon enough. However, many have presented, and continue to present, in a timely manner to the health service only to be turned away due to not being a low enough weight, despite showing clear signs of an eating disorder. Instead, their symptoms are often attributed to a mood disorder, or an ethnocultural 'norm'. I've received several reports of patients being sent away with only a BMI calculation, without any validation, enquiry or follow-up. Unfortunately, this results in the patients re-presenting later, by which point the symptoms and cognitions may have intensified, with there being greater bodily compromise too. Worse, there are reports of patients with atypical anorexia nervosa (all the symptoms of anorexia nervosa apart from not being underweight) being told by clinicians to *lose* weight. This is poor care and unacceptable on many levels.

There is a case to be had that this is partly due to a lack of clinician knowledge, as very little time is spent on eating disorder education in most medical schools. This is why I co-founded ed/md – the UK's first eating disorder conference for medical students. But it's also partly symptomatic of a broken system; one that has arbitrary cut-off points and in which funded care is siloed, instead of keeping the patient the focus of attention.

Race

Back in 2021, I tweeted, 'we need way, way, way more Black doctors in eating disorders' (Nwuba 2021). Someone then replied, 'And male I think!' While I applaud this comment (because it's true, we need a lot more male clinicians in eating disorders), this is typical of my experience in the eating disorder field; people seem quick to move the conversation away from issues of race. And as a field, we still seem massively uncomfortable talking about it.

In my years working in this field, I've only treated a handful of patients from minority ethnic groups – which is sad. Not because I have a particularly strong desire to treat members of these communities, but because evidence suggests that there are significant numbers from minority ethnic groups who would benefit from medical support. Which means that there must be many who are suffering in silence. Most of my eating disorder colleagues that I've spoken to also highlight a lack of minority ethnic patients amongst their respective caseloads. This is despite the NHS reporting a sharp increase in morbidity in these patients. For example, between 2017 and 2020, there was a 216 per cent rise in the number of Black people being admitted to hospital due to eating disorders, and 53 per cent among all minority ethnic groups (Thomas 2020). From evidence, we know that Black teenagers are 50 per cent more likely than White teenagers to exhibit eating disorder behaviours, such as binge eating and purging; we know that when Black people have anorexia nervosa, they may experience the condition for a longer period of time than non-Black people (Taylor *et al.* 2007); and we also know that Hispanic/Latino people are much more likely to suffer from bulimia nervosa than non-Hispanic/Latino people (Swanson *et al.* 2011). In a recent study, Asian American college students reported higher rates of restriction compared with their White peers (Uri *et al.* 2021).

Regrettably, clinicians still struggle to identify symptoms of an eating disorder in minority ethnic groups. Such groups are half as likely to be diagnosed or receive treatment (Deloitte Access Economics 2020). Often doctors fail to ask about eating disorder symptoms because assumptions are made about the patient based on their skin colour (e.g. the 'strong Black woman' stereotype has led to clinicians overlooking serious mental illness in Black women) (Kupemba 2021). Work led by Kathryn Gordon, Massachusetts-based clinical psychologist and author of *The Suicidal Thoughts Workbook*, highlighted that clinicians were more able to recognize an eating disorder in White patients than Black patients (Gordon, Perez and Joiner 2002). I believe that society's stereotypification and objectification of the Black body has left those with eating disorders either misdiagnosed or not diagnosed at all. Los Angeles-based family therapist Myeisha Brooks puts this down to society 'not acknowledging how systemic racism, overt/covert racism and all the forms of racism' play their part (Kupemba 2021).

Black women are less likely than White women to express discontent with their body shape and more likely to minimize their problems, but this is partly through fear of not being taken as seriously as their White counterparts and due to stigma (Sparrow 2019). Speaking about mental health issues is still heavily stigmatized in many minority ethnic communities. When it comes to eating disorders, it's almost as though there's perceived cultural incompatibility and immunity to developing one. Eating disorders are rarely talked about, and when they are, it's not uncommon to be met with an inappropriate response from either family or friends. Also, in some cultures, certain eating disorder behaviours (such as binge eating) are traditionally celebrated.

Two friends of mine, Johnny and Teresa, both consider their eating disorders as things of the past, but briefly answered a few questions I had of their experiences. Excerpts of the discussions are below. Johnny, 25, is a second-generation Black British male of East African heritage, who recovered from undiagnosed anorexia nervosa, and Teresa, 29, is a Black female from West Africa who recovered from undiagnosed bulimia nervosa.

Q: *When did your eating disorder start?*

Johnny: First, I should preface with the fact that I didn't recognize my experience as being disordered until much later in life. It started around the age of 12. I was never motivated to lose weight, and never had a body goal in mind. I never had body dysmorphia.

Teresa: I'm not sure, but I was doing it throughout my teens. I didn't even realize it was a problem until I confided in a family member and they talked me through how harmful what I was doing was; worried, but in love. This made me stop and think. All this while I just thought it was 'my little thing'. My habit. I didn't know it had a name. Growing up, there were always comments from strangers and adults in my life about weight, and I guess that's where it originated from.

Q: *What was life like?*

Johnny: I would go to [family] events. I didn't want people seeing that I wanted or needed to eat, so I never served my food first – I always went last. This was all unconscious by the way.

Teresa: In Nigeria, where I grew up, there seems to be this thing where people are never happy about their body. They're either too big or too skinny. People always talk about their weight. I always felt uncomfortable in my body.

Q: *Did you receive care?*

Johnny: Nope. I never received care.

Teresa: Eventually. I eventually spoke about it in therapy years later and received care. At the time, I used to throw up in secret and didn't want others to know. It wasn't very hard to hide because no one suspected it.

Q: *Was it not picked up? Were you ever misdiagnosed/turned away from treatment?*

Johnny: My parents never flagged it. Probably because I had always been a slimmer build, it wasn't noticed. They were more concerned about other behavioural issues I had at the time. And like I said, I never sought care. I didn't think of it as anorexia. I had a real lack of awareness. I didn't know that wearing jogging bottoms under jeans to do the belt up wasn't normal.

Teresa: I was never turned away from treatment because, for ages, I didn't let anyone know about it! No one knew apart from me.

Q: *Do you reckon there are a lot more Black people out there with disordered eating and eating disorders?*

Johnny: Absolutely! I reckon there are lots of people. I'm sad to say I don't know any other Black people that have eating problems, but I just know it can't be true. Once you don't fit the stereotype, people don't even ask the question. I used to jokingly get asked, 'You look skinny; are you anorexic?'

Teresa: Yeah, definitely, definitely, definitely. That's why I help women now with body image issues. I don't know whether they have eating disorders, but there is definitely a lot of dissatisfaction with their bodies, made worse by online pressure and Western beauty ideals, and it wouldn't surprise me if there are lots more out there like I used to be with issues with purging.

Wealth

I'll never forget being told off by a patient for assuming that she could afford the train fare home for a weekend's leave. She took it personally and made sure to correct me. She highlighted that her lack of finances was in fact part of her problem. And for me, this was a huge learning curve. Eating disorders are often trivialized as being 'illnesses of the rich'. In mainstream media, those with eating disorders are often portrayed as being wealthy. This belief has likely contributed to disparities in eating disorder identification and treatment, particularly among those of lower socioeconomic status backgrounds. But this couldn't be further from the truth. Recent research led by Kathryn Huryk, assistant clinical professor at the University of California San Francisco Eating Disorders Program, showed that there was no pattern of evidence for a relationship between higher socioeconomic status and eating disorders (Huryk, Drury and Loeb 2021).

Food insecurity, which is defined as 'a household-level economic and social condition of limited or uncertain access to adequate food', often results in individuals being unable to afford well-balanced meals, worrying that food will run out, and engaging in eating disorder behaviours such as not eating when hungry, cutting meal sizes, or skipping meals (USDA ERS 2022). Statistics show that young females from low-income families are nearly 1.5 times more likely to develop bulimia nervosa than those from higher-income families (Goeree *et al.* 2011). Early childhood experiences of food insecurity may lead to disordered eating habits such as excessive night-time eating, episodes of binge eating, hiding food and secretive eating (Tester, Lang and Laraia 2016). Research found that 17 per cent of children in the food-insecure group showed signs of an eating disorder, compared with less than 3 per cent of children in the non-food-insecure group (Darling *et al.* 2017). This is why the work of someone like Marcus Rashford, footballer for Manchester United FC, in engaging in food justice awareness and attempting to end UK child poverty, is much needed. Much more research is required to better understand the relationship between food insecurity and eating disorder psychopathology. Food insecurity is a problem involving individual access to food but also includes wider systemic, structural barriers.

Bulimia Nervosa

Diagnostic Criteria

1. Frequent, recurrent episodes of binge eating
2. Behaviours aimed at preventing weight gain
3. Excessive preoccupation with body weight or shape
4. Distress about binge eating and inappropriate compensatory behaviour or significant impairment in functioning
5. Symptoms do not meet the diagnostic requirements for anorexia nervosa

(Based on ICD-11)

One of my childhood friends had it at school, but I didn't know. She didn't talk about it back then. I didn't know till we were adults, in our early 20s. She told me about it because she had to change colleges because she was having problems with her eating disorder. She kept me up to date from then on. I wasn't sure at first how to talk to her about it. I just tried to listen and be there for her. My emotions changed over time as I realized how grave the situation was. I was so sad for her. The fact that it had gone on for so long and she hadn't overcome it was so sad. She eventually quit her job. I also didn't work for a couple years because I have depression, so sometimes we connect through our conditions. It's brought us a little bit together in a way.

Sylvia Butcher, a friend

Introduction

Professor Cynthia Bulik

Cynthia Bulik, PhD, FAED is the Founding Director of the University of North Carolina Center of Excellence for Eating Disorders, Distinguished Professor of Eating Disorders at the University of North Carolina at Chapel Hill, and Professor of Nutrition in the Gillings School of Global Public Health. She is also Professor in the Department of Medical Epidemiology and Biostatistics and Director of the Centre for Eating Disorders Innovation at Karolinska Institutet in Stockholm, Sweden. She specializes in testing evidence-based treatments for eating disorders and leads global initiatives on the genetics of eating disorders. @cbulik

In the summer of 1980, I received a Mellon summer research fellowship to work in childhood depression at the Western Psychiatric Institute and Clinic in Pittsburgh, Pennsylvania. The fellowship allowed us to shadow clinicians throughout the hospital, which was my first experience on an eating disorders treatment unit. Dr L. K. George Hsu was the attending physician and he recommended I read a paper that had been published the previous year by Dr Gerald Russell entitled 'Bulimia nervosa: An ominous variant of anorexia nervosa?' (Russell 1979). The paper reflected the observations of a master clinician, and the final words of the abstract – 'The main aims of treatment are (i) to interrupt the vicious circle of overeating and self-induced vomiting (or purging), (ii) to persuade the patients to accept a higher weight. Prognosis appears less favorable than in uncomplicated anorexia nervosa' – foretold a challenge ahead.

Soon after starting my clinical psychology training at the University of California, Berkeley, the very first patient I saw for therapy described episodes of eating 'enormous' amounts of food, and then, with great shame, she admitted to vomiting and 'wasting' all of that food. She had no signs of anorexia nervosa. The shame stemmed from the fact that her immigrant family would have been horrified if they knew how much money and food she wasted – especially when they had endured hunger and what we call food insufficiency, or insecurity, today. Hesitatingly, she also admitted that her binges were often accompanied by getting drunk – having experienced several blackouts and trips to the emergency room to have her stomach pumped. This was the first case of modern bulimia nervosa that many people in the clinic had seen – a departure from Russell's binge eating and purging within the context of anorexia nervosa – but potentially deadly, nonetheless. It was her case that led me to pursue the study of how eating disorders and substance use disorders track together in families, which eventually led to our current genetic studies.

In subsequent years, both the nature of eating disorders and what we call them have transformed. In the past, we treated more individuals with isolated anorexia nervosa, bulimia nervosa or binge eating disorder. Now, the majority of cases seem to come bundled with co-morbidities (such as anxiety, depression, PTSD, substance use disorder, autism, etc.) and other dysregulated behaviours (substance use, self-harm and behavioural addictions). In addition, the age range of our patients has broadened far beyond adolescence and young adulthood and in both directions, with younger and older patients needing care. To some extent, we have more tools now to treat these disorders – cognitive behavioural therapy, interpersonal psychotherapy, dialectical behavioural therapy – and some medications that do not offer a cure but can reduce symptoms. This being said, our outcomes are not yet as good as we would like.

Fortunately, we are learning more about both genetic and environmental causes of all eating disorders, including bulimia nervosa.

Remaining open-minded, and always considering biological, psychological and social contributions to every case, will allow us to further optimize treatments. We can use tools that we know are efficacious for many people and continue to work hard to find treatments that help those for whom our current interventions do not lead to remission or cure.

Detach the Stigma

Marilyn Okoro

Marilyn Okoro is a British track and field athlete and an Olympics, World Championships and European medallist. She is also a public speaker, life coach, mentor and champion of women and girls. She is Program Lead for the New to Career function at Equinix, the world's leading data infrastructure company. She is also an Association of Corporate Governance Practitioners (ACGP) governance practitioner. Driving change in professional sport and athlete welfare, she founded a podcast series, *Detach the Stigma*. In 2016, she was the sports category winner at the Igbo Women's Awards. She has a BA degree in Politics and French from the University of Bath. @mokoro4

I've just spent the last 20 minutes trying to get out of a dress I had no business trying on in the first instance. Is it just me? I marvel at how often I manage to squeeze and contort myself into a dress only to find that, at the midway point, perhaps this wasn't the best idea after all. But the sense of accomplishment, of fitting into it, overrides any momentary anguish – anguish you only recognize just as that final push is complete. But wait...oh, heck no, this is so not comfortable. Yes, well Marilyn, that's because it's a size S, for 'Something' you ain't no more!

It's been well over two decades since I was in my darkest place with bulimia and body dysmorphia. A teenage girl who, on the surface, had it 'all together', was flourishing academically and was a promising sporting talent. It's been a slow and steady journey since then. At times, I forget I even had such struggles. At other times, the slightest trigger reminds me that there's still a battle in my mind to fight and unhealthy thought patterns that need processing. Like the palaver with this dress.

As a retired elite athlete, these rude awakenings to my new normal have been a reminder of how much I once fixated on my body image. And the truth – and one of the hardest things to admit to myself right now in my retirement from sport – is that I still haven't fully accepted my post-track body.

One thing that I continuously need to remind myself, as I navigate adapting to my new body, is to buy clothes that fit around me! When it comes to clothes, though, I'm easy. I can quite happily flit from fashionista one day to joggers and t-shirt the next. I tend to dress according to my energy levels. How I dress has always been a good indicator of how I feel inwardly – I literally wear my emotions.

Body image and confidence are subjects I love to speak on because, as a young Black girl, I didn't hear enough about them – and definitely not in reference to bodies like mine. Serena Williams definitely changed that. People often looked at me, as an athlete, and thought, 'Black, muscular, successful, strong...how could you possibly have struggled with an eating disorder?'

❊ ❊ ❊

I have the happiest memories from my school days. For the most part, I was confident and happy in my skin. However, much of my formative years was spent as the only Black girl in the room. I spent these years surrounded by White female peers, and role models, whose somatotypes I could never emulate in a million years. I remember back then (mid-nineties and early noughties) that 'body goals', as they call it today, was to be skinny. Bonus points if you had a ridiculously large thigh gap. Well, my strong, athletic, Igbo physique could never!

First things first: I love food. I enjoy eating and breaking bread with others. In fact, fine dining is my second sport. I'm a proud London-born Nigerian, and food has always been at the centre of conversation and social occasions. You can't come to my mum's house, for example, and leave without having tasted something freshly prepared. Mum was always cooking and was amazing at it. But culturally, to be skinny was not the desired look. My mum and aunties would often remind me that it wouldn't help my chances of finding a husband. I can hear them now: 'All this running! You look sick. Are you eating?'

My life, away at boarding school, was the opposite. Skinny was life. And if you were skinny, you were cool. You could eat whatever you wanted. Oh, and you got the boys' attention – so no husband issues there. So I decided to take matters into my own hands, try to rail against my genetics and sculpt my body my own way. I had to be happy now, right?!

Well, fixating on everything that passed my lips meant mealtimes were no longer the enjoyable social occasions I knew them to be. Life became about secrecy, over-exercising, obsessing in the mirror, hoarding food and stuffing my face only to bring it all up again. Willing skinniness into being. Yeah, I definitely wasn't happy. But the thing is, no one knew that I wasn't happy. Looks are deceiving. If there's a degree in code-switching – not looking like what you're going through on the inside – I would graduate with a first class. For a long time, I battled in silence and shame, doing my best to hide behind my huge smile and vibrant personality.

Although I thought I hid it well, I clearly didn't do it well enough because my friend noticed. And looking back, I was so fortunate that she did. She knew that I wasn't being myself. Unbeknownst to me, she alerted one of our favourite members of staff, who also happened to be my tutor. I'll never forget both of them watching me like a hawk every time I rose from the table at meals.

One day, my tutor took me aside and asked me if I planned on wasting my talent by not committing 100 per cent to my dreams. I don't know what it was about that day, and that comment, but something stuck. Something within me decided enough was enough. I think fatigue played a big part in it because, for someone so extroverted, this life of secrecy was hard work.

I was a Black girl from a low socioeconomic background. Not a rich White girl. This is probably what surprised me the most to be honest; I thought I would've been exempt. But eating disorders don't discriminate. My podcast series, *Detach the Stigma*, which has since given me the opportunity to interview and connect with so many others who have struggled with eating disorders, reaffirmed this.

I would love to say I went on to become a successful athlete and my struggles ended with that, but that's not the case. I was still in the developmental stages of my sporting career, and a woman. Yes, I was motivated to take better care of my body as I chased my Olympic dream. But I still took all my disordered thoughts and behaviour patterns with me wherever I went.

Navigating the world of elite sport, again, I found myself feeling out of place on account of my physique. The British middle-distance world hadn't seen a 400/800-metre runner like me before and so didn't know where to fit me in. Probably because that should never have been the goal anyway: to fit in. I say all the time: I didn't need a system built *for* me but rather one that could *accommodate* me. The pressure to become the best, not just in the UK but in the world, re-awakened my anxieties around body image. Every time I lost a race, I never attributed it to wrong tactics or maybe that it just wasn't my day but, of course, to being 'fat and overweight' or that 'I never should have had that last thing I ate!'

I know I'm not alone in the sporting community, especially amongst runners who share this unhealthy mindset. But I'm encouraged to see more athletes who feel empowered to share their story. There is so much power and strength in this: not only for yourself, but also in knowing that you could be helping someone, somewhere, who may be going through exactly the same thing.

Much of the work I do today in this space is fuelled by the fact that, in my era of competition, you just cracked on. You didn't speak up or speak out. And besides, if I did, who would have listened to me anyway? At the time, all I would hear was 'she's too big to run the 800 metres' and 'why doesn't she stick to the sprints?' This truly bugged me. One day, I decided that it wasn't enough for my running to do the talking any more, but that I had to get talking about it. The advocate in me could no longer be suppressed.

Running was my escape and coping mechanism for many years. However, when I wasn't careful or attentive to my emotions, it would easily slip to doing more harm than good. In my early 30s, I decided to take more ownership of my career and the decisions that were made that affected me and *my* body. I had, for so much of my life up until this point, been dictated to. It's disturbing to think back now at how many decisions, in my sporting career, were made by men – and predominantly White men – who had so much power to police my body: a demographic who could probably relate to me the least, if at all. Having only ever had male coaches, I realize I never once trained from a female lens. It was in the years of being self-coached that I began to truly see how much damage I had done to myself both physically and mentally. I understood that I was constantly 'in the red' energy-wise, and that my energy deficiency was a result of me drawing from a depleted cup – relentlessly. The sporting culture still champions this 'win-at-all cost' mindset, even if it results in physical and psychological breakdown.

As I delved further into my quest for a more holistic approach to sport and competing, I connected with some incredible people along the way. Hope Virgo's #DumpTheScales campaign – which called for one's weight to not solely determine their eating disorder management – made me realize that even if I had attempted to get help, I may not have been taken seriously because I didn't tick the neat little box of what an eating disorder patient is apparently meant to look like. I began a journey of deep explorative work with Kaysha Thomas, a Black performance nutritionist, who facilitated my one-to-one nutritional therapy sessions. At first, I had no clue that nutritional therapy was even a thing. These sessions were a real eye-opener and massively supported me during the early phase of my transition out of sport. I finally began to process how my relationship with food had evolved over the years, and whilst I was no longer purging, my patterns of control and restricted eating were still dictating a lot of my life and identity. Also, it was refreshing to speak so freely to someone who looked like me and who I felt truly saw, heard and understood me. Post-competing, I connected with the likes of Renee McGregor. She has dedicated her life to supporting athletes who struggle with eating disorders and relative energy deficiency in sport (RED-S; a phenomenon of poor health and worsened athletic performance due to insufficient fuel to support the athlete's energy demands) to develop a healthier relationship with food.

Mental health remains the gargantuan elephant in the room of many Black homes. In fact, this was one of my main motivations behind starting the *Detach the Stigma* conversations. My own story speaks to West African culture and, more granularly, Nigerian culture. But from the discussions I've had with others, issues around stigma extend to other Black cultures, and so it somewhat appears that that's the normative Black experience. Discussions around mental health, if not ignored entirely, are often attributed to the individual failing in some way, or maybe not living a successful life. Often, it's labelled as something spiritual or demonic. As a Christian myself, I've struggled with coming to terms with the fact that I battled with an eating disorder, depression and anxiety. I used to think that my faith in God would render me exempt from such challenges and so I wasted a lot of time not seeking help because of the fear of being shamed: a toxic generational mindset that needed to be broken.

When looking for support, there were often financial and cultural limitations to the available options. But what set me in the right direction, to more stable ground, was finding the courage to:

1. admit something was not right

2. acknowledge I couldn't do it alone and needed help

3. begin to speak about it.

I often think of my mental health as a balancing act. Whenever I struggled most, it was because I was lacking somewhere or one of my cups was depleted. Language matters so much. I often struggled to say the words of the things I battled – let alone have full-blown conversations about them. But it was through *talking* that I learnt I wasn't a failure. I learnt to define what success meant to me. I learnt that despite being physically strong, true strength was recognizing when I felt weak and doing something about it. As hard as it may be, talking is so crucial. It's important to not suffer in silence, but instead to be empowered to find the courage to spark that necessary conversation.

Anyway, my recovery journey continues. But it's a far more informed and empowered one than when it began. Through acceptance, I'm grateful and accept who I am today. I have a daily decision to make: to love my body and my new shape, from the inside out. To be proud of myself. After all, we're constantly evolving in one way or another. Like life: you only have one body, and it is indeed my temple. My faith, as a Christian, grounds me, and I affirm myself each day with the following:

'I am fearfully and wonderfully made, Marvellous are your works' – *Psalm 139:14*

I do my best to never let the opinion of others dictate who I am, how I think or how I act, and I invite anyone struggling to do the same. Find your community, who can support and empower you, but above all: love and believe in *you* first!

When It Comes to Eating Disorders, Brown Girls Don't Measure Up

Smriti Mundhra

Smriti Mundhra is a multi-award-winning director and producer. Her film *St Louis Superman* was nominated for a 2020 Academy Award in the short documentary category, won a Critics' Choice Award and was named as one of the Documentaries of the Decade by the International Documentary Association. She is the Creator and Executive Producer of Emmy-nominated *Indian Matchmaking*, a Netflix original documentary series. In 2022, she directed *Shelter*, a Director's Guild of America Award-winning and NAACP Image Award-nominated documentary. She is the creator of *The Romantics*, a Netflix documentary series. She has won multiple Tribeca Film Festival awards. She is the Founder of Meralta Films, a Los Angeles and Mumbai-based production company focused on creating premium fiction and non-fiction content. @smritimundhra

An earlier version of this chapter appeared on Elle.com.

The soundstage at GUM Studios in Brooklyn, New York is washed in purple and pink lights, and a fog machine slowly spills a swirl of cloudy gas across the black astroturf floor. Athena Nair, a 19-year-old Tufts university student and Indian classical dancer, launches into a gorgeous kathak solo. I sit behind a bank of monitors and watch as the camera moves from the ghungroo bells on her ankles, to her graceful hands, to her face, luminous with joy as she makes the music come to life. The shot pulls out wider to give her more space to twirl and leap. Then, it happens. A rusted metal weighing scale, the kind you would see in a doctor's office, appears in the corner of the frame, like the shark in *Jaws*. Athena, mid-dance, freezes. Her expression changes, the joyous light extinguished in an instant. I see her visibly wince in pain. And, behind the monitor, I burst into tears. Someone has to call cut on my behalf as I take a moment to go outside and get some air.

We are on the set of the new Disney+ docuseries *Growing Up*, filming an episode about Athena's journey to self-love after years of disordered eating and body dysmorphia. This is a moment that Athena and I crafted to evoke the triggering feeling of panic and fear that metal doctor's office scale brings to anyone who has struggled with body image issues. Apparently, it was more effective than I realized – probably because when I looked at the monitor, I was really staring into a mirror.

Like Athena, I am a South Asian woman who suffers from eating disorders. My struggle with body dysmorphia began when I was told by my doctor, at six years old, that my BMI (body mass index) was too high, and I was put on the first of many diets that would come to define my life. Ever the overachiever and eager to please my concerned parents, I threw myself into controlling my weight. Calorie counting evolved into anorexia nervosa, which later evolved into bulimia nervosa. Since then, through adolescence and into adulthood, my self-worth has been dictated by numbers: weight, waist circumference, calories in, calories out, fasting blood sugar, ketones, dress size, jeans size, grams, ounces, macros, percentages. Like so many women, I have spent my life shrouded in shame over my inability to make my body conform to those numbers – the ones I was told meant I was healthy and that I belonged.

What I didn't know at that time was that those numbers were reflective of White, Eurocentric standards that never should have been applied to me. When I resorted to self-harm to bring my body into submission, I found that I also didn't fit the profile of a person who suffers from disordered eating. Therefore, I could easily hide my destructive behaviour from my doctors, my friends, and even my family.

Pop culture and even medical research would have you believe that eating disorders are the exclusive domain of people who are wealthy, skinny, cisgender female and White. I spent a lot of time as a teenager in the '90s watching straight-to-television movies about young women with anorexia or bulimia, but instead of looking at them as cautionary tales, I was taking notes. Eating disorder behaviour is so closely tied with Whiteness and wealth that for many – including many women of colour – the depictions of it can be unintentionally aspirational. When you've internalized generations of self-hate over your genetically given dark skin and curves, you'd do anything for Tracey Gold's pale skin, gaunt eyes and razor-sharp hip bones.

More than 20 years later, that image hasn't changed: from Lily Collins in *To the Bone*, Natalie Portman in *Black Swan*, or Rose Byrne in *Physical*, this White-washing of eating disorders in the media has real-world consequences for women of colour. In 2012, the National Eating Disorders Association (NEDA) reported that 'exact statistics on the prevalence of eating disorders among women of color are unavailable' because, 'due to our historically biased view that eating disorders only affect White women, relatively little research has been conducted utilizing participants from racial and ethnic minority groups'. More recent research shows that women of colour are as, if not more, affected than White women by anorexia nervosa, bulimia nervosa and binge eating disorder. Women of colour are also underdiagnosed for eating disorders, thanks to medical bias and lack of access to quality healthcare.

With *Growing Up*, I saw an opportunity to stop the erasure of the many types of people, like me, who fly under the radar of research, treatment and support. As South Asian women, Athena and I wanted to frame this topic through our specific cultural lens: from the subtle demands for perfection to the pressure to conform to White beauty standards to the earnest desire to unburden our hard-working immigrant parents of our problems, causing us to try to deal with our demons in secret.

I realize now that my burst of tears on set was catharsis; a recognition after decades of isolation that I wasn't alone in my struggle with my body. My own recovery began when I was in my 30s, after the birth of my daughter, and I realized if I didn't take steps to heal, my trauma would live through another generation. But recovery was jagged, and lonely. I never knew if I was doing it right, especially as dark thoughts crept into my mind about the number of carbs in a banana or whether or not oatmeal would make me gain weight. Athena taught me to look at eating disorder recovery as activism – a way to reject decades of bad science and colonialist beauty standards. Working with her to share her story moved me in profound ways. For the first time, I felt optimistic not only that recovery was possible, but so was radical self-love.

'What if you didn't have to hate your body before you could love your body?' Athena, now an activist and board member of The Body Positive, asks in one of the most powerful moments of our episode of *Growing Up*. That question struck me like a thunderbolt when I first heard it, and has stayed with me ever since. It won't be easy to deprogram ourselves of a lifetime of internalized ideals, but we owe it to ourselves, and to future generations, to try.

Hopefully, by sharing Athena's story, more young women – and men, and non-binary folks – who feel unseen by a system centred around the needs of White women will seek treatment and find community. Because being seen is the first step towards healing.

Pressure

Nigel Owens

Nigel Owens MBE, is a former international rugby union referee. He was one of the Welsh rugby union's first three professional referees. He took charge of the 2015 World Cup final, having become regarded as the world's best referee. He is a diversity and mental health ambassador at hasta World. In 2016, he received an MBE for his services to sport. His best-selling debut book, *Half Time*, was released in 2008. His second book, *The Final Whistle*, was released in 2022. @nigelrefowens

unanfeirniadol means self-critical in my mother tongue, Welsh. And I'm really, really hunanfeirniadol. I guess you sort of have to be when your individual performances can directly influence who wins and loses. Worse still, your performances are broadcast live on TV for the whole world to see. Literally. This being said, even before I became an international referee, I think I was just as bad with the self-criticism. And still am, to be honest, even though I retired a few years ago.

When I used to referee, I had a system: I typically refereed on a Saturday and travelled back on Sunday, and when I would eventually get in, it wouldn't be long before I was straight on it – reviewing my performance at home. Sometimes, I'd be away in, say, New Zealand. Maybe in a hotel room. And so the analysis would have to wait a day or two. But it would always happen, one way or another. It's a feeling you never really ever fully get used to. Seeing yourself back on TV, sometimes even catching snippets of yourself on someone else's social media next to you on a train; others already critiquing you before you've had a chance. This pressure, both internal and external, was something that I had become well accustomed to.

I think the first time I ever remember feeling overwhelming pressure, though, was in my 20s; pressure to hide my sexuality. The stereotype at the time was that gay men were camp and feminine. Growing up, none of my heroes were gay – my dad wasn't, Derek Bevan (my refereeing hero) wasn't and nor was Phil Bennett (my rugby hero). And so me being gay was something I felt was worth hiding. On the odd occasion, I secretly arranged to meet people that I'd been talking to online. Sometimes we'd go to the gay clubs, where I'd get to feel what freedom felt like for the night. But the limited time I had made it hard for people to get to know the real me, and the chances of actually meeting someone felt few and far between. Also, the scene was very much looks-based. People would fancy you based on your looks. The 'fit' ones would be attractive, not the 'bigger' ones. And I was very much one of the 'bigger' ones.

This wasn't surprising, to be honest – being one of the 'bigger' ones – because growing up, I really enjoyed food. I used to enjoy getting the groceries with my father – something I would do up until I finally left the house at 34. And when home, I wasn't one to shy away when it came to quantity. Whatever the food was, I would eat a lot of it. Instead of one, I'd have two. My mum being a good cook probably helped. She normally did the cooking, and I did the eating. We were both pretty good at what we did. I started getting bigger at 15 when I began going out a bit more without my parents, around town, drinking with my mates. By my late teens, I had started comfort eating. This comfort eating continued till I was 35. But my bulimia; I'm not really sure how that came about. All I remember is it starting in my 20s, when my body image sort of became a huge issue for me. I think I may have read somewhere that bulimia caused weight loss.

Bulimia ran the show for a while. The thought of being 'bigger' was enough to keep this secret habit alive. The thought of being 'bigger' was a huge trigger for me. Not just because I felt as though I ran the risk of never finding a life partner, but also because of the refereeing. Refereeing, knowing that millions of people across the world are viewing your every move, is pressure. An unspeakable pressure which I'm immeasurably happy that I don't need to deal with any more. There's obviously the aesthetics – of people not thinking you're out of shape running around – but also I don't think people realize the fitness testing involved in rugby refereeing. It's hard work. We had deadlines, lots and lots of fitness deadlines that we *had* to hit. We had to be ready. I remember in 2013, when the 2015 World Cup was on the horizon, that my bulimia made a vicious return (it had stopped when my mum was diagnosed with cancer in 2008). I felt I needed to lose a little weight to perform optimally at fitness testing, and hurried back to a habit that I felt I could rely on. From there it came back, off and on. It's only in the last couple of years that I've really got a grip on things.

And I've accomplished this partly because I've had such a supportive partner. I really don't know how he's managed over the years. He's been so, so supportive, and I can't thank him enough. At the worst of it, he would hear me in the toilet and pretend that he hadn't. Or he'd play along with me having an 'upset stomach'. I always felt guilty afterwards. Alongside him, I've had the most amazing support of my family (who also were accepting of my sexuality when many others weren't). But I also took part in a TV programme on the BBC current affairs series *Panorama*, called 'Men, Boys and Eating Disorders'. As part of the programme, I had a lot of conversations with experts in the eating disorders field, and I learnt a lot about my bulimia then. But I've never officially sought help with it as it were. I sort of dealt with it myself. A big thing for me was learning what my triggers were, my main ones being me and my body image, and the pressure of being fit for public performance.

Now, there are no deadlines. The pressure of fitness testing is no more, and with that, my dangerous habits have been slowly dying.

I was lucky my career had a natural end to it. Because, if not, who knows how long the behaviours would have continued at that intensity for. One thing's for sure, without retiring, I definitely wouldn't have had as much time to reflect. Reflection has made me realize that sometimes a lot of the pressure that we put on ourselves is needless. In my case, the pressure of the weight targets that I had set for myself wasn't necessary. Failing to reach these targets wouldn't have stopped me from being able to do my job, nor did hitting them necessarily enable me to do my job any better. In hindsight, it was pointless pressure. Because I already had what it took. Remember when I said I was self-critical? One of the many difficulties of 'pressure' is that it can draw out self-criticism. Self-critical traits, which I knew I had, rose up to the point of being overwhelming for me when I was put under the public spotlight.

I don't know what the general public's view is of bulimia. Believe it or not, I haven't had as many of those conversations with people as one might think. But what I *do* know, from my personal experience and the few conversations that I *have* had, is that it's stigmatized. So, my two bits of advice to those battling hard with this illness include to first seek professional help – regardless of what you think others might think. This may be help for an eating disorder, but this advice also applies to the young, aspiring referees – the mini-Nigels of this world making their way through the ranks – who might struggle with the pressure of performance. If I could have my time again, I would seek professional help. But I didn't. And I sort of feel that if I had, I would have been able to identify my triggers earlier. And that's my second point: identify your triggers. This one, when I made it happen, was a game-changer.

For me, 'recovery' is ongoing. It's when you may still be suffering from something, and may still be dealing with it, but you're putting things in place. I've reached a point where I'm not dealing with it all day every day any more. Not at this moment in time. I still could be much better at it. Making myself sick happens very rarely now, maybe about once or twice a year. But the difference now is that I feel liberated from pressure. I'm flourishing alongside this long-term eating disorder project that I'm continually working on. It's sort of hard to flourish when you don't know who you are, or aren't able to freely express who you are. I couldn't before, but I can now. I can enjoy love, and I can enjoy food again. I can have chips without feeling bad! I know how to be sensible and balanced in what I eat. Those days of being obsessional with what I eat are gone. Good thing too, because I can enjoy Christmas again. I love Christmas.

It Wasn't about Weight

Jasmine C. Perry

Jasmine C. Perry is a director, filmmaker and actress. With a BA degree in TV, film and media and an MFA degree in screenwriting, she worked as an associate producer on a NAACP award-winning docuseries, *Unsung*. She later wrote and produced *Being*, a docuseries highlighting dynamic entertainers in film and music. She has starred in commercials and print ads for major brands such as Nissan, Sony, Apple, Uber, American Express, Diesel, BlackPeopleMeet, Credit Sesame, Michelle Watches and *Elle* magazine. She also starred in the Lifetime show, *My Crazy Ex*. She co-produced a feature-length documentary, *The Invisible Vegan*, a film that chronicles her personal experience with plant-based eating. @theinvisiblevegan

I left my hometown, Washington DC, and moved to Los Angeles (LA), which is where I met my sweetheart, who wasn't the sweetest. Before I met my beau, I didn't know too many people in LA so I felt isolated and, socially, I struggled for my first few years. Sadly, isolation is the perfect breeding ground for abuse.

Like most relationships, our union was roses and lollipops at the beginning. He was mighty fine, and my ego was on cloud nine. Out of all the girls who wanted him – and it was about 95 per cent of them – he wanted *me*. Wasn't I lucky!

But my luck was nothing but smoke and mirrors. Early into the relationship, his temper would reveal itself more and more, and every time we argued he would push boundaries further and further. Until he realized I didn't have any. First, he'd yell. Then, he'd grab. Then, he'd push. And before I knew it, I was being punched. The worst part of it for me wasn't the physical pain. I can take a punch. The worst part was the mental and emotional state it left me in. This man was my biggest source of pain, but because I was in LA with no real friends or family, he was also my only source of pleasure. And with each hit, my self-esteem corroded. I hated what I had become so much that I couldn't even fight it.

In the midst of it, my appetite became ravenous, and I thought about food all the time. I was always pretty into food growing up, so I wasn't alarmed by my increased appetite. I just thought it was another stage in my development, so I ate. Instead of one big meal for dinner, I'd have four. I remember one night I went to The Hat to get a pastrami sandwich, Stix to get a plate of chow mein, Jack in the Box for a burger meal and El Pollo Loco for a Caesar chicken bowl. I didn't see anything wrong with what I was doing, but knew others might, so I'd only put on these elaborate spreads when my roommate was gone. Everything would be nicely spaced out on the floor, and then I'd gorge on everything like an animal. I used to call it 'my process'. Eventually, my body couldn't take all the food. I would eat until I became miserable so, to relieve my body, I would do anything to get the food off my stomach. At the time, I knew what I was doing was off, but I didn't look at it as an eating disorder. I wasn't trying to get skinny. I wasn't obsessed with weight. And I wasn't White.

I had learned about eating disorders in elementary school through the Lifetime TV network. They would show films about bulimia and anorexia and, because of the lack of diversity I saw, I thought eating disorders were something affluent White girls did when they wanted to join cheerleading squads. Lifetime University didn't properly unpack the complexities of eating disorders. So I thought it was more about vanity than emotions and, since I never saw people like me, I just assumed throwing up your food to get skinny was more of a 'White girl thing'. Like a lot of us who grew up in the 1980s and '90s, ignorance didn't escape me.

One night during 'my process', my roommate and her boy-friend showed up unexpectedly. I tried to make the episode into a joke, and told them I was out-of-this-world hungry. I think that's how I phrased it. Her boyfriend looked at my spread and said, 'Holy shit,' as he laughed at the crime scene. My roommate, on the other hand, stood in horror. After her boyfriend and I stopped laughing, she looked at me and said, 'Jasmine, this is not funny. Something is wrong with you. You are eating an unhealthy amount of food to try to cope with something and it's not good for you to do this to yourself.' I felt ashamed, embarrassed and weird. She made a connection that I wouldn't fully understand until a decade later. I was using food to try to curb an emotional hunger that would never be satisfied given the situation I was in.

I wasn't binge eating because I was some lazy and gluttonous person with no discipline, which is how people who struggle with overeating often get labelled. And I wasn't purging to look like a model, which is how many people are categorized when they engage in disordered eating behaviours. Being abused broke my spirit and caused me an immense amount of emotional pain, and to cope with the pain, I reached for the easiest source of pleasure at my disposal – food. I had an eating disorder, but because I wasn't aware of how disordered eating manifested outside of Lifetime stories, I didn't know what my problem was, or how to get help for it.

Lo and behold, when the relationship ended and the abuse stopped, so did the desire to eat myself into a coma. It wasn't until ten years later when I heard a woman talking about her eating disorder that I realized I had one. She spoke about similar attempts to get food off her stomach. When she highlighted that her struggle had nothing to do with weight, I finally understood my own past. An eating disorder can have nothing to do with food or weight. It can be the mind crying out to be soothed or helped, and I learned that the hard way. I had an eating disorder, and I didn't even know it.

I'm Searching for a Dance Partner

Dianne Buswell

Dianne Buswell is an Australian, professional, award-winning dancer. She has represented Western Australia in national and international ballroom and Latin events. She is best known as one of BBC *Strictly Come Dancing*'s pro dancers. In 2020, she launched Buswellness, a dedicated channel to share her passion for health and happiness with her audience. In January 2021, she launched her BBC Radio 1 podcast *Di's Salon*. She was featured on the cover of Superdrug's Spring 2021 *Dare* magazine. She has partnered with Lucy Locket Loves and Crash Bandicoot. She has a following of more than 1.5 million people across her social channels. Her debut book, *Move Yourself Happy: 21 Days to Make Joyful Movement a Habit*, was released in 2023. @dbuzz6589

It's when I get a quiet couple of weeks that I'm like, 'Oh, I *really* miss home.' Home is Bunbury, Western Australia – about two hours south of Perth. It's one of those places where most people know most people. A world away (literally) from my life now in England. I left Bunbury when I was offered a position in a dance company at the age of 21. No longer would I have to balance being both a hairdresser and dancing out of hours – I could *finally* focus on dance. With the company, I ended up touring around the world for seven years and, as you can imagine, got really good at living out of a suitcase.

I started dancing around four and a half years old and had dreamt of dancing globally from a really early age. I've played over and over again the dusty old home videos that my parents have done so well to keep. They are of my first dance exam in Latin and ballroom. I remember always loving dance – I lived and breathed it. I remember the excitement of Saturday mornings. I couldn't wait to get down to the local studio with what felt like lots of people (although probably not as many as I remember), all of us descending on a well-worn building. It felt like such a community. On Sundays, though, my mum would take me to Perth which had a completely different vibe. Perth was where I knew I wanted and needed to be. I had gotten good, and eventually began teaching kids older than me on Saturdays which felt pretty special. But it was Bunbury. Perth was where you went when you got good. I knew I was one of the better ones in my hometown, which made me feel great. But when I got to Perth, I was one of many, and felt pretty ordinary to be honest. I got quite competitive with myself from a young age, and badly wanted to learn from others in Perth. I wanted to compete.

I'm not entirely sure where my competitive edge came from, because I'm pretty sure it wasn't from my parents. They weren't your typically pushy dance parents. Perth was full of those. My parents were chilled, and never forced me into dance. The minute I fell out of love with it, I'm so sure that they would have supported me to do something else. My mum came to all the competitions; my dad to the big ones. They were committed. My dad used to take my brother to football too, and my mum would take my other brother – who also dances – to dance. At one point, my mum worked three jobs to help my brothers and me do what we loved. It helped fund what is an incredibly expensive sport. I think people often forget how expensive dance is: the dresses, the travel, the A$160 45-minute lessons. Paul (name changed), my dance partner; now *his* parents were pushy. But he turned out okay. At the time, I was over the moon when he chose me to be his dance partner. Back then, you needed a dance partner if you were going to compete, and he was the only available guy in Bunbury. Normally, if you weren't picked, you had to just wait patiently, or you could post online somewhere, 'I'm searching for a dance partner.' Fortunately, I never had to do that. Paul was my dance partner up until the end of my teenage years.

It was my dance teacher who first recognized that I was getting good. I was roughly 10 or 11 at the time and was in the top six in Western Australia for my category. I remember him suggesting that I go on an exercise regime to get 'game fit'. And so I also started to watch what I ate. I'm half-Italian, and you know what they say about Italians and food. We love it, basically. It's very much part of our culture. My family in Sicily are the definition of feeders. I can't speak Italian, but when Nan is waving a big plate of pasta con le sarde in my face shouting, 'Eat more, more!' I don't think I ever needed to. Growing up, my older brothers and I, we all loved food. So I wasn't too surprised when my teacher suggested an exercise regimen because I was slightly bigger than the other girls.

What surprised me, though, was how I reacted to a few people telling me, 'Oh my god, you look great,' after I had lost some weight. They hadn't said that to me before, and so I guess the teenage girl in me loved it. Also, initially, I felt much better. I was getting fitter, and felt like I was starting to look like the other girls. But the oh-my-god-you-look-great vicious cycle kicked in hard as I moved through my teens and went through all the hormonal changes that came with puberty. This took my issues to the next level. And I knew it too and was never in denial about it (the pictures from that time show just how dramatic the weight loss was). I moved from not eating enough for the amount my body needed (and I was doing *a lot* of dancing) to trying everything you could think of to try and keep the weight off. I went on some mad diets. Once, I had poisoning from having too much of the same low-calorie food.

The thing is, I was actually doing okay on tour for the first couple of years. But I think seeing some of the other dancers get fired, and not wanting to be the next, flipped a switch in me which led to a spiral. I also think that living with dancers 24/7 eventually got the better of me. Constantly comparing what I was eating to others. Constantly comparing what I looked like to others. Constantly comparing how much I weighed to others. Every single day, all body parts. All of it took so much of my time and was quite scary. Also, working where I got weighed wasn't the easiest. On weighing days, I did stuff that I shouldn't. Eventually, I stopped eating altogether, and whenever my body fought back with rage, in an attempt to keep me alive in the form of a blowout, I'd purge. My system started to malfunction, and I could see the effects it was having on my body. With my loss of weight came a loss of energy. I would get so anxious on the dance floor, panicking that my body wouldn't have the energy that it needed to get me through. And with my loss of weight came a loss of my love for dance. Bulimia had become my new dance partner.

❊ ❊ ❊

I get so busy with work now that I don't really have time to stop to think how much I miss my family, and so I feel okay about being this far away from them. Most of the time. But I can only be busy because my body allows me to be. I've come to realize that my body is my tool, and I want it to last as long as possible. I *need* a healthy body for longevity because I absolutely love my job now and would do it forever if I could. Not once have I ever felt judged (which is ironic). Never judged on looks, body size or shape. We maybe have a yearly costume measurement, but that's it. And even then, they don't even tell you what that measurement is. I never thought I'd be dancing in front of millions now. And even though I've done it for so long, I still get nervous. But never for me. Always for my dance partner – the celebrity I'm paired with. It's weird because this job isn't focused on me. There's the professionals' tour where I have to think about myself (and it's a nice thing) but for my day job in this industry to be one where all my mind, energy and time is on someone else for once is just great. I want *them* to be successful. But I need my body to be good for this. At times I think, 'What if I get injured?' It's a scary thought. Fortunately, in my life, I haven't had many injuries (touch wood). At one point, my hip got quite bad, and I was struggling to walk. An MRI showed a little wear and tear, but a few cortisone injections later and I was good as new.

I feel as though the illness thoughts are always going to be there, at the back of my mind. I feel as though 99 per cent of the time they aren't, but then there's that pesky 1 per cent of the time when they just pop into my thoughts for a second. But I also have at the back of my mind the people who used to pull me to one side and say, 'Di, let's have a chat.' The friends and family who called out the issues when they saw them and were there for me when I went back to Bunbury to recover. They saw right through me when I used to say, 'I'm fine, I'm fine.' (I'm a closed book in that sense and can get quite stubborn like that, and the illness made it worse.) I think about them and not wanting to let them down. I also think about the fact that I would love a family one day. Would the illness allow for that? Is it something I could live with long-term? These are questions I had to ask myself. I didn't make the toughest move of my life to the UK seven years ago, with no family or friends, to give in to this horrific illness.

Getting to know myself a bit better has helped. I've learnt so much more about myself as I've got older, especially over the last couple of years, through interviews and writing my first book. It's the most I think I've ever spoken about myself and the illness, and I would definitely recommend it. There's nothing like talking about the illness and understanding yourself, and your relationship with it, in the process. I've learnt that the minute I stopped comparing, beautiful things happened. I've learnt that the company picked me, to begin with, for *me*. To be authentically me, not to try and change myself to be someone else, and to be grateful for what I have in my own body (because I look back at certain points knowing I wasn't happy; yes, I'd had elements of success, but I hadn't been truly happy). I've also learnt the importance of self-care. I love massages, facials – anything that feels pampering and gives me that ah-this-feels-so-good feeling. I've learnt the importance of nutrition (back then, I didn't know much about it). And I've also learnt the power of my strong brain and mindset, and the importance of channelling it in the right way.

My time, energy and life is dance. And for that, I need the right dance partner.

Food

Dr Chuks

In 2022, during Eating Disorders Awareness Week, I was privileged enough to create and co-host #TheBigEDchat – a series of live audio conversations on Twitter. The discussions happened at the same time over the course of five weeks, each week with a different topic, and with a different selection of industry experts and popular figures. The general population could chime in too. The conversations proved popular, highlighting the need for more joint discussions between clinicians, those with lived experience and the public. The first week's topic was weight and diet culture, and what transpired caught my co-hosts and me completely off-guard. It would be an understatement to suggest that the first week's discussions didn't go according to plan. Things got seriously heated, emotions flared, and tears were shed (at least they sounded like they were over the audio). Fundamentally, there were differing opinions between the gastroenterology and diabetic physicians, eating disorder doctors and members of the fat community about how to approach the topic of weight, health (a vague word in and of itself which doesn't really mean much due to its huge subjectivity) and the relationship with our bodies. Fortunately, the proceeding weeks were less emotionally charged. But, as unlikely as it might sound, I found *that* week's discussions probably the most impactful. Over the years, I'd been so used to clinicians and guests on panels being all nicey-nicey. And, in a world where it can be hard to gather people of differing opinions, I felt as though good progress was made that day. A difficult conversation which needed to happen was had.

Yet, with all the differences of opinion, one viewpoint that was mutually shared by the guests was the fact that we live in a culture completely obsessed with food and dieting. Today's diet culture and widespread internalization of appearance norms makes recovering from an eating disorder feel 'impossible', as one of my patients once put it.

Diet Culture

It's pretty difficult to find two identical definitions of 'diet culture'. One of the best explanations that I've heard is by dietitian and former editor of SELF magazine, Christine Byrne. She describes diet culture as 'an entire belief system that associates food with morality and thinness with goodness, and it's rooted in the (very colonial) belief that every individual has full control and responsibility over their health' (Byrne 2022).

It wasn't always this way. The notion of thinness – particularly amongst the female population – mainly gained traction in the 1920s, at a time when Western women were making serious sociopolitical advances; notably, gaining the right to vote. Scholars describe a sharp, societal, patriarchal push-back against such progress, with women's bodies turned 'into the prisons their homes no longer were'. Dieting was driven hard on the agenda and ended up becoming 'the most potent political sedative in history' (Wolf 1991). A dramatic escalation of thinness standards then occurred across the latter half of the 20th century, when fatphobia – the implicit and explicit bias against fat individuals that is rooted in a sense of blame and presumed moral failing (Boston Medical Center 2023) – rose in popularity. In the words of Sharlene Hesse-Biber, Professor of Sociology at the University of Michigan, being fat began to represent 'the inability to delay gratification, poor impulse control, greed, and self-indulgence', whereas slenderness depicted 'restraint, moderation, and self-control' (Hesse-Biber 2006). In her book *Fearing the Black Body*, Sabrina Strings, Associate Professor of Sociology at the University of California, Irvine, makes the case that fatphobia was 'a means of using the body to validate race, class, and gender prejudice' (Strings 2019).

Statistics would suggest that those who experience normative discontent – a term used to describe weight dissatisfaction – are more likely to diet (NEDA 2014). This is despite overwhelming evidence that, in general, dieting doesn't work very well (Ge *et al.* 2020). It is also one of the biggest risk factors for developing an eating disorder (Barakat *et al.* 2023). According to research, young girls can begin to express concerns about their weight by the age of six (Smolak 2011). In another report, 24 per cent of boys avoided taking part in activities like physical education due to worries about their appearance (Be Real 2017). These figures become even more concerning when we find that six in ten 13-year-old girls, and four in ten boys of the same age, are afraid of gaining weight or getting fat (Micali *et al.* 2014). Even worse, more than half of women aged 18–25 would rather be hit by a truck, and two-thirds would rather be unintelligent or unkind, than be fat (Gaesser 2002). As it stands, it would appear that outward appearance falls higher on the social hierarchy than inward character development.

Normative discontent is also reflected in negative conversations about weight, often referred to as 'fat talk', which is the intelligent name of New York-based journalist Virginia Sole-Smith's latest book, in which she details parenting in the age of diet culture. Based on the aforementioned statistics, such a book seems timely. Children are internalizing complicated ideas about 'good' and 'bad' foods from an early age. In *The Body Project*, American social historian Joan Brumberg noted that young people 'are on guard constantly against gaining weight, and, as a result, appetite control is a major feature of their adolescent experience' (Brumberg 1997). Eating disorders thrive in environments where there is widespread bodily discontent and self-degradation, eating disorders being one of the most extreme manifestations of such debasement.

This isn't necessarily helped by recent American Academy of Pediatrics guidelines which suggest referring children as young as two years old to 'intensive health behavior and lifestyle treatment' programmes if they have a BMI above the 'normal' range (Hampl *et al.* 2023). What may be needed instead are weight-inclusive approaches. This may mean unpicking deeper issues that families may have surrounding health prioritization and challenges. A number on a scale, in isolation, won't get to the root of what may be going on.

Food is often at the heart of most social interactions. Whether it's meeting friends for a coffee, going to the pub with work colleagues or to restaurants with a partner, birthdays, holidays or Thanksgiving with the extended family, food seems to be the guest that's always invited. But never have we known so much about it. Today's obsession with nutritional intake has led to an explosion in the health and wellness industry, as well as the genesis of organizations such as the Anti Diet Riot Club, a UK-based non-profit, trying to act as an antidote to said diet culture and a balm to those at the receiving end of body shame and fatphobia. At any one time, there seem to be multiple books that relate to food or dieting in bestsellers lists. This makes sense, as research shows that 49.1 per cent of US adults try to lose weight in any given 12 months, with 53 per cent of dieters already at a healthy weight yet still trying to lose weight. Thirty-nine per cent of women said concerns about what they eat or weigh interfered with their happiness (UNC 2008; NHNES 2018).

Heightened focus on diet and exercise has led to the increase of weight loss jabs, and the ever-increasing popularity of diet and exercise apps such as MyFitnessPal and Noom. Other platforms such as TikTok have seen an increase in 'What I Eat in a Day' videos. These videos – in which vloggers detail the entirety of their nutritional intake within a day – can increase the intimacy between the vloggers and their audience. However, a concerning potential outcome of such videos is for the viewer to be misled into thinking that these diets ought to be copied; that there is a specific *amount* and *type* of food that is 'normal' to eat. The most appropriate examples of such videos come with disclaimers highlighting that nutritional intake is indeed individual and depends on the individual's context (e.g. prefaced with 'what may work nutritionally for me may be completely inappropriate for you'). In April 2023, YouTube updated its approach to eating disorder-related content in an attempt to protect viewers from harmful content (Graham 2023). I appreciate that. Unfortunately, the wellness industry is full of many organizations who wouldn't act with such consideration. Quite frankly, it's also full of a lot of people who don't know what they're talking about. I've looked after countless patients who have been ripped off, left in a bad way with musculoskeletal injuries perpetuated by inadequate nutrition plans, or swamped with faddy diets. I reckon I wouldn't be the only medical doctor who feels the industry could do with some sort of regulation. I've looked after so many patients whose lives have been absolutely decimated by dieting.

Regrettably, as a by-product of societal dietary misconceptions, issues such as orthorexia nervosa – the unhealthy obsession with eating 'pure' food resulting in food restriction and sometimes malnutrition – have also grown exponentially. The obsession with counting calories is another. There are serious risks when food becomes less about taste and more about numbers.

Calories

On 6 April 2022, large businesses in the UK – those with more than 250 employees – were legally required to display calorie information on physical and online menus, food delivery platforms and food labels. This came 18 months after a similar intervention was introduced in the US (Petimar *et al.* 2019). I remember where I was when I first heard the news that this was going to be implemented. Ironically, I was at a restaurant at the time. My wife had nipped to the toilet, and when the alert hit my phone, I almost choked on my fish and chips out of shock.

I felt at the time (and still do) that this move was potentially disastrous. And so do virtually all of those in the eating disorders community who I have spoken to. With eating disorders such as anorexia nervosa and bulimia nervosa, attempting to stay on the streets of a more balanced approach to food, and avoid being trapped along the back alleyways of number crunching, can be difficult. Eating disorder recovery can be such a delicate affair anyway, with the most unexpected of things precipitating regression (or at least stalling progress), which is what calories on restaurant menus continually threaten to do. Placing more focus on calories may in turn lead to a deterioration in health in these individuals: ironically, the very thing that the government is trying to avoid.

The optimists in the room may argue that if someone with a restrictive eating disorder is able to see, yet disregard, the number of calories within a particularly difficult meal, then that would be a triumph in that person challenging their fears. But though ostensibly sound, this shouldn't be used as justification. First, from my experience, those in recovery probably have a rough idea of the number of calories in the food already – so any additional emphasis just feels cruel and unnecessary. And second, are we truly to suggest that although we know what may trigger an eating disorder relapse, we shouldn't take as many measures as possible to avoid it? That if we know where one's weaknesses may lie, we shouldn't jump in to avoid failure? Is it not our duty of care, as a society, to minimize the psychological pressure pent up within an individual's closed system so as to prevent them from cracking? Although an inexact analogy, calories on menus are akin to opening a bar fridge to an alcoholic, showing them the contents within it and then closing it again: the self-destructive cogs may have already started to turn, and it may be an uphill battle from there.

Despite several campaigns against its introduction, including a nationwide survey of people with existing or past eating disorders that found that 93 per cent thought that it would have a negative or extremely negative impact on them (Beat 2021a), the move went ahead anyway. Andrew Radford, chief executive of Britain's leading eating disorders charity, Beat, said that this move risks 'causing great distress for people suffering from or vulnerable to eating disorders, since evidence shows that calorie labelling exacerbates eating disorders of all kinds' (Beat 2021b). The government's caveat was that those who may find viewing calorie information more difficult should be enabled to have a menu without calorie information on (GOV.UK 2021). However, it failed to acknowledge the logistical impracticalities of this, especially in busy eating environments where default menus (with calorie information on) are likely. I've been told of countless examples where people were left frustrated when unable to access calorie-less menus.

But those with eating disorders aside, one of my major concerns was (and still is) for people who don't care about calories in the same way that some of my patients do. The sort who would ordinarily pick a meal from a restaurant menu in carefree fashion. The sort who, although living in a society where calories are hard to get away from (they are literally everywhere you turn in supermarkets), would not give calories a second's thought when dining with friends. Restaurants are typically used as spaces to relax, commune and socialize; to experience new cuisines with familiar people, familiar cuisines with new people, and everything in between. But the reality is that they often serve up food that has more calories than one might expect, with research suggesting that approximately 92 per cent of both large-chain and local restaurants exceed recommended calorie requirements for a single meal (Urban *et al.* 2016). Now, for these calories to be displayed so evidently on menus, without proper nutritional education to those reading them, is to run the risk of precipitating irrevocable changes in attitudes to food in these settings. Essentially, a fresh wave of calorie-counters may emerge. And, when this is superimposed on the backdrop of society's already rampant diet culture, it may lead to a widespread increase in the levels of disordered eating, body image concerns and malnutrition.

Prior to this implementation, the now defunct Public Health England – a body that in the past was heavily criticized for downplaying mental health – carried out a survey which found that 79 per cent of respondents said they thought that menus *should* include the number of calories in food and drinks (PHE 2018). I'm assuming that this was one of the justifications for its introduction. But, in my opinion, the outcome of that survey is symptomatic of a society ignorant of the pervasiveness of eating disorder psychopathology. There is such little awareness of the full extent of the damage caused by a weight- and calorie-focused dialogue. Currently, £9.4 billion is calculated as being the cost of eating disorders in the UK (HMGCED 2021). I reckon most people would probably assume it to be less.

The UK government said that menus with calories on would 'help the public to make healthier choices when eating out' (GOV.UK 2021). This is highly contentious. What does 'healthier' even mean? In conversation with TV doctor Dr Ellie Cannon, a self-declared 'straight talking GP', she said to me that she thought that 'the concept of "healthy" food is a complete fallacy...different for different bodies and illnesses...as a word, it means nothing' (Cannon 2022). The number of calories is not a reliable indicator of health. Indeed, I can think of very few circumstances where food choices should be made with the number of calories in mind. And I know many competent dietitians who would say the same. The concept of a calorie is relatively new; less than 200 years old in fact. Humans have been around eating for a little longer than that. The thing is, if calories accurately reflected the nutritional value of food, then one would understand their importance. But they don't. A calorie is simply a unit of energy. Instead, focus should be on nutritionally balanced meals, of balanced sizes, at balanced intervals throughout the day. Not necessarily calories.

This perpetuates the dangerous narrative that lower calories means healthier. For many of my patients, the opposite was true: by consuming higher calories, they were becoming healthier.

So this narrative needs to change. In a discussion with Florida-based dietitian Summer Kessel, she told me, '[we ought to be] teaching nutrition in a way that's realistic, adequate, nourishing, enjoyable, culturally satisfying, evidence-based, beneficial, self-caring, practical and affordable' (Kessel 2021).

Nourishment is more than just calories, and there needs to be more education about the limitations of calories. There should also be education around food groups (in particular, carbohydrates and fats, which are often avoided by those with restrictive eating disorders) because they all have their physiological importance.

Orthorexia

Orthorexia nervosa, more commonly referred to as orthorexia, is the fixation on the consumption of foods perceived as healthy. It's a relatively new but exploding phenomenon, and there's still no consensus between the American Psychiatric Association and the World Health Organization (producers of the DSM-5 and ICD-11 respectively) as to whether orthorexia nervosa should be regarded as a mental health disorder or just an unhealthy eating habit (especially since many of its symptoms fall within normal parameters).

Orthorexia nervosa shares some of its features with anorexia nervosa, such as perfectionism and need for control. However, those suffering from orthorexia nervosa primarily focus on the *quality* of food (including food preparation), while those with anorexia nervosa tend to focus on the *quantity* of it (Niedzielski and Kaźmierczak-Wojtaś 2021). In orthorexia nervosa, typically, products containing synthetic substances (such as preservatives, colour additives and pesticides) and other common substances (such as fat, sugar and salt) are eliminated. Unfortunately, this obsession can gradually escalate to the point of overwhelming one's daily life. I've seen patients riddled with stress, guilt and shame at the thought of deviating from their strict regimens. In the most extreme cases, paradoxically, orthorexia nervosa can result in *ill health* – most commonly in the form of malnutrition. There is also the risk of experiencing other short-term symptoms such as fatigue, difficulty concentrating and digestive issues, and long-term health complications such as osteoporosis, anaemia and testosterone deficiency. Orthorexia nervosa also exhibits some symptom overlap with generalized anxiety disorder, obsessive compulsive disorder (OCD) and avoidant/restrictive food intake disorder (ARFID).

Estimates have orthorexia nervosa as impacting 1–7 per cent of the general population (Luck-Sikorski *et al.* 2019). However, because there is no uniform measure of defining orthorexia nervosa, most of these estimates should be treated with caution. One thing is for sure, its prevalence is believed to have increased hugely in recent years, and the scientific community is certainly paying more attention to its impact. A recent study found that 49 per cent of those who followed 'healthy eating' accounts on Instagram met the criteria for orthorexia nervosa (Turner and Lefevre 2017). Another found that 85 per cent of college students who studied a health- or fitness-oriented subject experienced symptoms of orthorexia nervosa – far higher than other unrelated subjects (Malmborg *et al.* 2017). A different study, which showed that 86 per cent of yoga instructors showed symptoms of orthorexia nervosa, supports the idea that this is a condition endemic in the health and wellness community (Herranz Valera *et al.* 2014).

Veganism

In January 2023, the city of Edinburgh, Scotland, became the first city in Europe to endorse the call for a 'Plant Based Treaty' in response to the climate emergency. The move would see 'schools, hospitals and nursing homes move to plant-based meals, and includes a controversial proposal for a "meat tax" to halt farm expansions and new slaughterhouse developments'. The report highlighted that one of the main drivers of climate change is food systems, suggesting that a transition towards plant-based diets would see a significant reduction in offending greenhouse gas emissions (Bovingdon 2023).

When I heard this, I must say, I instantly thought, 'Oh no.' Memories of the countless episodes of my colleagues and me pulling out our hair through frustration when it came to veganism flooded my mind. Now, please don't misunderstand me; I don't think there is anything wrong with veganism. But context is important. In the context of eating disorders, veganism can be a socially acceptable way to obsess over food (such as reading food labels) as well as restrict food groups. Popular eating disorder recovery coach Tabitha Farrar stated that her 'eating disorder would have been in seventh heaven' if she allowed herself to be vegan. She said that she believes that veganism is in fact food restriction and should be avoided in those susceptible to eating disorders, highlighting, 'it doesn't take a rocket scientist to work out that this is not something that a person with an eating disorder should do' (Farrar 2015). Veganism can also result in the intensification of moral perfectionism, often already a problem in those with eating disorders.

However, according to the latest guidelines, veganism is to be regarded as an individual's belief system which is to be acknowledged and respected (RCPsych 2019). Just like a religion, for example. This makes challenging eating disorder-driven veganism much harder. Some say that if a patient with a restrictive eating disorder chooses to accept a higher-calorie vegan option over a lower-calorie non-vegan option, then they have passed the 'vegan test'. And while this *can* work, it's not normally this straightforward. As Maris Degener, a manager at the virtual eating disorder treatment programme Equip says, 'whilst veganism or vegetarianism can often complicate [eating disorder] recovery, it can also be an important or valid part' of one's recovery journey (Degener 2021). However, as I often tell my patients, vegetarians and vegans need to ensure that they do their due diligence to make sure that they are not falling short on micronutrients. They need to ensure that all food groups are accounted for. For example, fats are vital; up to 35 per cent of our nutrition should be from fats (Liu *et al.* 2017). They help protect our organs and keep our nerves healthy, and help with the absorption of essential vitamins. Unfortunately, due to dietary restriction, patients with anorexia nervosa, for example, often lack polyunsaturated essential fatty acids, and 45 per cent of them suffer from at least one micronutrient deficiency (with vitamin A and vitamin B9 deficiencies being most common) (Achamrah *et al.* 2017).

There is a push for humanity to improve its relationship with, and stewarding of, the planet. Veganism is on the increase, especially amongst generation Z and the upcoming generation alpha (KKB 2021). And it's not going away. More people than ever are concerned about the bioenvironmental impact of their dietary choices, and thus more and more patients will inevitably present to eating disorders services stating that they are vegan. Those working in eating disorders can't shy away from it any more. So, the question is how do we navigate this? How do we deliver good care and remain future-focused, whilst at the same time challenging destructive forms of veganism used to mask eating disorders? In the words of Degener, 'to be kind to animals and the earth, we first have to practice being kind to ourselves. Sometimes, especially in recovery, that may mean choosing to eat meat or meat products' (Degener 2021).

Insight from Bailey

During my adolescence, veganism felt like a trend. It was introduced to me by my eldest sister, who turned vegan in protest of animal mistreatment in the US. Struggling with my weight and appearance all my life, I saw veganism as an opportunity to cut a few pounds. It led to me restricting myself from having many important food groups. Veganism slowly became my everything, and I started to see a decline in not just my weight, but also my health. After one year of veganism, I was anaemic. But the decrease in weight pushed me to continue on. I was consuming far less than my body needed, but wouldn't stop because of the 'results' I was seeing. My hair started to wither, and when I got up too quickly, I started seeing stars. As a competitive swimmer, my performance decreased, and after a race my vision, along with hearing, would fade and return after a while. The lack of iron was causing me fainting spells after the intense cardio I was putting myself through. No one had told me about the importance of fuelling your body properly, and so my way of eating continued. Eventually, I realized the extent to which it was affecting my body. Four years was more than enough to seriously affect my health.

'Ethnic' Foods

Unfortunately, a victim of today's narrative around food is food from minority ethnic groups. In a push for 'healthier' eating, there has been the systematic shunning of foods from non-Western diets, often described as 'ethnic' food. First, I find the term 'ethnic' – when used in a way to marginalize people of colour – lazy. It's often used clunkily and synonymously to mean non-White; an attempt to describe the vast array of global communities, colours and cultures as one homogenous lump. I guess my biggest problem with it is that inherent within it is a definition that elevates White food as being the 'norm' – as though White food is not 'ethnic'. Lavanya Ramanathan, senior editor at Vox, said that the term 'ethnic' is applied selectively 'to cuisines that seem the most foreign, often cooked by people with the brownest skin' (Ramanathan 2015).

The problem arises when we consider how 'ethnic' cuisines are perceived in modern society – often held in lower esteem than their European counterparts. Diners often expect 'ethnic' food to be cheap; likely part of the reason they're also perceived as unhealthy. The myth that you cannot be healthy and enjoy non-Western foods needs urgent debunking. The Eurocentric lens – through which we often view health – can be hugely damaging. Tamar Samuels, a Black registered dietitian and the co-founder of Culina Health, said that 'what is considered healthy is often associated with thinness, and thinness is often associated with whiteness…we need to redefine what healthy looks like to include different body shapes, colors and sizes' (USA Today 2021). In an interview about his award-winning book *Black Food*, Bryant Terry, American chef and author, said that one of his main aims was to 'elevate and embrace' the aspects of African-American food that are often neglected (CBS Mornings 2021). Psyche A. Williams-Forson's *Eating While Black* is also a powerful argument for embracing non-racist understandings and practices in relation to food.

Jon Kung, Detroit-based chef and content creator, said, 'Growing up in the West, we're conditioned to assume that certain foods are healthier than others, and certain foods – especially "ethnic" foods – tend to be unhealthy' (USA Today 2021). Kung, along with others such as Dr Kera Nyemb-Diop (also known as 'The Black Nutritionist') and Jessica Wilson, MS RD, are doing their part to increase the ethnic mix among dietetic, nutrition and wellness influencers – a sector notoriously lacking in diversity. In a sample of more than 100,000 dietitians, 74.8 per cent identified as White, whilst only 4 per cent identified as Asian, 3.3 per cent as Latino/a and 2.5 per cent as Black (Taylor 2018). Such ethnocultural imbalances can have real-world repercussions in eating disorder care. Unfortunately, such lack of diversity may be part of the reason why many Black, Indigenous and people of colour (BIPOC) feel unsatisfied with the eating disorder care that they experience when they do present to services (Kupemba 2021). The few patients of colour that I have looked after in an inpatient setting have all made comments on the food availability; one patient in particular mentioned that the food was 'too White' for her. In the world of nutrition, dietetics and wellness, the indifference to underrepresented ethnic groups is deafening (Russell 2021). It represents a wholehearted negligent attitude to the very things that nutrition stands for – variety and sustainability.

Anorexia Nervosa

Diagnostic Criteria

1. BMI < 18.5 kg/m2,[1] or rapid weight loss (> 20% of total body weight within 6 months)
2. Behaviours to keep body weight low
3. Excessive preoccupation with body weight or shape

(Based on ICD-11)

" Being the parent of a person with anorexia nervosa means you experience every emotion, sometimes all in one day, but for a long time the overriding feelings are of fear and guilt. You have the constant fear of receiving that phone call, the one that destroys your world, the one to tell you your child has succumbed to the illness. You feel guilty because you always question yourself; what did I do wrong, could I have done more to understand, could I have done more to help them eat? That guilt, for me, is as false as the anorexic voice that destroys your child, but that doesn't stop it gnawing away. There is one other feeling that is welcome, though, and that is pride. I have been lucky enough to see my daughter battle through, against all odds, to be in a position of recovery. She is eating and starting to enjoy life again. She still has her demons with food and her illness, but I have an overwhelming sense of pride in her strength and determination to beat this horrific illness. Never give up hope.

John Rogers, a father

---

1   BMI-for-age under 5th percentile in children and adolescents; low body weight is not due to a medical condition or food scarcity.

Introduction

Clare Steedman and Rachael Alder-Byrne

Clare Steedman is a leading specialist occupational therapist in eating disorders, a systemic psychotherapy practitioner, an eye movement desensitization and reprocessing (EMDR) therapist and the Co-founder and Clinical Director of The Eating Disorder Specialists (TEDS), an innovative online service offering a blended approach of therapies for individuals in the community presenting with an array of disordered eating. She is currently Co-chair of the Royal College of Occupational Therapists Eating Disorders Specialist Interest Group. @claresteedman

Rachael Alder-Byrne is a specialist art psychotherapist in eating disorders, an EMDR therapist and Co-founder of The Eating Disorder Specialists (TEDS), an innovative online service offering a blended approach of therapies for individuals in the community presenting with an array of disordered eating. Having worked in mental health for more than 17 years, her experience includes forensics and palliative care. @rachael-alder-byrne

Our paths as therapists started very differently within the field of eating disorders; however, the challenges of treating this client group were all too similar. As an occupational therapist and an art psychotherapist, our experiences of working alongside individuals with anorexia nervosa, within the UK's National Health Service and private sector, highlighted to us not only the sheer exhaustion of existing with this serious mental health condition, but also the complexities in effectively treating this illness within a contemporary healthcare system lacking in resources, funding and a variety of therapeutic approaches.

Anorexia nervosa can engulf an individual's identity, roles and relationships. It can provide a person with a sense of meaning, purpose, control, confidence and sometimes a sense of escapism, albeit maladaptive. This illness can also give an individual a means to communicate, to the outside world, their own internal distress. Every client who we have had the privilege of walking alongside has had their own unique narrative as to how anorexia nervosa stepped into their lives, sometimes enabling them to survive, but also negatively impacting on their everyday functioning: from being unable to prepare and eat meals, to difficulties regulating emotions and forming healthy attachments. Also, as part of each client's unique story lie the often devastating effects on the interpersonal relationships with those in their network.

In our experience, anorexia nervosa is an extremely complex mental health condition and thus requires a dynamic, integrative, multifaceted therapeutic approach to support clients. Yet we have observed clients being limited to accessing one specific type of therapy, as set by care pathways or rigid guidelines. We have also witnessed clients who are ready for change being unable to access support due to not meeting specific referral criteria. Lastly, we have sadly borne witness to many – due to a lack of funding and resources – forced into life-threatening positions before accessing specialist eating disorder treatment. When we meet a client in this space, we often find someone – due to untimely intervention – lacking in identity, detached from meaningful life roles, routines, relationships and activities, and limited in their motivation to change.

As therapists working together, we have come to understand the importance of three concepts that provide the most beneficial outcomes in recovery. First, a multitude of therapeutic approaches are needed to address the complexities that anorexia nervosa presents. This informs the way we currently work with clients. We integrate our core professions of occupational therapy and art psychotherapy, as well as additional therapies such as eye movement desensitization and reprocessing (EMDR), which allows us to adjust to meet the needs of our clients rather than restricting them to a 'one size fits all' approach. Second, individuals need to be able to access support when they are ready for change, rather than only when they are in crisis. And third, the therapist–client relationship is crucial for healing, as well as the therapist–therapist connection for avoiding conflicts of interest regarding their mutual client.

We have often heard the term 'treatment-resistant' used to describe people with longstanding anorexia nervosa. However, in our clinical experience, we understand this to mean that an individual has lacked the appropriate interventions to support a move towards their own version of recovery. An integrated approach offers an alternative way of exploring attachments and the past, current and future challenges that may be preventing an individual from connecting with their identity and aspirations. We have witnessed clients who were deemed untreatable go on to establish full and meaningful lives, free of healthcare settings. We have seen the power of holding hope for our clients. When they are afforded the opportunity to gain the right support, at the right time, it can be the difference between surviving and thriving.

Eating Disorders Don't Just Disappear When You Get Pregnant

Hope Virgo

Hope Virgo is an author and a multi-award-winning eating disorders advocate. She is a recognized media spokesperson, having appeared on various platforms including BBC's *Newsnight* and *Victoria Derbyshire*, ITV's *Good Morning Britain*, and *Sky News*. She is the founder of the #DumpTheScales campaign which put eating disorders on the UK government's agenda. Her book *Stand Tall Little Girl* was released in 2018. @hopevirgo

Having children was something I wanted eventually. But not even a life-saving year in a mental health hospital (which I appreciate I was extremely lucky to get) – where I learnt so much about myself – can prepare you for pregnancy. I honestly don't think anything can really set you up for pregnancy, whether you've had an eating disorder or not. Inevitably, there will be challenges.

I was 13 years old when I met her. She came running over to me one evening when I lay in bed ruminating. At first, I didn't know who she was. But all I knew is that, with her, life felt somewhat easier and seemed to make sense. Her voice numbed the emotions I didn't want to feel and gave me what I thought was this real sense of certainty. At the time, I thought she was it: the solution to life. The answer to everything.

So, when I sat there on the bathroom floor, aged 31, having been out of hospital for just over a decade, on that fateful November night, I felt afraid. I was scared of the heightened emotions I was already beginning to feel; emotions that, for so much of my childhood, I had run away from. I was afraid of my body changing, afraid of the impact on my life, the sheer uncertainty that I was about to embark on, and the 'what ifs' that gradually began to take over. The thought of the next few months ahead filled me with an intense fear. I knew that eating disorders can use news of pregnancy to rope a person back in; a concoction creating a perfect storm for the eating disorder to thrive. Statistics showing the high eating disorder relapse rates in pregnancy and postpartum left me terrified.

Fast-forward four years, and I'm sitting in a cold, rather bleak-looking hospital waiting room, waiting for an assessment. Around the room: leaflets of various mental illnesses, a boy sitting opposite me lost in his thoughts, and some kids' toys shoved in the corner.
   'Jennifer Hope Virgo.'
   The icy, piercing voice of the receptionist cut through the deathly silence. My mum looked at me in an encouraging way as we got up and headed down the corridor. The man in the office exuded warmth, his room decorated with cards. What followed was an hour of me sitting, looking at the floor, feeling uncomfortable, with my walls shooting up to protect me. It was following this appointment they told me that her name was anorexia.

Pregnancy is full of rules; things you should and shouldn't eat. Cue eating disorder: 'You could probably add a whole lot more to the no-go list to get away with things.' There are rules on how much weight to put on. Eating disorder: 'You need to put on the minimum, if that.' And then the fear and uncertainty of what is happening. Eating disorder: 'I can numb the emotions and give you a sense of certainty, if you listen to me.' A constant battle with an incessant fear that perhaps I'm actually harming the baby through my behaviours, or from my past.

But I was so sure they had got it wrong. So sure that they were making things up. I couldn't accept what was going on and, over the next six months at my weekly appointments, I lied and lied and lied. She had a way of convincing me that I didn't know her. And also, that the only solution is to be secretive. It became second nature to put on a mask and say, 'I'm fine. Life's fine. Yep, everything is just fine.' But behind the exterior was a broken person. Someone so desperate to be like others. Someone so desperate to just be happy. I spent a year, in the end, living in an in-patient unit – and it saved my life.

The shame I felt during pregnancy was huge. The shame of not being able to work out how to feed my body, to keep my baby safe, consumed me. And in that first trimester, it was this shame that stopped me speaking up. Shame and judgement that I was afraid of receiving, combined with the guilt that I should have been blooming through pregnancy. I should have been loving it. I felt so guilty that so many people want kids but can't have them, yet I was lying there unsure of whether I could even do it.

The inevitable discharge loomed as I approached my 18th birthday. How can it be so clear-cut? One day a child, and the next an adult and no longer able to access support. Anyway, I had always planned to go to uni, and after taking my A levels in hospital, I was desperate for a change of scenery, so the hospital and my parents agreed that they would support my decision to go. On a Thursday morning, over the summer, my mum and I drove up to Birmingham to meet the adult eating disorder team that would be supporting me during my time at uni. I felt lucky to be able to get this assessment.

Eating disorders can so often come like a hurricane, impacting entire networks. When I told my family I was pregnant, they were all so happy for me, but there was also fear and a question about how I would cope. My husband, my family and close friends weren't naïve – they all knew that my eating disorder had not simply disappeared. As the weeks progressed, and my body began to change, I would often lie awake at night feeling my stomach. By night, my brain would make me anxious about what I looked like. I would lie awake for hours comparing my bump to others on social media, jealous of those doing 'so well' at pregnancy, worrying about what would happen to my body after the baby was born.

My coping mechanisms at uni were simple:

1. Stick to my meal plan.

2. Have at least one day off from exercise a week.

3. Remember that my feelings about food are in my head and not my reality.

4. Remember my motivations.

5. Remember how the eating disorder ruined my life.

It was about taking one day at a time and making sure that I didn't slip into bad habits.

It certainly felt easier when people looked at me and could tell I was pregnant. Whilst I enjoyed feeling the baby kick, I would often take one look at myself in the morning mirror and be disgusted. My eating disorder has never been just about my body, but so much else. But in these moments, my brain did what it could to distort how I was feeling. Seducing me, pulling me into those dark places, using my body to project so many emotions. So many things I just did not want to feel. That nagging voice in my head trying to tell me that if I just did certain behaviours, then I would experience that short-lived numbing of emotions that I longed for in so many ways. Then everything would be okay.

Anyway, despite these rules, and despite managing to keep putting one step in front of the other throughout university, and subsequently travelling the world, 14 years later in 2016, I relapsed. Finally, it took a global pandemic, and some major life changes, to make me start realizing that there was so much more to life. I realized that I had to start challenging my own recovery more. I had become stuck in this space of just settling, allowing her to still have an impact on me.

From the first appointment with my midwife, my pregnancy had been categorized as a risk to both me and the baby. But it wasn't until my second trimester that I was able to access support – predominantly due to the lack of services available. And the age-old issue arose – that because I was a healthy weight, everything 'must be fine'. In my second trimester, I knew that I was finding things harder. I was under the perinatal mental health team and, with issues around the baby's growth, now had more scans. I also received additional support from a dietitian. I was scared about the baby, scared of hurting it, and of letting down those around me. With all this going on, I had to sit down and talk honestly to my husband, mum, sister and aunt about what was going on, and discussed the details of my thought pattern that I was so ashamed of. Whilst I was terrified of opening up, I knew that I had to. Full transparency was the only way that I was going to get through things. I knew that I never wanted to get unwell again and so needed a plan of action. I didn't want this any more.

I didn't want her any more.

With my medical team, which at that point included a midwife, key worker, consultant, dietitian and two therapists, we worked out my 32-week mental health plan. It included triggers, ways to cope with emotions and ways that others could spot I was struggling. I was able to share all of this with my husband and family who, by then, knew what they needed to do to offer any additional support. But even with all these plans in place, there was still fear, worry and concern around what was going to happen. I was still scared of relapsing, scared of what would happen to the baby. At times, the uncertainty completely consumed me.

✻ ✻ ✻

I write this sitting on my sofa at home after taking my three-month-old son for another round of jabs. I still have fears about the future and of not moving around as much on some days. But I always hold on to the hope that I'll fully recover – and I'm so close to that point. I know what I need to do to get there. Meanwhile, in between changing nappies, I campaign full-time for those affected by eating disorders. Because every single person deserves justice.

Entire Life in a Grain of Rice

Megan Jayne Crabbe

Megan Jayne Crabbe is a best-selling author, digital creator and presenter with more than 1.3 million followers across her social channels. She built her online platform creating content around body positivity, eating disorder recovery, mental health and feminism. In 2017, she wrote her first book, *Body Positive Power*, a manifesto on all the reasons why we hate our bodies, and how to challenge these reasons. She has been a featured speaker at events hosted by Spotify, Instagram, *Stylist* magazine, *The Sunday Times* and The Body Shop. In 2019, she co-created and toured a sell-out live show called *The Never Say Diet Club*. She has worked with the BBC, The BRITS and Channel 4 as a presenter and podcast host. @meganjaynecrabbe

I've never understood how people can love rollercoasters. Voluntarily propel myself through the air in a metal contraption that I don't understand or have any control over? Legs dangling? No sense of up or down? Hard pass.

The same goes for horror films. Or obstacle courses. Or jumping off a cliff into the sea. Anything designed to destabilize or simulate fear is something I can do without. I'm far more comfortable with my feet planted firmly on the ground, a clear idea of what's coming next and all the details possible. That stuff helps me feel safe.

And I don't necessarily mean just physically safe – but safe from the unknown, the overwhelming, the unpredictable. Or in other words: life.

My eating disorder came along (as it does for so many of us) on the cusp between girlhood and womanhood.

In my pre-eating disorder world, I knew how everything worked. I knew the morning routine before school. I knew the flow of the day. I knew where the cartons of milk were kept for break time. I knew that working hard on homework meant reward. I knew how to interact with my friends, say the right things to adults, how to get everything as perfect as possible.

Life was contained between the chalk-painted paving slabs I skipped over – every day the same.

And then growing up happens.

Suddenly, you know nothing.

You start spending your days in a completely new place, three times the size of the last. All kinds of different people flood in, each with opinions about who you should be. The bar for being 'good' at things has shifted, starkly. And within all this newness, you're supposed to be able to point out into the endless expanse of what your life could be, and choose.

If you're lucky, that's all you have to deal with.

But if you're a girl (increasingly, a young person of any gender), and if you happen to be aware of all the extra things the world expects from you in order to fit that role well, you're really in for a ride.

Because now it's time to fit every ideal about what a woman should be: how you should look, what you should eat, how you should behave and what you should want. The world has started to see you differently, even if inside you still feel the same.

I started studying for womanhood young. I soaked up every cultural message about what beauty was while my friends were focusing on whether they could do a cartwheel. I studied my body and spent hours imagining what it might become, quietly learning ways that I could get there.

I observed that beautiful women won the attention of men, and that was important. Being wanted was very important.

I thought I'd be prepared for when that shift happened. I'd have the perfect body to satisfy the male gaze. (In my imagination I would naturally transform into a thin, White woman with blue eyes, like the ones on the TV. My brown skin and Jamaican heritage didn't seem to factor into the equation.)

I'd have the kind of femininity that wouldn't disturb the patriarchal order of things. I wouldn't have feelings that were ugly or loud or complicated. I had it all planned out.

Except you really can't plan it out. You can't prepare for that shift from child to something else – the way it seems to happen overnight, the way suddenly people want things from you that you don't understand, the way everything from your weight to your taste to the way your voice sounds couldn't feel more wrong.

The way you have control over none of it.

The way your feet are no longer on the ground.

I think I held on quite well at first. I re-learned how to be perfect in my new academic arena. I kept up with shifting friendships and I stayed good at home. I adopted fresh layers of femininity and found the time to obsess over boys. I also dieted, with increasing intensity. And I kept quiet about all the new ways I was starting to hate myself every day.

Balancing all of that at the age of 13 is a precarious game. I'm not sure I could point to the one thing that tipped it over, but I remember lots of conversations around me about what was coming next, how everything was going to change soon and that I had choices to make. I felt terrified.

And then there was food.

Food that I already understood how to manipulate to change my body into something 'better' (according to societal standards of femininity). Food that could be easily measured, added up, taken away. Food that I could build a routine around, and be contained by. Food that I could control.

I might not know what's coming next, but I can plan every number in my next meal.

I might not understand why it feels like my body doesn't fully belong to me any more, but I'm in control of how it looks.

I might not know what I want to do with my life, but I know I need to be less.

Every day that I listened to my eating disorder, my world – the things I cared about, my thoughts, my goals – got smaller. And within that smallness, I knew how everything worked.

I knew how to avoid breakfast during the morning routine before school. I knew how to plan food into the flow of the day. I knew the exact numbers inside every snack for break time. I knew that working hard at exercise meant reward. I knew how to avoid concern from my friends, say the right things to adults, how to get everything as perfect as possible.

I learned how to fit my entire life into a grain of rice, and I felt safe. Which made no sense to anyone around me, because clearly I was destroying myself. But brains aren't always the best at distinguishing self-protection from self-destruction.

It took me a long time to see reality.

To see that listening to the eating disorder (because it feels like the safest way to live) ends with barely living at all. Because the best parts about being alive – feeling things and exploring places and tasting flavours and being present – can't exist at the same time as the eating disorder. The eating disorder takes away all of those parts while telling you that it's for your protection.

To see that listening to the eating disorder might feel like being in control (and it is being in control of one very small part of your life), but if you listen for too long, it leaves you completely out of control. You are no longer driving your life. You don't feel like you have a choice. You don't feel like you. And when you get to that point, defying the eating disorder is the only way to truly be in control again.

To see that reducing your life to a series of numbers might seem like the only thing you can do to manage everything that's unpredictable, unknown, overwhelming, unspeakable. But you are more capable of managing those things than you realize. And if you stay in your eating disorder, you'll never even give yourself a chance to find that out.

While I was recovering, I had to turn my eating disorder into a beast. I needed an enemy to rage against. I needed it to not feel like a part of me. I mentally war-cried, 'FUCK YOU ANOREXIA' before every meal, and defied every disordered thought she threw at me. And it worked.

It wasn't until years later, long out of the woods and living in a softly rounded body that I'd learned to love, when a therapist suggested that my eating disorder was a way my brain had tried to protect me.

It made absolutely no sense.

How could this thing that burned down everything around me, and nearly took me with it, be trying to keep me safe?

It took me a while to accept that she was part of me. That she developed as a result of life feeling unbearable. That she was my response to fear. To not knowing. To living in a culture of impossible expectations and normalized self-blame.

My eating disorder was a coping mechanism when I couldn't cope. I understand that now.

I also understand that choosing recovery doesn't mean you magically know how to cope with all the things you didn't before.

There will still be endless unknowns, changes you can't control, expectations that feel unbearable sometimes. But you'll know better than attempting to find safety from them in self-destruction.

You'll learn that everyone feels like they don't know sometimes. That everyone needs coping mechanisms in this world and that you can learn better ones. That you don't always have to be in total control to be safe.

You'll see that life on the other side of an eating disorder is big, and messy. It includes mistakes and overwhelming moments. It also includes sunsets, and Subway sandwiches at 2 a.m. after you've been dancing at a festival all day. It includes books that will change your life and kisses that feel like you're floating above the world. It includes being held and seen in ways you thought nobody would ever see you. It includes every emotion.

It might even include taking your feet off the ground sometimes, and letting go.

One thing that the eating disorder will never tell you though (but I will) is that you were never supposed to be able to handle it all. It was always too much. It was never your fault. You did your best. You deserve to be here. And you deserve to be okay.

It's safe to be okay.

Keep Smiling

Lara Rebecca

Lara Rebecca is a mental health and eating disorder awareness advocate, creator and public speaker. Her self-titled YouTube channel has accumulated over 50,000 subscribers and 8 million views. She is the host of *The Keep Smiling Podcast*. She has collaborated on international campaigns and worked alongside the BBC, ITV, Channel 4, S4C, and Snapchat. @lara__rebecca

It ravaged my teenage years. The 'harmless' coping mechanism – for my co-existent anxiety, perfectionism, insecurities and destructive inner dialogue – eventually became an addiction. It gave me the control my young, impressionable, vulnerable high school self was so desperate for. I took comfort within my ability to fixate, modify and customize my lifestyle to encourage my habits. But slowly, the insidious disease overwhelmed my identity and daily motivations. Throwing school packed lunches away, intentionally walking longer routes to class to encourage energy expenditure, and spending hours learning how to vomit and celebrating when I finally did, became my new normal.

This was worsened by the innocuous square of glass I had just discovered. My worth now lay in its fluorescent blue digits, which I could use to calculate my body mass index. Just like math class, everything became about the numbers. Calories, circumference of body parts, weights, steps, training duration. Everything, numbers.

I was anorexic.

Alongside this, academic stress was becoming increasingly triggering. I had to live up to the seemingly unrealistic educational standards I had set for myself. Anything under 100 per cent, or an A*, was a failure in my eyes.

School life became increasingly hostile. My sense of confidence was disintegrating into nothingness, and sitting amidst groups of schoolmates was replaced by hiding away in toilets. I insisted on finding additional work as an excuse to avoid any social contact. I hid away. Teachers reorganized my seating position in classes to ensure I was within easy reach of the door to provide an escape when I suffered anxiety attacks. I'd run through the corridors, searching for a quiet space to control my erratic breathing. Then, I'd simply cry. Humiliated and hopeless. I isolated myself. This normally giggly, young, karate-loving kid was slowly vanishing. And in its place: an empty, sad, lonely girl.

❋ ❋ ❋

I was recommended a school counsellor to help with my debilitating social anxiety and non-existent confidence. Despite initially being hesitant, our conversations consisted of me confessing how I never felt good enough, exploring my horrendous self-esteem and discussing my unmistakable obsessive characteristics. As the weeks progressed, and trust began to form, I became more comfortable disclosing the true extent of my mindset. My warped perspective of my body, and food, became increasingly obvious. And my counsellor waved a red flag. This is when everything changed. I was referred to my GP who diagnosed me with anorexia nervosa. My secret, my hidden comfort, and my independent control, was now externally recognized. And I wasn't happy about it.

But despite the terrifying prospect of attention, the label provided yet another motivator. The name gave it this unbelievable power and expectation, exacerbating the illness further. I lied a lot. Outside of school hours, I became immersed in online communities sharing tips, tricks and advice on how to 'succeed' in this eating disorder and how to maintain this aggressive weight loss cycle 'efficiently'. My weight was falling off. I lied a lot. The numbers on the scales were dropping. I'd managed to convince myself that I'd be happy upon hitting a certain number – but that was never the case. Nothing was ever enough. I kept pushing it, further and further. I lied a lot. My eating disorder was now controlling *me*.

❉ ❉ ❉

Looking back now, I hardly recognize that person. Visually, there was nothing of me. My face was totally sunken. My fingers were blue from lack of circulation, my eyes lifeless, and hands skeletal. Psychologically, I was empty. I felt numb and valueless. Lost and hopeless. I was stuck in an aggressive, life-threatening cycle that I couldn't escape. So much so that my parents were becoming increasingly concerned about my safety, and ended up taking me to hospital where medical staff finally responded.

The control was slipping from my grasp. I was taken out of school, put on a meal plan and monitored. Life was miserable, still. My daily purpose now revolved around eating within a caloric surplus, gaining weight and facing up to countless 'fear foods'.

I'd write pages of self-loathing, bitterness and anger in my A5 journals – of how disgusted I was in myself, the disappointment, the hopelessness and the confusion. I'd write of the frustration I felt towards those allegedly trying to help me, and how appalled I was seeing the digits on the scale climb steadily.

❉ ❉ ❉

Months and months down the line, I witnessed a gradual transition in my mindset. My perception of life began evolving. I was gaining clarity of thought and fresh perspectives, and started noticing the opportunities that anorexia had stripped away from me.

Rather than solely focusing on the *symptoms* of my disorder and weight restoration, I finally began considering the psychological *triggers*. The work started from the roots, up. This is when my transformation truly initiated.

I was no longer exhausted, freezing cold and drained. I had unfamiliar energy. When given the medical go-ahead to walk my newly adopted greyhounds, it felt freeing. The brisk wind brushed against my skin as I slowly strolled around the perimeter of my local park, alongside my incredible dad, watching my baby sister innocently giggle as she threw herself down the slide in the playground. *Life* – this is what I had been missing. These small, yet highly meaningful moments gradually accumulated, all of which inspired me to keep pushing towards recovery.

❊ ❊ ❊

My motivation gathered pace. Following discharge, I had the opportunity to do it for *myself*. I was driven, dreaming of a life of freedom and happiness. I was exhausted by the years of restriction, isolation and hiding. Instead, I wanted to authentically laugh again, create wholesome memories, and live without all-consuming anxiety.

Food transformed into a creative outlet. No longer the enemy, but instead an enjoyment. A social event and an opportunity to experiment with textures, flavours, cuisines and colours.

I focused on establishing respect and acceptance towards my body, by lightly introducing exercise back into my weekly routine. Fitness faded from being an abusive tool – to encourage my disordered tendencies – into a celebration. An empowering and healthy instrument for my mental health.

The same year, I took part in my local 5k 'Race for Life' with my stepmum. I remember the crowds of women, hundreds of beaming smiles, umpteen pink tutus, painted faces, groups of encouraging spectators and a humbling sense of community. The sense of togetherness, connectedness, and wholesome positivity totally captivated me. I hadn't smiled so much in years. Lara was coming back.

Interspersed among inevitable wobbles and fragile moments – days where I felt that I was taking steps backwards, and periods where I'd feel discouraged and overwhelmed – were the sprouts of a more optimistic and happy future.

❋ ❋ ❋

My newfound mindset motivated me to launch my self-titled blog: a platform to share my experiences. It was my safe space – my corner of the Internet – to explore my creativity, write openly and honestly with vulnerability to a global audience and, most importantly, create beneficial content for others in a similar predicament. Writing was therapeutic, and engaging with others was humbling. Building a community of kind individuals made me smile, and provided somewhat of a purpose.

I (somehow) cultivated the confidence to launch a YouTube channel the year following. The objective was to continue the conversation around mental health and eating disorder awareness, and spread a little positivity. From this came the public-speaking opportunities, live TV and radio features, documentary recordings and various panel discussions. I became accustomed to applying myself in uncomfortable and unfamiliar circumstances, with the hopes of growing, learning, evolving, connecting, networking, building knowledge and confidence. The insecure, anxiety-ridden Lara – from a few years prior – would never have contemplated this ever being a reality.

At the beginning of 2020, I launched *The Keep Smiling Podcast*: a platform of honest and authentic discussions, exploring an abundance of topics ranging from fitness to mental health, mindset and wellbeing. I've been so fortunate to interview some incredible guests regarding how they've flourished in spite of trauma and adversity. These conversations have benefited my personal recovery journey and continue to motivate me.

Embarking on these creative endeavours, putting myself out there and continually leaning into discomfort inspired this ever-continuing process of self-discovery. Steadily, I was re-establishing my values, discovering my true passions and connecting with likeminded others. It was empowering.

❊ ❊ ❊

Today, I'm 22. Am I 'fully' recovered from my eating disorder? Not necessarily. But over the past decade, I've cultivated an understanding of how my mindset works, and I have learnt to implement healthier coping strategies when my mental health is more fragile.

You see, life isn't supposed to be simple. But its complexities provide a catalyst for progression. The process has been slow, turbulent, challenging, yet remarkably gratifying. I've grown, learned, and continue to do so. My experiences have shaped me, revealed my true capabilities and forced me to push boundaries, allowing me to acquire new skills, a healthy purpose, enhanced social relationships, a greater appreciation for life and a recognition of new possibilities.

A few years ago, I was asphyxiated by my over-consuming panic disorder, and I felt empty. However, my life is no longer dictated by disordered routines and addictive unhealthy tendencies.

Rather, I enthusiastically engage in conversation, smile with authenticity, push myself into unfamiliar, growth-provoking environments and prioritize my psychological wellbeing. I have accepted the adversities of my past. I have reconstructed previously held assumptions, narratives and beliefs, and now possess refreshed perspectives, and hope for an optimistic, happy future.

I am no longer trapped by the label of 'anorexic'.

I am Lara.

Comedy for Coping

Dave Chawner

Dave Chawner is an award-winning stand-up comedian, number-one best-selling author, presenter and mental health campaigner. He has presented for BBC's *Tomorrow's World* and has appeared on BBC's *Breakfast*, ITV's *Lorraine* and *Loose Women*, and Channel 5's *Jeremy Vine* as well as made appearances on BBC Radio 1, BBC Radio 2 and BBC Radio 4. His best-selling book *Weight Expectations* was released in 2018. He has also written for *The Guardian, The Telegraph, Metro, Cosmopolitan, GQ* and *Reader's Digest*. As a stand-up comic, he has performed six solo shows at the Edinburgh Fringe Festival and received an award for his show *Normally Abnormal* at the Houses of Parliament in 2014. @davechawner

A couple of years back, I was asked to be a guest on the sofa on *BBC Breakfast* talking about eating disorders and comedy. The producer called the day before, began by thanking me for my time and followed up with 'I'm really excited to talk to you, because I've never had any mental health.'

I was confused. 'Sorry? You've never had any mental health?'

Without missing a beat, she replied, 'Nope. I've never had any mental health, my family have never had mental health, nor have any of my friends. In fact, I don't know anyone with any mental health!'

I wish I'd said something cool, sassy and funny in that moment, but I just burbled something incomprehensible while my brain buffered and then eventually moved the conversation along. But it kinda pissed me off. Everyone has mental health. But why do we always talk about mental health as an illness rather than a state of mental wellbeing? Why do we always focus on the negative rather than the positive? And it's things like that which meant that, when I was a teenager, I'd rather have waxed my scrotum with duct tape than talk about mental health.

So, no wonder I didn't talk about my anorexia when it began. But also, part of the reason was that I didn't really know what was happening. It took years to develop and slowly became my normality.

I once read this weird article which said that if you pop a frog in a pan of water and slowly heat it, the frog doesn't realize the water's getting warmer and even though it could hop out of the pan any time it wants, it boils to death. Now, obviously if you do that, you're a Grade A bellend who should probably be on some government watch list. But this particularly callous experiment shows that sometimes, when things happen slowly, we can be the last person to see what's going on. It's like being really close to a massive picture – you can't see the wood for the trees. That's what happened with my anorexia. People around me noticed before I did. It took me a long time to realize that my eating disorder was in control of me rather than the other way round. And it took me a hell of a lot longer to get treatment.

It took me over half a decade before I was diagnosed as severely clinically anorexic and had to have fast-tracked treatment. I'll save you the sob stories, because I do worry that sometimes this sort of thing turns into mawkish pity-porn. When talking about eating disorders, it seems to become some unspoken competition about who was more ill than who! Especially with anorexia, there's this subliminal competition to try to outdo others on their BMIS, weights and sizes. I'm not bothered about that shit to be honest, so if you're looking for my 'tale of woe', you ain't going to find it here!

All I will say is that I was reluctant to get treatment. Of course I bloody well was! The anorexia filled a void; it was a diseased coping mechanism. Over time, I realized I had an eating disorder. Sure, it took time to realize – and even longer to accept – but I got there in the end. Yes, I knew that I was damaging my body. Yadda, yadda, yadda. Of course I knew that it could kill me. Yes, yes, yes. In fact, I wanted it to. I tried to speed that up. For me the eating disorder was a passive suicide attempt. So trying to scare me into treatment was about as much use as tits on a snake. So I didn't want to 'recover' because there was nothing in it for me. After all, everyone talked about recovery as 'taking the anorexia away'; no one talked about giving anything back. I had everything to lose and nothing to gain from treatment, so why in God's name would I even think about it?!

So, what changed? The answer is simple – my perspective.

I slipped into depression. I went to the GP telling them that I didn't want to be treated for the anorexia, just the depression. I refused treatment for the anorexia four times and played the system so that they couldn't make me do anything I didn't want. People kept on focusing on the eating disorder, which frustrated me. I genuinely saw that as something separate. To my befuddled mind, them focusing on my eating disorder was like getting a hearing test when you've gone in for a sprained wrist. However, as one frustrated nurse put it: 'Bottom line, you wouldn't expect your laptop to work if you don't charge it, so why would you expect your brain to work if you don't feed it?' She had a point! I didn't think about it that way.

So I had a choice: let the anorexia take its course and push everyone away, as the depression would get worse, or do something about the eating disorder with a view to getting rid of the depression.

I chose the latter route. I was lucky enough to get 2.5 years of therapy. I can't complain; the treatment was incredible. To be completely honest, I feel bad about that. I know I got lucky. While I was going through therapy, I was also creating a stand-up show all about my anorexia. I'm lucky enough that stand-up is my job, but I was amazed by how similar writing comedy and going to therapy were. I suppose it shouldn't have been a shock because, after all, humour has the rare ability to break things down into manageable chunks and look at them in a different way. In fact, if I was to get all 'Stephen Fry' about it, the word 'comedy' itself is believed to be from the Ancient Greek 'kōmos' meaning 'to reveal'.

OK, that might be a bit highfalutin so let's take it down a notch. The fact of the matter is, it's hard to be scared and laughing at the same time. That's why you don't find many 'knock knock' jokes in the middle of *Scream*. Humour has the power to take big scary things and make them less threatening.

So, comedy provided a unique opportunity to try to understand my eating disorder so that I could try to build better, more sustainable coping mechanisms while also creating something that could help inform, educate and (hopefully!) entertain people who might have experience of eating disorders. Or, perhaps, it might even be able to reach those who were lucky enough to have no experience of eating disorders at all.

And, of course, that always raises the question 'Surely you can't laugh about mental health?'

Over recent years there has been increasing debate about what you can and can't say. Debates about freedom of speech, cancel culture and de-platforming have increased. Personally, I don't think anything is off limits for comedy. Anything is fair game when it comes to humour. But intent is a lot more important than content. You have to think about the joke teller's relationship to the topic: is the joke aiming to demean, belittle and bully or is it using humour to engage, analyse and explain?

For example, if I was to joke about how hard it is being a single Canadian mother living in the UK, you would, quite rightly, think that I don't know what I'm talking about. On the other hand, if the wonderful Katherine Ryan jokes about it, the joke comes from a place of knowledge rather than ignorance. And meaningful comedy should always come from a place of knowledge rather than ignorance. Which is why I used my experience to engage people in the topic of eating disorders in a positive way, to help spot the signs in other people and to give help to those who might need it.

Now, I get it, you might still be worried that I'm joking *about* anorexia. But I'm not: nothing could be further from the truth. Comedy is the hook to make people interested. In fact, I think comedy *should* turn its attention to mental health. After all, what is *good* mental health if it doesn't involve smiling, laughing and not taking things too seriously? So, rather than using mental illness statistics to shock, appal and anger people, we should celebrate good mental health to reach a whole new audience and lead with positivity rather than negativity.

That's why I've created a six-week comedy course aimed at people with eating disorders to teach stand-up to build their confidence, communication and that connection with other people, to combat loneliness while literally giving them a platform to stand up for themselves. After all, stand-up was integral to my recovery, and now I want to help other people. I want to engage people who might not see themselves represented in services, to provide a low-cost, high-impact method of help that can change the tone around mental health.

Because it's not only that producer who thinks they 'don't have mental health'. I would never have cared about looking after my noggin before I got ill. So let's make it interesting. Let's make people passionate rather than reluctant about eating disorder recovery. Let's look forward with positivity, rather than staring backwards with negativity. And let's have a bit of a laugh...because who doesn't enjoy that?!

Hormones

Ro Mitchell

Ro Mitchell is a content creator from the UK. After battling anorexia nervosa in her teenage years, she chose to document her recovery journey on social media. Through her YouTube channel, she has built a community of more than 500,000 people across all social media platforms looking to improve their relationship with food. She is passionate about helping those with eating disorders to recover, and believes that making a full recovery is possible. @romitchell

Here, Ro discusses the complicated nature of hormone-related issues in eating disorder recovery. The endocrine system, which is response for our hormones, can be affected by all eating disorders. Other conditions that affect hormones, such as polycystic ovarian syndrome (PCOS) and diabetes mellitus, can increase the likelihood of eating disorders. Hormonal issues in men with eating disorders are often overlooked and so it's important that males get reviewed by a professional.

Perhaps my delusions about how 'fine' I was at the height of my illness played a part, but I didn't feel *that* unwell during the worst of my battle with anorexia. Deep down I knew I was sick, of course, but it was starting recovery that caused me to experience all the awful symptoms. The hair loss, the night sweats, the stomach bloat, the crazy hunger I felt. For months, I'd been a freezing cold, weak girl. Yet, after choosing what everybody told me was right, I felt a million times worse.

We all anticipate the emotions that come with allowing ourselves to eat again, and the pain of gaining weight, but nobody ever warned me about the extreme hunger. It took me by complete surprise. I'd never struggled with bingeing, yet suddenly I felt this alien need to eat, and eat, and it was terrifying. Extreme hunger is a part of anorexia recovery that needs to be spoken about so much more. Not a single professional discussed it with me. Personally, I felt that the only way through it was to listen to my body. Over time I learned that it was sending signals for a reason. So, if I wanted three bowls of cereal, I had three bowls of cereal. I felt immense guilt and an overwhelming sense of being out of control, but knowing I was regaining control over my life kept me sane. Extreme hunger didn't last long for me. Maybe because I didn't ignore it. I rolled with the punches, pushed anorexia's boundaries, and the bottomless pit feeling started to wane.

When somebody close to you suffers with anorexia, or you get unwell yourself, you realize that no stereotype of anorexia will show you the real side-effects of restriction. My skin stayed dry no matter how many times I moisturized it; my hands were cracked and sore. I started losing clumps of my once thick, healthy hair. With every wash I'd see more and more fall out. As if I wasn't self-conscious enough of my changing body, I was now hyperaware of how thin and damaged my hair looked, how dull and dry my skin had become. In treatment this doesn't seem to be commonly discussed either. The impact that being underweight has on hormones is immense, and I paid a big price for neglecting my body. Anorexia is so much more than just losing weight.

Not every sufferer will lose their period, but for many it's yet another thing that is destroyed by malnutrition. There was such a huge focus in my treatment on gaining my period back, but I was terrified to. I know I'm not the only one. Losing your period is a huge indicator that your body is struggling and ultimately unhealthy, but 'healthy' was what I was running from. And I didn't want to be womanly either. After choosing recovery and accepting that, to live fully, I needed to menstruate and allow my body to function as it should, I worked to get it back. It started off slow. My emotions were all out of whack as my body got back to normal and, the week before my period, I always found myself a wreck, never having hated my body so much.

I wish treatment teams were more educated and had also educated me more on all the horrible symptoms that came with weight restoration. I wish I'd known that I'd wake up soaked in sweat as my body struggled to regulate its temperature, that my stomach would bloat to the point of intense discomfort, that my periods would be so erratic and strange, and that, most of all, it happened to almost everyone in recovery, and I wasn't alone.

Family-Based Treatment

Kristina Saffran

Kristina Saffran is the Co-founder and CEO of Equip, a virtual programme that delivers modern eating disorder treatment through family-based care that promises lasting recovery at home. Prior to Equip, she founded Project HEAL, a leading grassroots eating disorder non-profit dedicated to treatment access. She is an Ashoka Fellow, a *Forbes* 30 under 30 social entrepreneur, and an honouree on both *Inc.*'s Female Founders 100 and *Insider*'s 30 under 40 in healthcare recognition lists. She graduated from Harvard College with a bachelor's degree in Psychology. @kristinasaffran

Here, Kristina discusses the importance of family-based treatment, which is one of the most successful treatments for eating disorders in children and teens with other specified feeding or eating disorder (OSFED), bulimia nervosa and anorexia nervosa. She also highlights the optimism which we should all hold for the future of eating disorders care.

When I struggled with anorexia nervosa two decades ago, people viewed it as a vanity problem that made sense in afflicting a thin, White, upper middle class, cisgendered teenage girl. Doctors told me that I'd never recover from this illness; even if I went on to lead a fairly normal life, I'd still be overwhelmed with negative thoughts of food and my body. I cycled in and out of hospitals and missed my entire freshman year of high school. When I came home from my fourth hospitalization, and inevitably started to slip back into the disorder, my family was instructed to send me to a long-term residential facility across the country, and not have much hope of a full recovery.

My mum didn't feel comfortable sending her teenage daughter across the country for another year, and after researching other alternatives, she came across F.E.A.S.T. – an international grassroots group of parents of children with eating disorders – who told her about family-based treatment. Family-based treatment involves the immediate support network of an individual in structuring the home for pro-health. It understands that eating disorders are brain disorders and that, for an illness that requires you to fight your brain upwards of six times per day, it's not only ineffective but frankly cruel to treat it as an *individual* illness. This was the early 2000s, and family-based treatment was just making its way over from the Maudsley Hospital in London to academic centres in the US. My mum found an out-of-network family-based treatment specialist 30 minutes from where we lived; my parents arranged to finish work early twice a week to accompany me to appointments. It was the single hardest year of my life. It was also, undoubtedly, the thing that got me better. My parents took away the option of me turning back to my eating disorder, and as I settled into my new nourished body, I also settled into a life larger than my eating disorder. When they started to hand back control many months into my eating disorder, it was tempting to relapse, but I had already built up enough good things in my life that there were now real consequences to doing so.

Certain traits that make one vulnerable to an eating disorder – such as perfectionism, drive and focus – are wonderful when channelled appropriately. And that's exactly what I did. In recovery, upon learning that 80 per cent of the 30 million Americans with eating disorders don't get treatment, I made it my life's mission to change that. I founded Project HEAL to raise funds for people who couldn't afford treatment. I was fortunate to learn from leading clinicians and academics in the field, along with thousands of patients and families struggling. This further opened my eyes to the myriad of barriers that folks face when trying to recover.

In addition to those who don't receive treatment, a minority of patients get treatment that works (Hart *et al.* 2011). For example, in the US there's a large shortage of qualified outpatient providers, with many not taking insurance (Blackwell *et al.* 2021). It's challenging enough to find one specialized provider but near impossible to find an entire team that is coordinated and on the same page, which is the gold standard. In the absence of outpatient providers, facility-based care has emerged as a go-to treatment in the US, despite it not necessarily being the most effective. The treatment space is also incredibly homogenous – often with lots of thin, White women who don't reflect the diversity of the eating disorder population. And, of course, public insurance rarely covers eating disorder treatment, leaving most people shut out to begin with.

Despite the injustices and lack of understanding in the field, there is reason for optimism. There is more awareness than ever before that eating disorders are brain disorders, and that they don't discriminate. Public attention is driving increased investments in treatment, including family-based treatment. More people are accessing recovery. And when people with eating disorders recover, they often channel their amazing traits into doing incredible things in the world, paying it forward and improving the field so that even more people can recover too.

An Unconventional Recovery: A Vegan Story

Hana Brannigan

Hana Brannigan is a content creator, freelance copywriter and vegan activist. She uses her online platform, with nearly 20,000 followers, to discuss mental health, veganism and eating disorders. She shares her passionate, creative and collaborative attitude to help others on their journeys, and always strives to bring out the best in the people around her. @thishanabee

obviously can't generalize for everyone, but growing up in *my* Asian household, I was taught two main things when it came to food:

1. Never waste food – when you're prepping, cooking and eating.

2. Never refuse food if you're offered it – because food is our love language and you risk offending the person offering it.

So you can imagine my internal conflict as I stared at the plate of eggs my partner had just made me, right before we decided to watch an animal-rights speech by one of the world's most well-known vegan activists. It was a really compelling speech, and he made me think about things I either chose to be ignorant about or that I just had never thought about before.

Needless to say, I was sick to my stomach after learning about the horrors that happen behind the scenes of factory farms. And I knew right then that if I still wanted my goal in life to leave a positive mark on the world, there was *no way* I was going to eat animals ever again.

The video had taken the rose-tinted glasses off me, and I wouldn't be able to ignore what an innocent animal had to go through to get on my plate for my own taste pleasure.

What about all the animal products in the fridge? What about the plate in front of me? All that will go to waste, I thought.

But then I got hit with an even bigger dilemma.

Will this undo all the work I've done in my eating disorder recovery to heal my relationship with ALL foods?

We watched this video and decided to turn vegan cold turkey (tofurkey) during the COVID-19 pandemic. So I had a *lot* of time to think about how turning vegan would impact my recovery.

For context, I had been in eating disorder recovery for five years by this point. And, after going to therapy, I discovered that I had eating disorder and body dysmorphia tendencies since I was very young. It manifested because of many different factors:

- the messaging I (probably) heard when I was super young (although I don't remember any of it, the things I hear from the people I know *now* are very diet culture-infused)
- the type of beauty standards that were popular at the time (no one was talking about body neutrality or positivity)
- the culture I grew up in (I felt pressure to stay thin, even as half-Asian)
- not knowing how to express my emotions (I bottled everything up and needed an outlet)
- being a people pleaser (I absorbed implied expectations and never wanted to let anyone down)

- family history (genetics can play a big role in developing mental health disorders).

Every factor played a part in developing an eating disorder. And I've found this to be super common in other people I've talked to because eating disorders are highly complex and not just something that manifests for vanity's sake.

I was concerned about undoing all the hard work I had gone through with therapy – unlearning diet culture messaging, reframing my negative self-talk into more positive self-talk, gaining more confidence, and understanding this disorder and how it manifests in me.

It was a really long journey full of relapses, anxiety and a lot of mental turmoil.

So I knew I needed to consider this decision carefully. Here are the main things I considered:

1. I was at a point in my journey where I felt confident to make choices that felt best for me.

There comes a stage in recovery where you are healed to the point where you can finally make choices that make you feel the best. In 'intuitive eating', a non-diet approach to healing your relationship with food that was created by the registered dietitians Evelyn Tribole and Elyse Resch and is now supported by over 120 studies, this is called gentle nutrition.

It's the last principle of ten principles because, in eating disorder recovery, you can't jump to making dietary choices that benefit you mentally, physically and emotionally without first learning how to reject dangerous diet culture behaviours, making sure you have enough to eat and aren't mentally or physically restricting yourself, and overall taking care of your mental health first (Tribole and Resch 2012).

I realize that not everyone with an eating disorder has this luxury of choice. And so I had to dig deep to reveal what the situation was with me. It's hard to be honest with yourself about these things because, in many cases, if you're not fully recovered, there's a part of you that wants to hang on to some eating disorder tendencies since it makes you feel in control. At least, that was the case for me.

At this point, I felt I was *nearly* there. I was still holding on to some food rules, but it wasn't affecting my life nearly as much as it did before.

But, there were other criteria...

2. I no longer viewed animal products as food.

Animal products were no longer food for me. I now viewed every piece of meat on a plate as a living being who didn't ask to be raised and killed to feed a human.

I also learned the concept of 'speciesism', which is a term used in philosophy to describe 'treating members of a species as morally more important than members of another species in the context of their similar interests' (Duignan 2013). Just as people treat different races with contempt or with a 'lesser than' attitude, we treat animals the same.

I had to ask myself, 'Why do I love my dog so much and I would never eat her, but I would eat a pig, who has just as much sentience as my dog and is even smarter than my dog?'

It didn't feel right to me that we had these arbitrary rules for what animals we could eat and what animals we couldn't eat. If I loved animals so much, I would need to view them with the same lens, so I wasn't a hypocrite.

Since, in my eyes, animals weren't food any more but actually living, sentient beings who can't consent to what is being done to them (such as being shoved in small cages with barely any room to move their wings or being artificially inseminated to produce babies and therefore milk), I didn't even have a reason to consider them in my diet.

3. This was an ethical issue – not simply a food issue.

Before going vegan, or learning about the true intentions of veganism, I knew that vegans typically avoided *all* animal products – from those in household items to food to clothes – because my uncle was vegan and he would warn everyone to not buy him anything leather. However, since I wasn't a part of the movement and I didn't talk to my uncle a lot, it never occurred to me *why* or how important a topic it was.

Since I had just been exposed to the horrors of *all* animal industries, I finally understood why.

It's not a dietary restriction.

It's a way of living, a philosophy and a moral code. Vegans usually don't want to contribute to animal suffering and exploitation, which is why many don't want to increase demand for animal products. We typically don't buy wool socks, leather boots *or* beef (cow) burgers because that would mean investing our money in an industry we believe leads to immoral outcomes.

This was a huge game-changer for me because, suddenly, the movement was about so much more than simply *food*.

4. I could support my health by being vegan.

Although veganism isn't normally just about the food, food is, understandably, a big part of the conversation because most people eat at least three times a day.

Being severely malnourished before, and dealing with what I suspected to be irritable bowel syndrome (IBS) symptoms, I had to make sure that humans could be healthy whilst being vegan. I wanted to make sure that I could get an adequate amount of nutrition by eliminating meat, dairy and eggs from my diet.

It turns out that the Accreditation Council for Education in Nutrition and Dietetics (ACEND), part of the Academy of Nutrition and

Dietetics, and a 'reliable authority on the quality of nutrition and dietetics education programs' (ACEND 2023), said this about vegan and vegetarian diets:

> It is the position of the Academy of Nutrition and Dietetics that appropriately planned vegetarian, including vegan, diets are healthful, nutritionally adequate, and...are appropriate for all stages of the life cycle, including pregnancy, lactation, infancy, childhood, adolescence, older adulthood, and for athletes. Plant-based diets are more environmentally sustainable than diets rich in animal products because they use fewer natural resources and are associated with much less environmental damage. Vegans need reliable sources of vitamin B-12, such as fortified foods or supplements. (Melina, Craig and Levin 2016)

That was the confirmation I needed to know that it was safe to move forward since I wouldn't be risking my newly restored health.

I thought I was already eating a varied diet before the transition but it turns out I was missing out on some really delicious fruits, vegetables, grains and legumes.

I ate more mindfully, became a lot more connected with my plate and was genuinely enthusiastic about food, and I started experimenting in the kitchen with new recipes, which also helped me recover from my eating disorder in a way I never expected.

Nearly three years later, I'm still so happy I made the switch. Although sometimes I still get questions from my Vietnamese grandma, such as 'Can't you eat just a *little bit* of chicken?', she and my whole family have been very supportive of my decision to switch. Meat is considered a luxury in Vietnamese cuisine since it used to be very expensive, but we're living in different times now, and I think my family understands that. My grandma even makes me vegan meals during our weekly family Sunday dinners, and it's the most loving gesture.

✻ ✻ ✻

Today, I feel the best that I've ever felt in my life, because I'm synchronized with my beliefs, aligned with my values, doing a compassionate thing *and* completely healed from my eating disorder. And it's the most *freeing* feeling I've ever experienced.

Hypervisibility

James Downs

James Downs is a mental health campaigner, peer researcher and expert by experience in eating disorders. He holds roles at the Royal College of Psychiatrists, NHS England and a number of universities and charities. His work includes co-writing the medical emergencies in eating disorders (MEED) guidelines, and peer research projects with UCL and Mind. He is an associate lecturer in psychology at the Open University, and is a yoga, barre and mindfulness teacher. He has written extensively about his own experiences, from textbook chapters and peer-reviewed research to blog posts and mainstream media features. He recently co-authored papers on eating disorders in *Lancet Psychiatry* and the *Journal of Eating Disorders*, and co-edited *The Practical Handbook of Eating Difficulties*. @jamesldowns

Growing up, the only times I ever heard about 'eating disorders' was amongst the parents of other children, in hushed tones – something not to be spoken about for fear of them catching a hold, or sowing the seed of an idea that could become manifest in their daughters as the dreaded diagnosis called 'anorexia nervosa'. Eating disorders were rarely named and awareness was scant – least of all, beyond a very narrow idea, of what kinds of experiences these conditions might involve; the kinds of people they might affect.

Eating disorders don't take root via whispers on the wind or after flicking through a teen beauty magazine in a waiting room. Neither do they occur in a vacuum. But when I was diagnosed with anorexia aged 15, it seemed to me like nobody else in the entire world who was having this experience was like me. The invisibility of other men with eating problems made my own seem hypervisible – like I was an anomaly, a special case to be gawped at by professionals, or a rare specimen that could get some special kind of attention through being unusual or different.

In reality, I wasn't really seen for who I was when I became unwell – for my distress at not understanding my differences as an undiagnosed autistic child with ADHD. Just like I didn't later fit the stereotype of who might get an eating disorder, I also wasn't a 'typical' child with ADHD and autism, either – if such a thing exists. I had elaborate language from a young age, and an ability to fit in and hide my differences that meant they went under the radar – not least because I was still able to achieve well without really trying in every exam that came my way. But under the surface – far more hidden than the physical impacts of my eating disorder – there was a fallout from this suppression of myself and masking of my differences simply in order to feel safe in the social world.

I went from being a free-spirited and naturally content child, who had always been so happy in his own skin growing up, to living with a deep-seated dis-ease and dislocation from those around me. I didn't understand the rules of the tough social world of high school, and the chaotic noise and threatening sensory nature of it all combined with being tethered to a chair for hours on end made it all physically so unbearable for me. More recently, I have also been diagnosed with a genetic connective tissue disorder called Ehlers Danlos syndrome, which helps me to make sense of how growing up I had a huge amount of chronic pain and a whole array of physical health problems that were easily dismissed as growing pains and which I chose not to make a fuss about, but which made life really difficult on a physical level day by day when I couldn't simply move around as I wanted to at home or earlier in primary school.

I didn't really have anyone to talk to about any of these things. Because, on paper, everything was going well for me, nobody could really understand why someone so apparently competent and successful might find something like sitting still in a lesson so difficult. This was so lonely and confusing, and the feelings my experience gave rise to often felt too difficult to bear.

But feelings are felt in the body, and so, in the short term, I found a new strategy for survival. I didn't have to feel the feelings if I shut down the vessel through which these difficult feelings were conducted from the outside world into my inner experience. I would stop eating and drinking, from before school to the moment I got home, avoiding as much of the school day as possible by putting off going in and literally running home to appear the most joyful child when I raced through the door, wolfing down two dinners one after the other. No wonder my parents never suspected anything was wrong. My body would flush with warm energy and I would get lost in all my obsessive hobbies and accepting family environment until the dread of school came around the next day.

This only lasted so long, though, as my difficulty with school only increased to the point that I found it simply too hard to go at all. It didn't help that I was bullied for my appearance as a tall, lanky adolescent who stood out from the crowd for lots of reasons, including being very academic and bookish with a passion for classical music in a school where this really wasn't the norm. I had a very early puberty, too, and so I stood out on the basis of my appearance, and this was quickly picked on with the particular cruelty that only children show to one another. I learnt quickly that, in our society, how you look really does matter, and minimizing my physical differences also became part of my strategy for social survival.

By the time that I had missed a lot of school, it all came out to my parents. I am quite impressed by the ingenuity I showed in covering up my truancy for so long – and unfortunately this capacity to adapt, deceive and work around even the most impossible-looking of obstacles has been a running thing in living with an eating disorder for the many years that have followed. It was clear to everyone – once I could no longer continue to keep up the appearance of coping or fitting in – that I needed help. And this is when I was referred to child and adolescent mental health services (CAMHS) – a moment that took my life in a direction I couldn't have expected.

The doctors in CAMHS were the people I thought would 'get it'. After all these years of coping on my own and being in a vacuum of understanding, I had hope that – finally – someone would listen, see me for who I was and help me to comprehend what was going on. But it's clear to me now that the same blindness to my differences was there. I was told that I had everything going for me, was a bright child with the world ahead of me in the palm of my hand – 'you can do anything you choose to do!' A few weeks of therapy for what I was told were obsessive compulsive disorder (OCD) symptoms, a few tablets to take the edge off the anxiety, and I'd be well on my way to Oxbridge.

Whilst this sounded all very reassuring, I met this response with terror. The very people who I thought would understand were seeing only the surface of my experience, and the rest was a quirk, stress or bad behaviour. But if they didn't understand, then who would? Who could? And what did I have to reach for, for them to understand that I was not well?

This is when the eating disorder stepped in. Something they did seem concerned about was my behaviour when it came to food – this shutting down of my body that had helped me get through the difficult days of school and my already slight frame which struggled to maintain its stature. I didn't quite understand what the fuss was about. I always loved food and would eat well at home, even though I had a repertoire of foods I tended to fixate on and particularly relish. I understood more clearly when they introduced me to the concept of anorexia nervosa, something that was so deadly serious and almost impossible to conceive of in a male but which we had to watch out for with the utmost of vigilance. Now *that* would be serious.

So, of course, I chose to lose weight. 'This will show them,' I thought: that something was truly wrong, that something deeper had gone unattended to. And it did – they sat up and paid attention. My weight status, blood results and food intake started to be pored over like a rare specimen. My inner world remained totally eclipsed – not now by my apparent ability to fit in and succeed (this had expired), but by the near-impossibility of being a boy with anorexia. Now it was the eating disorder, rather than my intelligence or ability to act normally enough to get by, that stood out so much as to overshadow the other conditions I had been struggling with for so long in the first place.

But some attention was better than no attention at all. It was better to be attended to for my potassium levels and body mass index than for nothing at all, even if it didn't really increase the chances of me being seen for my humanness. Later in my life I have seen in painful ways just how much society stigmatizes asking for help – having 'cried for help' when telling people about my private pain and asking politely had failed to get a response for years. We too easily blame people for not seeking attention in the correct, acceptable ways that society finds palatable. We prefer ways that aren't too messy, demanding or inconvenient. The reality is that the problems I and many others seek help for are messy in their nature. The bulimia nervosa I have lived with ever since finally having treatment for anorexia over six years after being diagnosed is inherently messy, dirty and dysregulated. Expectations of perfect help-seeking or 'normal' expressions of mental and emotional distress that leave no room for difference leaves people like me without many avenues at all to get the attention that we all, as human beings, need and deserve.

Words had failed me when it came to speaking to the very people who would have had the capacity to understand me if only they had looked beyond the surface. What did I have left but action, and to make the unseen, seen? In making my body so visibly unwell with anorexia, I demanded the attention that I wasn't getting, even if it still wasn't focused on the deeper things I needed it to be. The almost violently shocking impact of seeing my skeletal form was something physically 'real' that was unmissable, and perhaps even a way of punishing those who I felt, somewhere inside me, had let me down in not responding to me in the way I had so desperately wanted them to.

The Odd One Out

Molly Bartrip

Molly Bartrip is a professional footballer for Tottenham Hotspur Women. She has done various interviews and promotion on mental health – more specifically anorexia from her own experience, but also depression and anxiety. She has been featured on the BBC's *One Show* as well as a mini documentary on Sky Sports. She has a BA (Hons) degree in Sports and Exercise Science. @mollybarts

This piece is written in the style of a football match. Molly vs Anorexia nervosa.

'The footballer'. That's what I always got called at school. Football has always been my passion, my release. I fell in love with the game at an early age, kicking the ball at the local park with my dad, playing with the boys, and even being lucky enough to travel the world. Truthfully, though, football sent me to some scary places. The thing with football is that when it's good, it's *really* good, and you're on top of the world. But when it's bad, it can end up with you feeling seriously low. For me, I experienced both. Football was both my enemy, and my saviour.

0–0 (1')

I was 14 playing for a local girls' team at Charlton Athletic FC. It was a centre of excellence at the time so I was training with the best girls from the area. The level was good. I loved it. I remember, at the time, shrugging off advice – from a coach I knew – to trial for Arsenal. Growing up, it was Arsenal, and the rest. *Arsenal* was the biggest women's team. Arsenal was the dream. Arsenal was also a million miles away from the level I thought I was playing at. But my parents encouraged me to trial anyway. I seriously didn't think I was Arsenal standard. That was, of course, until I was offered a place in the team. Getting to train, and play, with some of the best – if not the best – footballers around, for my age group, was a dream come true. I remember being a bag of nerves on my first day; a bundle of emotions, made easier by the warm welcome I received from the girls. They were great.

0–0 (13')

I can still recall that first email. This was big: an England U15s call-up. I was in shock, so proud, and overwhelmed. To represent my country was something I never thought possible. I was only a young girl, still at school. Well, barely. The call-up meant I had a lot of time away from school. Because of this, I massively struggled with friendships. I felt like an odd one out – always here, there and everywhere, with probably the year's worst attendance. My mum was on it, though. She made sure that I caught up on all the school work I missed out on. But missing school? I wasn't complaining.

The future felt bright, yet unknown.

0–0 (18')

My hamstring gave way in the training session before the game. I was away on international duty with England at the time, and just my luck: I got injured. Despite me being just 14, I knew exactly what this meant. It meant I'd blown it. Had my only chance of being successful as a footballer gone?

Why me?

What was worse was that my whole family had travelled to watch me. I felt like I hadn't just let myself down, but them too. I felt a kind of guilt that I had never experienced before, and I was absolutely gutted.

0–1 (25')

Not eating gave me back some of that lost control. I had no control over whether I'd be selected to play for my country again, but I *did* have control over my body and what I put in it. The behaviour took hold, and I was officially in self-destruction mode. The voice in my head was very, very strong. I knew I had to eat to train, to live, to survive. But it wasn't as easy as that. I couldn't. I started throwing my lunch away at school, and couldn't stop.

0–2 (41')

My mum recently told me that before I turned 14, I had never sworn. Basically, I was an angel of a child. But I started exhibiting behaviour so out of character that my family didn't recognize me. I told my family I hated them, I hid away in my room, I harmed myself. My thoughts had complete control over me and played me like a puppet. Before this, I was a happy, bubbly girl. After, a manipulative, deceitful monster.

Half Time (HT)

The illness was talking loudly and left no room for Molly. I know that now, years later.

1–2 (51')

My recovery was a slow burner. From the start, it took about eight months before I was eating regularly. And by eating, I mean enough to survive, not enough for anything serious. *Definitely* not enough for intense exercise. Football was a long way off; not even in my thoughts at all. My mind was too preoccupied with the illness. By now, I could reel off the calories in most foods and was closely tracking fat and sugar content. I continued to throw away food, and getting better and better at hiding the fact that I was doing so.

2–2 (66')

I visited a counsellor weekly. Honestly, I hated it. Probably because it made me realize how ill I was. I would always leave the sessions feeling like a freak. I struggled to express, out loud, how I felt. Really struggled. So one day the counsellor told me to write instead; to write *to* the illness. One thing that I've always enjoyed doing is writing, so, for me, this was a much simpler way of explaining what was going on in my head.

To this day, I still have the letters I wrote, and the letters between me and my family. On the odd occasion, we read them through together, sharing emotional exchanges on how far I've come.

2–2 (70')

My family didn't trust me to eat at school, so they made sure I didn't. I was always picked up at lunchtime, and rarely ever returned the same day because I'd normally throw a tantrum of some sort (honestly, I don't know how I managed to get good grades at school; a miracle really, as I was never there!). Who would have to deal with me alternated between my grandparents and my mum.

A moody teenager with an eating disorder; I was not nice to be around.

2–3 (76')

I had a few wake-up calls that made me realize what I was doing to myself. Like when my parents took me to the local general hospital. To be honest, this was probably my lowest point. I remember, clear as day, the nurses weighing me and beginning to set up the nasogastric tube equipment, whilst my parents left the room. The thought of being alone on a hospital bed terrified me. I screamed out, 'Let me do this! Let me try and fight it!' Before this point, I wasn't fighting anything except my family.

3–3 (89')

I started to want to *fight* the voice in my head, instead of just wanting to *listen* to it. Don't get me wrong, it wasn't a click-of-the-fingers moment. Not at all. It took time. A big thing for me was when I slowly began seeing my dreams fade. I began to process the idea that my dream of becoming a professional footballer may never happen. I began to process my reality that I was potentially never going to kick a ball, professionally, ever.

4–3 (90')

After around a year, I was able to tolerate a very basic diet, enough to perform, but I still had my small issues. I was back playing football so I knew I simply had to eat. I started to get traces of the old Molly back, the sociable, entertaining side. If I didn't have football to drive me, I really don't know where I would be today.

5–3 (90'+2)

It was a long time before I was able to eat bacon again, my favourite food since I could remember. It took me five years, but I was finally able to eat it without feeling guilty. That's when I knew I had really beaten the illness. It was such a relief.

✳ ✳ ✳

Extra Time

I sit here now, knowing I could have died. The smallest of injuries almost shaped my life. Almost caused me to give my life away. But now, I have more time, extra time. My life goes on. And I'm grateful for it. I've beaten this illness. I'm currently a professional footballer living my dream, but it could easily have been a completely different story.

At the core of it, I think my anorexia stemmed from rejection. That's *my* fear: rejection. Others will have their own fears. Although I know, in my mind, that this is part of life and learning, I feel that I will always have this fear. For me, it's the feeling of not being good enough and failing that makes me feel so ashamed. It probably comes from a lack of self-esteem; still, to this day, I'm working on it. I have my good and bad days.

I'm very aware of anorexia triggers, and can sometimes even see them in others. It's almost like a sixth sense. I want to be able to help those struggling, or offer advice and support to family and friends watching a loved one struggle. It's a horrible illness but I'm living proof that defeating it *is* possible; like winning a football match. There is light, but you have to run towards it.

The pressure of football caused me to go into a dark place, but also gave me the fight to get back to Molly. Sport, and the pressures that come with it, can sometimes feel like a rollercoaster. You win, you lose, you play, you don't play. Every day you're competing for one position. Sometimes even competing against friends. You have to be the best footballing version of yourself to get a place in the starting 11. If you aren't, you probably won't be picked. More stress. Many factors, different triggers, different reactions. It's taken me ten years to train my brain to be able to handle this part of the game, because for so long I had developed some unhealthy coping mechanisms. And the training is still ongoing.

These days, women's football is growing and the expectations from the outside world are naturally building. More pressure. With that, there are more modern things to consider, such as comments on social media and much larger crowds. These things come as part and parcel of where we want our sport to be. Learning to deal with these quickly – not allowing these pressures to negatively affect us – will be important.

I currently play football for Tottenham Hotspur in the top division of the women's game in England. Looking back at 14-year-old

Molly, I would never have thought I would be in this situation. I've truly grown up through my struggles and they've shaped me into the person and footballer I am today. I'm not perfect (not by a long way!) and I still have my down moments, but doesn't everyone, hey?

Befriending the Hunger Monster

Amalie Lee

Amalie Lee is an eating disorder recovery coach, and mental health and LGBTQ+ advocate. Her work has been featured on platforms including NBC's *Today*, *Fox News* and *Cosmopolitan* magazine. She is the founder of the recovery platform Let's Recover and hosts the podcast *Recovery Talk*. @amalielee

And so it hit me: The Hunger Monster. As the Snickers advert goes, 'You are not you when you are hungry', and I surely did not feel like me, raiding the kitchen cupboards for anything vaguely resembling food. It felt like I was in a haze, possessed by something wild and primal that I could not quite tame. I found a gift bag of fancy mint chocolates that was not mine, but my eating disorder made me no stranger to lying and stealing. 'Perfect,' I thought to myself. Chocolate is what I usually ban myself from, and forbidden fruits do taste the sweetest.

Looking back almost a decade later, as someone who now has recovered from anorexia nervosa binge–purge subtype and works with eating disorders for a living, it was pretty obvious what went down on nights like this one: I was really goddamn hungry. It is as obvious as why you feel tired all the time when you are sleep-deprived, yet I blamed what was triggered by the absence of food on the presence of food. Feeling unable to control myself around food (especially those pesky mint chocolates) was, in my head, used as an argument as to why I had to continue restricting it. The fact that my bingeing coincided with restriction went over my head. We often look for solutions and answers where we want to find them; in my case, I desperately wanted the solution to be more restriction, more perceived self-control, and more eating disorder. That is exactly what I did. Until I could not any more.

People often ask me what made me recover; what was my light-bulb moment, my revelation where I saw the light and accepted recovery as my saviour? Truth is, there was none. My lightbulb moment was realizing there was no lightbulb moment. Instead, I had to put in the bulb myself. I had support, guidance, tools and direction from my treatment team, but I had to screw it in, often in what felt like a bottomless pit of darkness. For so long, I had been waiting for that lightbulb moment: the magical future moment when I would wake up one morning, fully ready to recover. Except that is not how recovery, or readiness, works. You don't wait to do something until you are ready; instead, you become ready by doing. Action creates motivation, not the other way around. I never felt fully ready to recover, and the closest thing I had to readiness was realizing and accepting it would not happen. Motivation in itself is fluctuating and unreliable. Instead, I had to rely on determination and commitment.

When working with clients with eating disorders, I often compare recovery with going to the dentist with a cavity. As far as I am aware, nobody wakes up excited about 25 minutes of a stranger prodding and poking in your mouth with various unidentified medieval-looking metal tools, whilst engaging in the awkward small talk you cannot reciprocate due to said metal tools. If anything, you are secretly hoping your appointment gets cancelled, and you look for any reason to reschedule. Still, you (hopefully) make yourself go in the end. Why? Because the alternative would be far more miserable. You know your cavity is not going to go away by itself, and the longer you wait, the worse it gets. What started as a small cavity might develop into an aching infection in need of antibiotics and expensive root canal treatment. By attending the appointment, you are enduring short-term discomfort for long-term relief, instead of the opposite.

From my observation, people with eating disorders are often very able to understand the concept of short-term discomfort for long-term relief in any other arena of their lives. These are often (but not always – sometimes it is the complete opposite) the type of people who are very sensible and future-oriented. They will revise for their exams, put money into their savings account and attend that dentist appointment, all because they know these are actions that will benefit their future selves. If anything, their sensible future orientation may at times be excessive to the point where it is no longer sensible at all, such as excessive perfectionism and overdoing it at work or in school, or becoming so frugal that they avoid treating themselves to anything nice. Yet, in respect of recovery, this future orientation often goes straight out the window, despite very few of them explicitly saying they see a future with the eating disorder.

The harsh truth is, the future is created in the current. Nothing changes if nothing changes. When I went to purge after a binge, I maintained a cycle of overeating and compensating, because in my case, the cycle was set off by restriction in the first place. I wanted to break the cycle by simply stopping the bingeing as if it was a conscious, thought-out choice. 'If only I could have some self-control,' I thought to myself. Reality check: bingeing has nothing to do with self-control. I was hungry because I was hungry. The energy deficit had been ongoing for a prolonged period of time, constantly signalling to my body that food is a scarce resource and thereby activating physical and psychological famine mode. I was so angry at my body for sabotaging me when it was in fact trying to protect me all along. I was hungry, and I was not myself because of it.

With reactive hunger in eating disorders and recovery, or 'post-starvation hyperphagia' as it is scientifically called, it is important to be aware that 'hunger' may not present itself as a familiar guest when it comes knocking. We often think of hunger solely as a physiological sensation, with a growling orchestra from the abdomen and an overall sense of physical emptiness. In recovery, that is often not how hunger manifests, at least not all the time. Instead, it can often manifest as a mental hunger and a hyper-focus on food, from suddenly becoming a dedicated baker to endlessly scrolling through food hashtags online. People may find themselves not physically hungry, yet with an endless drive to eat, eat and eat, almost like they are on autopilot. The hunger manifesting more mentally than physically means people often confuse it for emotional eating or 'not real hunger', and justify restrictive, compensatory behaviours in response to punish their 'gluttony'. These compensatory behaviours then signal to the body and brain that food is scarce, triggering more bingeing, especially on high-energy, previously forbidden foods. It is a vicious cycle that some people spend years, decades, even a lifetime, being stuck in.

Diet culture has a way of demonizing hunger, similar to how Western capitalistic 'hustle culture' has a way of demonizing rest. Yet even with the latter, we understand that if someone is about to nod off from sleep deprivation, they will not be fully present. We understand that if someone stays awake for three nights straight, they will probably go on a sleeping bender as soon as they go to bed. We know that if you are tired at a party, all you can think about is going home to your warm bed. None of these makes you a sleep addict (well, we all are, to some extent – it is a biological need!) or an emotional sleeper, and no amount of psychotherapy discussing *why* you are tired would make the tiredness go away if you are tired because you are tired. You need to correct the sleep deficit because you are not you when you are tired. Now imagine this, but with a caloric deficit. Now tell me, how long have you been restricting again?!

To beat my bingeing, I had to correct my energy deficit and get my body to a weight it was happy with. In order to get there, I had to eat. A lot. I had to give myself unconditional permission not just to eat enough, but also to eat all the kinds of foods I had previously banned myself from. Those minty chocolates I stole that afternoon tasted so, so sweet because they were forbidden fruit (in addition to me being *really* goddamn hungry). I had to eat them over and over until they were just mint chocolates, as opposed to the godly creation they looked like from the pedestal I had put them on. With these mint chocolates, I had somehow managed to demonize and pedestal them at once, both for the same reason: I *really* enjoyed eating them.

When working on breaking the binge–restrict/compensate cycle, it can be tempting to simply eliminate certain 'trigger foods': foods you are convinced you simply cannot control yourself around as, from your perspective, they tend to 'cause' a binge. You may find yourself more likely to binge on a bag of chocolates than a bag of carrots, thus deciding chocolates are unsafe and carrots are safe. Unfortunately, treatment professionals sometimes echo this sentiment, perhaps in part due to their own ingrained beliefs from living under diet culture. From 'Have you lost weight?' being used as a compliment to self-deprecating jokes about being 'bad' for eating cake, we live in a fatphobic society where the script and social code suggests less is good: less food, less weight, less calories, less you, less life.

What if instead what we blame as a problem (the food) is part of the solution? What if the best way to stop bingeing on a specific food was to give yourself access to said food? What if you are hungry because you are hungry, and you are not yourself because of it? What if there is nothing fundamentally wrong with you, and instead bingeing is a sign something is *right* with you; your body doing what it is programmed to do when famine is detected?

I am a morning person. My favourite time of the day is getting out of bed and making myself a nice, creamy decaf coffee. Alongside my coffee, I love having some mint chocolates – whoever named 'After Eight' must have meant eight in the morning! I will grab a few. Sometimes a couple is enough to satisfy my sweet tooth; other times I will empty the box. Sometimes I eat fast, other times I eat slowly. I eat until I no longer feel like eating them, and put them back in my fridge (chocolate belongs in the fridge: I *will* die on this hill). I don't spend my time hyper-focusing on the chocolates, or feel like I must throw them out of the house to prevent a binge. My brain can focus on other things because it knows it can access minty chocolates whenever it wants, and my body can relax knowing I will feed it regularly.

Getting to this point was not an easy, linear journey. In fact, it was a long, messy rollercoaster ride where I kept falling off and getting back on, often heavily doubting that the journey would take me to its final destination at all. The pendulum had to swing in the other direction for a while – I remember eating so much of my previously forbidden 'fear foods' that I felt sick of them. I had to let go of all control in order to regain it, and it had to be stormy before it got quiet. I had to sit with a lot of self-doubt and feelings that recovery was possible for everyone but me; that I was the unicorn that the rules somehow did not apply to. Instead of trying to get rid of all the doubt, I had to learn to sit with it and do what felt wrong until it felt right. Eventually, it did. Turns out the Hunger Monster did not need to be tamed; it was my friend all along. And guess what? An unrestricted life tastes the sweetest.

The Recipe for My Eating Disorder

Becky Excell

Becky Excell is a four-time *Sunday Times* best-selling author, food blogger and gluten-free home cook. She openly talks about her IBS (irritable bowel syndrome) and anorexia nervosa diagnoses. Through her gluten-free cookbooks and online recipes, she has been able to develop a more positive relationship with food, using it as a way to help those like her with special dietary requirements. @beckyexcell

If anyone ever asks me why, or how, I got an eating disorder, my first response is always, 'I don't know.' And whilst that's not entirely true, I guess what I really mean is that the answer is far too complicated to summarize in one convenient sentence.

Mental healthcare professionals, who also tried to discover the root cause of my eating disorder, would ask things like, 'How is your relationship with your parents?', 'Is everything OK at home?' or 'Did anyone ever mistreat you in your childhood?' But my answers to these questions were always 'Fine' or 'No'. There's nothing overt in my early life that a professional could point to and be like, 'Oh, that's why she has an eating disorder.' Nor could I really tell them exactly why, or how, I embarked upon that path. To me, it just happened.

But much like any accident or event, where things go wrong, there's rarely just one sole factor that causes it. For example, if you accidentally slip over on a rainy day, it's easy to blame the rain for making it slippery. But what about the worn-out soles of the shoes you were wearing? What about the fact you were in a hurry? What about the heavy bags you were carrying that made you off-balance? In reality, in this example, it was more likely a combination of all of the above in varying degrees rather than one lone factor. And, for me, the same thinking probably goes towards explaining how my eating disorder developed.

After much personal reflection throughout my eight years of recovery, these are the key things I can think of that, for me at least, formed the 'recipe' for my eating disorder. The combination of them all is what eventually became the foundation of my eating disorder.

1. Past stress

It wasn't until years into eating disorder recovery that my boyfriend asked me, 'When was the first time you ever remember bingeing on food in a stressed way, even to a small degree?'

I recalled the time when I was 13 and my dad was in hospital. We were all so worried about him, and I genuinely believed he might die. Unable to cope with the stress at that age, I remember going to the biscuit jar in the kitchen and eating every single biscuit in there. Though it didn't change the situation, I'm guessing that, at that age, I experienced some comfort through food.

This behaviour continued on and off for my entire childhood and into my teens, even long after my dad thankfully recovered. I never really thought anything strange of it. It was just something I did. After all, every kid loves to eat more biscuits than they should, right? Somehow, my brain had made hardwired connections between stress and binge eating.

2. Life stress

My eating disorder properly began at a time when I was going through a lot of change in my life, aged 18. I had just moved 300 miles from home to university, and my degree was incredibly intense. My bingeing habits would return occasionally (though to a minor degree when compared to what they would later become) and I eventually dropped out and enrolled in a different degree at an entirely different university. This general stress would continue throughout my university life, as I'm sure it does for most students.

3. Isolation

During my second attempt at university (now 'only' 100 miles from my home), things were very different to my last – and not in a positive way. This time, I made zero friends. This is, despite my efforts to try. My course was a bit less demanding, meaning I had a lot of free time to myself, but unfortunately this meant that I was alone 95 per cent of the time, seven days a week. This is where my disordered behaviours really began to develop and my binge eating habits spun out of control. Eventually, I thought to myself, 'If I'm going to be alone and miserable here, I might as well use this time to get into the best shape of my life.'

Although it wasn't a direct or conscious choice to balance out my binge eating habit, that's what it later became as I began to exercise more and more. But little did I know, this is how I would establish the cycle of bingeing and purging through exercise, which would form the core of my eating disorder.

4. Being told that I wasn't underweight enough to have an eating disorder

As my cycle of bingeing and purging developed further, it was beginning to affect more areas of my life. It made me a horrible person to be around and I came to the realization that I actually needed professional help. It took me a couple of years, but I went to my local

GP to try to explain. I could barely get a word out before I burst into tears, purely from the stress of what I put myself through every day. I eventually did explain my eating behaviours to her and she referred me to a counsellor. Long story short: the counsellor weighed me and told me that I wasn't underweight enough to have an eating disorder, so I should be fine. And that was that.

It wasn't until years later that I realized that the denial of my eating disorder by a professional, based on my weight, was a huge driving factor in my eating disorder progressing from an emerging problem to a life-threatening one. The counsellor basically told me that I needed to get worse before I deserved help. I needed to prove that I was mentally ill via my weight to receive any attention – which is exactly what I set out to do. Bear in mind that I was far from the point of rational thinking at this point and semi out of control of my own thoughts (which was part of the entire reason I sought help in the first place).

I was still at a 'healthy'-ish weight at the point I tried to seek help (though quite a lot less than what I once weighed). So, I was turned away. With professional help and support at that point, I feel I could have potentially avoided the following years of awful things I would put myself, family and loved ones through. It took so much mental strength to ask for help in the first place (something I had very little of at the time) and the 'me' today still can't believe I was turned away like that. Without a doubt, this was one of the key triggers that set me on a very bad path – a path that eventually led to doctors telling me I might die in my sleep if I continued my behaviours. And even that didn't stop me from continuing anyway.

5. Competitiveness and comparison

I'm a naturally competitive person. As a kid, I loved participating in competitive sports – you name a sport, I played it. I was in the school team for everything and my hobbies outside of school were nearly all sports-based. It made me feel happy and alive. Also, in my day job, I'm very competitive! If I'm going to compete in something, I have to be the best. I have to win. Though I'm sure this is regarded as a positive trait, somehow this translated into me wanting to be the 'best' at my eating disorder.

So putting me in a day unit surrounded by ten other people with eating disorders was, looking back, probably one of the hardest things to happen to me during treatment. Now, I had people to compete with. What made this even worse is that, from my experience, others with eating disorders often want to be the best at it too.

For example, if I leaned against the radiator in the day unit because I was cold (I was so thin at this point and always felt the cold), another girl would complain that I was standing whilst the rest of them were sitting. Or, during scheduled mealtimes, there were elements of certain meals that I was allowed to pass on as I was on a gluten-free diet. But this didn't go down well at all with the others, who had no choice but to eat everything. Being gluten-free certainly didn't make me popular with the other girls.

You can't be competitive without comparing yourself to others. I always compared what I ate to other members of my family, I compared my behaviours to fellow eating disorder sufferers, and it seemed like everyone else did too.

I feel like the competitive and comparative elements of an eating disorder are sorely underestimated and ignored, especially when they can provide further fuel to the fire of weight loss and, ultimately, encourage one to be 'the best' at getting worse. Whilst I agree that peers with shared experience often understand your struggles better than anyone else, this competitive element can be profound enough to significantly impact on eating disorder support and recovery.

6. Regularly checking my weight

Most people are capable of looking at their own weight. However, the numbers on my scales went on to become a huge trigger that constantly fuelled my disordered behaviours. If it was up, I would starve myself and excessively exercise. If it was down, it would only spur me on to lower it further. Starving myself meant I was so hungry that I'd compulsively binge, weigh myself immediately, then starve myself all over again for days and go back to over-exercising – thus, repeating the cycle. I'd set weight goals that I'd need to get to, then, once achieved, I'd set a lower goal, being the competitive person I am. The goals just kept getting lower and lower.

I haven't weighed myself in eight years and I'm still too scared to do so.

7. Body image and IBS

What young female isn't concerned with body image to some degree? Mine was my stomach. I always wanted a flat stomach. However, likely due to some of the ill treatment I'd given to my stomach through binge eating over the years, my stomach was almost permanently bloated, constantly cramping and in pain. This would later lead to my GP diagnosing me with IBS and instructing me to follow a gluten-free diet, which helped to subdue some of the pain.

Irritable bowel syndrome made my desire for a flat stomach pointless. So many foods disagreed with me, meaning that I was (and still am) bloated almost 90 per cent of the time. But that didn't stop me from trying. Every time I'd look at my stomach, it would be bloated, which would instantly trigger thoughts that I needed to go to the gym or starve myself.

Being on a gluten-free diet, although it helped to alleviate my painful symptoms, only made the mental battle harder. Being on a gluten-free diet gave me a genuine reason to restrict certain foods, which I found very difficult to responsibly manage during my eating disorder. I'd often use it as a reason to eat even less than I already did. During binges, I would also sometimes purposefully eat gluten knowing it made me very unwell, meaning I would experience some of the most intense bloating possible. Looking back on it now, it's hard to say exactly why I did it. I don't think you truly know what you are doing when in the depths of an eating disorder; essentially, though, it was my form of self-harm.

Now, I rarely ever look at my stomach in the mirror any more, and I always shower in the morning as I don't want to risk looking at my bloated stomach after I've eaten.

※ ※ ※

These became the individual ingredients that would form the recipe for my eating disorder. Although I can now list and explain some of the factors that led to it, I had absolutely zero awareness of them collectively uniting forces at the time. In fact, I only realized most of these contributing factors years and years later; back then, I rationalized them as being normal. This acted as a cloak that my eating disorder could hide behind whilst it grew into something that had full control of my life.

I feel that if we think about eating disorders more in terms of their *collective* causes, then we'll be more able to understand each person's unique contributing factors and better act upon the various elements that create them.

So, how did I go from being told my eating-disordered behaviours might soon result in me dying in my sleep (because ECG tests showed that my heart rhythm was so poor) to being eight years into recovery? For me, the turning point that finally made me realize that enough was enough was when my GP told me that if I continued, she would section me under the Mental Health Act.

To this day, I can't say why being told that I might die didn't stop me, but being told that I was going to be sectioned finally got through to me. Maybe it was the final validation I needed (in my warped way of thinking) that corrected what that counsellor said all those years prior, and that I now *was* indeed ill enough. Maybe I just didn't want to be back anywhere similar to the day unit again. I can't say for certain why I suddenly saw sense, but again, just like the reason my eating disorder started, I'm sure there are multiple reasons which I may only fully realize in years to come.

After my GP sternly told me that, I rushed home, cancelled my gym membership (my way of purging) and manically exclaimed to my mum that I was going to get better from today. Understandably, she was sceptical. But that became the exact point where my road to recovery began. However, I still had a lot of work to do.

Over many years, I slowly counteracted all the things that contributed to my eating disorder in the first place. I stopped looking at my weight and totally abstained from looking at my stomach. I limited being competitive to the places it belonged – work and sport. I'm no longer isolated, as I graduated from university a very long time ago. I take antidepressants to help me manage everyday stress and control my bingeing tendencies, and I now never look at calories on food – which was another persistent trigger for me. I can only imagine what would have happened if I started doing all of these things earlier. Ironically, my job is in the food writing industry, which seems like a terrible idea for someone recovering from an eating disorder! But by creating recipes for others on a gluten-free diet and helping them reunite with foods they couldn't otherwise eat, I've been able to develop an entirely different, positive relationship with food: food as a means to help others.

※ ※ ※

Eating disorders can happen to anyone for their own very different, personalized reasons. You don't need one painfully obvious reason, or to fit any sort of stereotype at all. Because the cause of my eating disorder wasn't obvious to me or anyone else, this allowed it to get worse and worse and only made it harder to reverse. But, by recognizing that eating disorders can have multifaceted, personalized causes, I feel we can be better equipped to combat and counteract those specific causes, instead of hopelessly searching for one, lone reason.

It's important to know that as eating disorders themselves are very personalized to the individual, recovery can be just the same and without any set path or timeframe. For me, eight years on, I would say I am most definitely still in recovery and possibly will be forever. I've experienced relapses to varying degrees over the years, I still have to manage my thoughts on a regular basis, and my digestive system may never fully recover. That's just my journey, though, and for others it will be different.

But what should be the *same* for everyone is that weight alone should never be used to diagnose an eating disorder. I feel extremely strongly about this. My disordered way of thinking began long before I was ever diagnosed with anorexia, when I was still at a 'healthy' weight. Being anorexic was a by-product of all those years of practising disordered eating habits. Only supplying help to those at a much lower point merely guarantees they'll be harder to treat by giving them more time to cement their behaviour. Just like me.

So, although my answer to the question 'How did your eating disorder start?' will still probably always be 'I don't know,' as you can see, the cause of an eating disorder can be much harder to explain than one might first think.

The Model Industry

Q&A with Emme

Emme is an award-winning American supermodel. She has been recognized for more than 20 years for her innovation. She has twice been chosen as one of *People* Magazine's 50 Most Beautiful People and has been dubbed the 'Godmother of the full-figured industry' by *The Oprah Magazine*. She is a respected voice in the news, fashion, wellness and beauty sectors and is acknowledged on a global scale as a leading influencer for positive body image and self-esteem. Her passion has led to the development of the True Beauty Foundation – a 501(c)(3) non-profit organization whose goal is to strengthen youth mental wellbeing by offering initiatives and activities that support healthy body image and self-esteem for members of the whole family. @theofficialemme

Emme is a pioneer in the modelling industry, with over 30 years' experience. She has been a National Eating Disorders Association (NEDA) ambassador for decades. With latest evidence suggesting that 40 per cent of models engage in disordered eating, and 62 per cent have been asked to lose weight or change their shape or size by someone in the industry, Dr Chuks was keen to hear her thoughts and experiences regarding issues within the modelling industry – an industry infamous for body pressures and eating disorders.

Q: So, Emme, what got you into modelling?

'You should model...you've got the looks,' friends and a few adults told me when I was growing up. 'No,' I said. 'I'd have to lose half of my body. I'm not interested. I'm a jock. I'm fine.' I was a marketing director for a real estate firm in New York City at the time, trying to figure out how to market temporary office space to travelling business people who did a lot of flying. 'On-flight magazine!' I thought one day. When thumbing through an *American Way* magazine, I saw this article where a plus-sized agency was being featured. I remembered my friend's brother was dating a full-figured model before I moved to New York: 'full-figured' meaning the fuller side of the fashion industry, which was relatively new. I decided to check the agency out. One day during my lunch break, I put on a black and white polyester pant suit with a thick patent leather belt and thought, 'Why not? Let's go investigate and see what happens.' It seemed like a big deal to me back then, but I did it anyway. I walked in with my red lipstick on, I'll never forget it. After knocking on the agency's door a couple of times, I realized everyone was out to lunch until I heard a woman in the back say, 'Hi! Hold on, I'm coming.' When she turned the corner, she looked me over head to toe and said, 'Have you ever modelled before? I want you to model for us.' Nothing like this ever happened to me. I jumped into a cab back to the office and thought, 'What just happened?!'

Q: *How was life with that agency?*

I left that modelling agency after six months because they weren't paying me in full for whatever reason and I got introduced to and started working with Ford Models, which made all the difference. In 1994, I was chosen as one of *People* magazine's 50 Most Beautiful People and again in 1999 while working there. My life literally changed when the first article was published, thanks mainly to my bookers at Ford and to Carol Wallace, *People* magazine's editor-in-chief, who was determined to reflect a more inclusive beauty for the Most Beautiful issue, and my life was never the same. I began working, and worked consistently and consecutively for years in domestic and international catalogues and some big print campaigns, then signed with the commercial division at WME (William Morris Agency). The exposure I received was a game changer. There were clients like Revlon and Clairol working with me, along with industry icons such as Cindy Crawford, Halle Berry and MTV's Karen Duffy.

Q: What was your relationship like with your body before, and during, life as a full-figured model?

I was a Division 1 (D1) rower and was awarded a full athletic scholarship to Syracuse University and, during the summer of my senior year, was invited to the Olympic rowing trials at Princeton. I was extremely athletic all my life, even today. I need movement and nature like blood. So, regardless of the push-back my fellow models and I received from stylists, photographers and the industry as a whole, I knew that my body was healthy and strong, which gave me the confidence to continue to show up when it was subject to another's opinion or judgement. On the crew team, we were all D1 athletes. We'd walk into restaurants, and they'd wonder if they had enough food to feed us. Being very strong, and hungry, was our superpower! I also come from a family of athletes. My brother is 6′ 7″, my sister is 6′ 1″, I'm 5′ 11″, the shrimp in the family, my daughter is 5′ 11″, and my niece and nephews are all very tall. We are descended from trees. So there's nothing strange or unusual about us when we're together. I'm a curvy Amazon. That's just who I am. However, when I'm on my own, my strength and height is called out quite frequently, especially by men. I admittedly stick out like a sore thumb in a thin-centric fashion industry. I'm Norwegian, Swedish, more like a Viking, and nothing could ever change that. As a result, when I entered the full-figured industry, I witnessed many of the straight-sized models seemed discontent, smoking cigarettes and refusing to eat lunch with us, while, more times than not, getting paid double and being featured on covers of magazines. On the other side, the full-figured models were also like, 'I gotta be careful of not gaining too much weight or losing too much weight.' It was thoroughly confusing. Both sides of the fashion industry were unhappy.

Q: During your time as a model, did you experience any body pressures?

So, I was an average US size when I first entered the field in the 1990s. I was told to purchase body pads so that I would fit into the larger clothing better. I thought in all seriousness, 'How bizarre is this?' I'd heard, 'Be careful, be careful, you're going to be too large!' throughout my life, and now here I am, working in a field that requires me to be bigger! But that was only a portion of the situation. Early in my career, because I was full-figured, high-end fashion photographers would not shoot me due to the hierarchy of the fashion industry. At the time, I was deemed much too big to work with them. I'd heard they were concerned that if others knew they were photographing a full-figured model, it would cast a negative light on how they were perceived. 'I'm not going to shoot this fatty,' exclaimed a photographer one day, at my most lucrative shoot up to this point. My hair in curlers, and eyelashes fluttering – Emme was in the house! And I remember thinking, 'Are you kidding me? I'm too old for this kind of stuff,' *and* it was my first time getting this kind of exposure. Where did this photographer come from to speak to me like that? It was a pivotal moment for me as a young adult and I took a nine-month hiatus, to my modelling agent's chagrin, and got my New Jersey massage therapy certification.

Q: You said, 'I'm too old for this kind of stuff,' so how old were you when you started modelling, and what would be the typical age to start in the industry?

Typically, you would enter the modelling industry around the ages of 14 to 18. Then there's a very short window. You can come and go. When you hit it, savour the run till the next 'flavour', or look, is on its way. The girls in the full-figured industry, on the other hand, generally start later and last longer. I came in at 26, after a two-year stint being a TV journalist. Modelling was my second career. By the time I exited, some of the top-tier girls' pay scales were getting pretty much on par with the straight-size girls, which made me happy. It was about time, and billions were now being made in the plus-sized end of the fashion industry.

Q: *So, at some point, you became a major voice for inclusivity in the industry?*

There were very few people speaking out about the need for inclusive reflections of beauty within the fashion and beauty industries. With the help of my agents at WME and Sarah Hall Productions, I was brought right into everyone's homes and hit the mainstream as a commercial spokesperson and woman's advocate, TV personality, model and mother. I began to share body-affirming data that called for the need for more diverse images of beauty, inclusive of the current ideal. No one left behind. In my mind, inclusivity was where it was at. When I was on location, or hosting fabulous fashion shows, there were beautiful diverse images of female customers reflecting back to me at every stop. And it was to this audience, on the covers of magazines, articles, newspapers and television shows, that I shared what I was learning from NEDA (National Eating Disorders Association), doctors, nurses and other advocates. We were all shining a light in our own ways on the issue of body image and how to improve it, and the self-esteem in young girls and women. By the way, more research on men and boys is greatly needed! When I realized I wanted to share my stories, and the stories of others, to motivate and shine a light on a counter point of view, I knew I was exactly where I needed to be, on the cusp of change.

Q: *What sort of things did you used to speak out about in particular?*

I thought, 'I don't want to diet ever again or put myself down.' An epiphany of sorts got to a tipping point and it felt good to drop the dead weight of shame. I used to share that when we don't trust that we're exactly how we're supposed to be at any given moment, and something comes between us and our body – whether it's friends from home, parents, family, the environment or marketers – we become disconnected from our power, a power that no one can take from us unless we let them. I made it my business to pass along new information each time I was asked to speak, go on air, or be interviewed. It was beautiful timing. Almost like planting seeds where now, 20 years later, younger generations are kicking down the door in the name of change. Love the energy they bring to the table. Totally inspires me, and boy, do we need today's advocates!

Q: *You said that you 'don't want to diet ever again'. Did you experience diet culture messaging growing up at all?*

My parents always battled with their bodies and the weight game was a real one at home. I had preconceived notions around a person's value being tied to the size of their body. I grew up on low-fat cookies and sugar-free soft drinks. Those lovely low-fat diets of the 1990s were not only nutrient-scarce, but the worst mind game. Growing up through the 1970s, '80s and '90s, I was susceptible to ideas that my body was not to be trusted to develop on its own. To find a great life partner, land a great job and live a life filled with happiness, you had to look a certain specific way. Sadly, rarely did I meet a girl or woman who was happy with the body, hair and face they were born with. When I moved into my life after college, I began to realize that what was going on in my home was happening in other families' homes and that society and industry kept validating the toxicity. First, I asked,

'For what?' But the question became a resounding 'For whom?' The diet-related industry is a mystery in and of itself, making hundreds of billions off our backs because we let them each time we pay for a powder, bar or drink that promises to deliver the world.

Q: Were you ever diagnosed with an eating disorder?

No, never diagnosed, but when negative emotions would arise and I lacked the emotional tools to redirect them to a much better feeling place, I thank God for a handful of excellent therapists who listened, handed me tissues and led me in a better direction. I knew something was not right despite travelling to these beautiful palatial hotels in the most incredible locations and earning good money. I was constantly hearing an old record: 'Oooh, don't eat too much, don't eat too little, don't be too athletic.' It was perplexing because I had a successful life going on, but when I was alone, I was beating myself up over the smallest of things, which spilled over into how my body looked, which was a bit jumbled. It was through therapy that I was able to understand that what I absorbed in childhood no longer was serving me as a young adult. I applaud NEDA. They were the first to point to information that I could relate to, and made me realize that I was not alone. Thankfully, today there are excellent doctors, nurses and master therapists in the eating disorders community, and there are resources and individuals igniting activism around the issues. I am hopeful the Band-Aid has been pulled off, for good.

Q: So, in your opinion, how rife do you think eating disorders are in the fashion industry?

Candidly, I have not been near a runway in a while, but based on history, sadly, eating disorders are everywhere at all levels of society, including the fashion industry.

Q: *Nowadays, in the modelling industry, is it easy to flag issues? Do you know whether they have in-house medics, dietitians or psychologists?*

To the best of my knowledge, agencies do not have in-house medical doctors, therapists or coaches as of today. Several times, I've taken my hat off to the work done by Models Trust (MT), based in the UK. Models Trust is an organization that advocates on behalf of models to improve all work-related boundaries, health and safety issues. I am sure if there are agencies that have in-house medical doctors, therapists or coaches in the UK, MT will know about them. There are agencies like True Models in New York City that support a beautifully diverse model roster, and I'm sure there are plenty more here and overseas. In the United States, I am on the advisory board for the Model Alliance (MA). The MA has worked tirelessly to establish laws and regulations around health and safety for models in the US with the leadership of Sara Ziff and the MA staff. Models in the US have the rights they have today because of the work Sara and MA have done. Yes, there's much more work to be done. But step by step, with good pacing, we continue to get closer to equity.

Q: *I know that you navigated some serious health issues at one stage. How was that for you whilst working in the industry?*

When I was undergoing chemo in 2007, I understood that even though I wasn't feeling well, I should try to attend a red carpet event, if I felt up to it. Although some folks knew I was going through intense chemo treatments which meant I lost a lot of weight, I had one of the strangest things happen. I attended a woman's magazine Pier59 event while sporting my incredibly sparse short hair and dramatically reduced bod and several of the regular event photographers who were present said when I walked in, 'Emme, my god, you look so great...what the heck are you doing?' Their positive cajoling caught me so off guard, I remember getting a full body chill. I wanted to say to them, 'Do you have any idea what I'm going through!?' But, of course, I didn't. I just smiled and moved on. The whole experience was completely eye-opening until it happened a couple more times after. Showed me how programmed we are to celebrating thinness.

Wow.

Truth.

Q: *As you've got older, has your relationship with your body changed? Do older ladies experience different pressures, or fewer pressures, than those who are younger?*

Sixty is unquestionably today's 40. A 60-year-old woman has more vitality and youthfulness than her parents ever did. However, retailers have passed up an exciting opportunity to honour her. A woman over 50 has more money and wisdom to do more for herself than when she was younger. Then why don't we see more beautiful older women in campaigns, in movies or in positions of power? Until we embrace and ask for a full array of beauty, like a bouquet of flowers, we will be provided a limited curated beauty. I will remain hopeful that one day we will embrace and honour women – period. Let women be honoured for who they are, diverse, complex and beautiful.

Q: *That would be great! Speaking of diversity, you set up a new initiative, right?*

Yes, Fashion Without Limits (FWL). It was founded as an educational solution for the lack of inclusive designers and companies within the fashion industry. Bacon's 'knowledge is power' rang true for me and I felt for real change to take hold, fashion design schools and programmes needed to teach an inclusive fashion education. The True

Beauty Foundation was founded later and now has FWL under its um-
brella to promote youth mental wellness through various programmes,
including FWL. Parents were outraged when we first introduced FWL
at Syracuse University. They were saying to professors, 'How dare
you teach our kids to make clothes for fat people!' Happily, the press
felt otherwise. That year we were featured in a cascading variety of
news outlets and fashion magazines, including *WWD*, *Vogue Italia*
and *Business Insider*. The news outlets agreed that inclusive fashion
was long overdue.

Q: *What advice would you give to a young person aspiring to be a
model today?*

I'd ask a few questions. What are your goals once you're signed by an
agency? Know what they are prior to your go-see interview. Second,
what do you feel modelling will give you, other than money? If you
need to be told you're beautiful, walk away from the modelling industry, immediately. Really important. You'll be told you're beautiful
until the next model or flavour is all the rave. So, if you find yourself
signed to a top agency, know who you are and don't let anyone tell
you differently. Third, how will modelling help you? Will you be
providing for your mother, father or immediate family? If you are
charged with providing for your family, stay far away from the modelling industry because you don't want to be faced with a potentially
compromising situation. Enjoy your journey, stay tethered to your
family and friends, show up authentically, save and have fun!

Q: *So, what do you think the future has in store?*

The future is bright. The best part today is the younger generations
owning their inclusive selves. They are the change agents. So, rather
than demanding inclusivity, they're simply fully embracing themselves and those around them. In the next ten years, this mindset

will be the game changer seen reflected in advertising, social media, billboards, movies and all reflections of life. While some people still believe that beauty and fashion are exclusive rights, I'm excited for a hopeful and inclusive future. Today, I embrace this fresh perspective and will allow the process to unfold, whilst having fun working with the True Beauty Foundation providing programmes to support this important work. One important lesson cancer showed me: Life is short, time to enjoy every bit of it!

Avoidant/Restrictive Food Intake Disorder
(ARFID)

Diagnostic Criteria

1. Avoidance or restriction of food intake that results in either, or both, of the following:
    a. The intake of an insufficient quantity, or variety, of food to meet adequate energy or nutritional requirements
    b. Significant impairment in functioning (e.g. due to avoidance or distress related to participating in social experiences involving eating)
2. Eating behaviour not motivated by preoccupation with body weight or shape

NB: Eating behaviour, weight or other physical health impact are not due to unavailability of food, a medical or mental condition, or the effects of a substance or medication.

(Based on ICD-11)

" My daughter developed ARFID following a throat infection of already enlarged tonsils. At some point fear took over from pain and she was convinced that she would choke and die if she swallowed any food at all. She lost weight dramatically and the impact this starvation had on her brain and body was scary. Trying to get someone to listen and understand the seriousness of the situation was frustrating. I felt that the situation was being minimized, that the impact of the starvation was being overlooked, and that I was just an overanxious mother. As an eating disorder clinician myself, I couldn't understand why our situation was not being prioritized in the same way as someone with anorexia. Different cause for the fear of eating, but same impact on the body and brain. Just as serious, and just as devastating. We eventually got support and she is thankfully now recovered.

Anita Jones, a mother

Introduction

Dr Eva Trujillo

Eva María Trujillo Chi Vacuán, MD, FAED, CEDS, Fiaedp, FAAP, is Executive Director and Co-founder of Comenzar de Nuevo, A.C., a Mexican-based facility specializing in the treatment, education, prevention and research of eating disorders. She is a Clinical Professor of Paediatrics at the Tecnologico de Monterrey, Escuela de Medicina y Ciencias de la Salud. She is the Founder of Habilita A.C., a national non-profit organization dedicated to supporting carers and families affected by eating disorders. She has held many advisory and board roles, and authored extensively on eating disorders and adolescence. She has given more than 350 conferences and workshops on these topics worldwide, receiving numerous awards and recognitions for her world-leading work. @etrujilloch

'Now everything makes sense to me.' This is the most common statement I hear from our patients and families when I explain their ARFID diagnosis and how we need to approach it.

I have been in the field of eating disorders for a quarter of a century and, as a paediatrician, I get to talk to many parents of children, adolescents and young adults with food issues. For many years, one regular observation in clinical practice was that many patients with restrictive eating disorders did not fulfil the criteria for anorexia nervosa as described in the *Diagnostic and Statistical Manual of Mental Disorders* (DSM). They showed no fear of gaining weight, and often their reason for consultation was for this very reason – help to gain weight. Unfortunately, on many occasions, clinicians failed to help. Some dismissed any eating disorder diagnosis because patients had a 'normal' weight or were able to eat a lot of carbohydrates. Those of us who have been working with patients for a long time know that the big, grey area between normal eating and an eating disorder diagnosis is often full of suffering, pain and hopelessness for many people.

In Mexico, where I live, about 25 per cent of adolescents are affected by a mental health problem, and, unfortunately, less than 50 per cent of those will get the correct mental health support. In most Latin American countries, economic resources are very limited, and mental health services are usually not integrated into primary care services; less than 30 per cent of primary care services will have a treatment protocol for mental health issues. With all that said, the diagnosis of ARFID is often a real challenge.

Most families and patients affirm that they have been navigating a world full of mishearing, misunderstanding and misdiagnosing. Our patients have been easily dismissed as picky eaters or treated inappropriately as patients with anorexia nervosa. ARFID is not really a new diagnosis; it has existed for decades, maybe more, and has gone unrecognized for much of this time. This is why in 2013 – when the latest publication of the American Psychiatric Association's DSM (fifth edition) named and described a syndrome that reflected what many of our patients had been struggling with for years – many of us welcomed this change with open arms: a change desperately needed in our field. Even better, a few years later, Dr Jennifer Thomas and Dr Kamryn Eddy developed a therapeutic approach (cognitive-behavioural therapy for avoidant/restrictive food intake disorder (CBT-AR)) based on their research and clinical evidence, which helped us give hope to our patients. Other tools have been researched by others, too. We can now tell our patients that we have evidence-based solutions, and we have been adapting these to the Latin community. So far, we know that this syndrome is not culture-bound (limited to any specific society or culture).

ARFID is still not totally understood, and our field needs to work in the coming decades on research, treatment innovations and sub-represented populations. We still hear professionals who have never heard of ARFID. It is imperative that we translate the research literature into an accessible and authoritative resource for those who suffer from this illness, their families, friends, loved ones, health professionals, educators and the public. I hope that we can bridge the gap between this urgent problem that affects too many people – children, adolescents and adults – and what we know about it. Bringing ARFID to light is the first big step towards helping patients, carers and professionals be seen and heard, and feel accompanied.

Pizza, Again?

Lindsey Holland

Lindsey Holland is a full-time plus-size fashion content creator who speaks openly about her experiences with ARFID. She has more than 200,000 followers on her TikTok account. She is also known for the YouTube series *Fat History*. @im.an.adult

I'm fat and completely happy with how I look. For my job, I'm a full-time social media content creator who advocates for loving your body at any size. I'm also at the beginning of (hopefully) a successful modelling career. I have nothing but love for my body, and myself, and don't feel the need to change anything intentionally. I also have an eating disorder – ARFID.

ARFID largely relates to the restriction of particular kinds of food due to the sensory experience around them. Those restrictions can look like specifications around texture, temperature, smell, colour and even time of day. There may also be issues with fear around choking or being sick. These things lead to skipping meals and cutting out entire food groups, and, if left untreated, can lead to health problems from lack of proper nutrition – which is why it's especially important to recognize and address ARFID symptoms in developing children.

I was 28 when I first heard of ARFID. I can remember sitting in complete silence for 45 minutes not believing what I had just read. I'd been struggling with eating for so long, and had never felt comfortable saying that there was a problem, because no diagnosis ever felt like it quite fit.

People often ask me how I went so long without knowing that I had a problem. Well, things changed so gradually over time that recognizing that there was a problem wasn't super obvious.

I've always been fairly particular about what I eat. Whilst I didn't care for a lot of types of food, eating wasn't that difficult because I would just go for larger portions of the few things that I *did* like, and would skip the parts of the meal that I didn't like. I didn't really pay it any more mind than that.

My parents also have a lot of similar specifications and quirks. We always liked to laugh about how, in the summer, my mother lives on tomatoes. With a salt shaker in one hand and a tomato in the other, she bites into the tomato like an apple, sprinkling a little bit of salt on each new bite. She will gladly eat tomatoes by themselves, every meal for days on end. We never thought of this as odd, just that she loves them so she eats them all the time.

Similarly, I can tell you my parents' pizza order. Because it's the exact same order they've got every single time they've ordered a pizza, my entire life, with very few exceptions. Having very strong preferences when it comes to food was always seen as completely normal.

When I think of family road trips, I think of snacks. They were the secret to any road trip, or vacation, going smoothly because we would get so focused on whatever we were doing that we would completely forget to eat. If we didn't eat the occasional snack, everyone would get grumpy. Forgetting to eat for really long periods of time, by accident, was another funny little quirk that seemed to run in the family.

Within the context of how I was raised and what 'normal' looked like to my family, I thought things were completely normal for me for the vast majority of my life. During my young adult days, I thought I was 'just a bit picky' and felt I had a few, very normal and completely reasonable preferences.

I mean everyone likes fast food because it's predictable and consistent, right?

Everyone struggles with keeping a container of salad greens before they go bad, right?

It's normal to prefer not to eat fish because you're really scared of choking on a bone that may have got missed while preparing it, right?

It's normal to not be very good at noticing you're hungry until you feel sick, right?

It's normal to get as close as you can to the exact same meal every time you go to a restaurant (I just really knew what I liked), right?

Everyone has a fridge full of leftovers they won't eat, right?

Everyone would rather not eat than eat something that's not the exact thing they had been wanting, right?

Everyone worries about mould on their food, right?

Everyone prefers to eat alone, right?

I don't know but, to me, individually, all of these seem fairly normal. So, when was the turning point? And when did it get serious?

I could say that there was some significance to when I was 23 and went vegan 'just to try it out'. I was completely surprised at how little of a struggle it was. I would have never imagined it to be so easy considering how picky I was normally. But it felt effortless and was my first experience cutting out large sections of food.

I could also see a turning point being when I was 25. I found out that I was going to need back surgery, had lost my job and went through my first heartbreak – all within a six-month period. I fell into a consuming depression and could barely find the strength to make myself eat most days. When I *could* eat, it was almost always one of a handful of things, usually only once a day, likely in large portions, and almost certainly not nutritionally balanced by any means. It was like my body was trying to get my entire day's nutrition in one meal. I knew I needed to eat. I also knew I didn't hate my body and wasn't trying to intentionally not eat. But I knew that I wasn't *able* to eat properly. The thought of eating things outside of a few specific meals made me feel physically sick. It all felt very mechanical.

This is the point at which I wish I had known what ARFID was. I've always been known as 'the fat girl that likes herself', which made me hesitant to talk to anyone about it. The first, and only, time I tried to talk to someone about it, their reaction devastated me. They told me that they thought I was lying, and that they thought I had another restrictive disorder and had clearly been dishonest about my confidence and feelings towards myself. I trusted their opinion, and I didn't know ARFID was a thing, so I believed them. I must have had it wrong. I must have been doing this intentionally without realizing it, or too scared to admit it anyway.

I spent years trying to completely dismantle every remaining aspect of internalized fatphobia and self-hate, and at the end of all of that, I *still* wasn't able to eat. The hardest part of ARFID to articulate is how upsetting it is to not be able to eat even if you want to. Even if you know you need to. It can make you physically sick if you try to force yourself to eat, so even if you want to, it still feels impossible. I felt like such a failure. But I felt like I had to hide my feelings because the most important thing to me was showing people what it looks like to live in a fat body whilst also being happy and loving yourself.

How could I do that, though, if I couldn't eat? How could I tell other people to love themselves if I couldn't even eat? How could I tell other people they could eat, if *I* couldn't? I looked in the mirror and truly loved who I saw looking back. I looked at myself with the purest of love, so why couldn't I take care of myself?

One day, I was researching autism symptoms because I was at the beginning stages of figuring out that I am autistic. I came across an article talking about various issues with eating and ARFID. All I could think, as I spent hours researching everything I could and listening to other people share their own experiences, was: I wasn't lying. I wasn't making it up. This is real and it's not all in my head. I was shocked that I had never heard of ARFID before. I felt more understood than ever in my life.

Even before I knew about ARFID, or sought out recovery, I found ways that I could work around my needs. For example, when I couldn't eat salads, I added a scoop of greens powder to some water in the morning and felt safe knowing that I was still getting some vegetables in. Or I convinced myself to drink more water if it had flavouring in, on days when drinking water was difficult. While I didn't feel like I had all of the answers, I felt like I was managing the best I could. Once I knew about ARFID, though, I made it my mission to learn as much as I could. I realized that there was hope of actually thriving!

※ ※ ※

Some days are more challenging than others, but the biggest difference is that, even on my hardest days, I know I'm still getting the important parts of nutrition. I've found effective ways of living with it and it's made my life better.

On my best days, I can eat balanced meals. I still have periods when I'm more affected by symptoms, but now I have a ton of systems in place so that – no matter what – I know I'm taking care of myself. In general, these are some things that I have found to be the most helpful in managing symptoms:

- Eat what you can manage to safely eat *without force*.
- Give yourself compassion and don't shame yourself for what you can't manage to eat.

- Find a range of foods that are typically safe when more nutritious foods are either out of stock or feel impossible to eat.
- Keep safe foods stocked in your pantry so that you have them when you need them.
- Try new foods when possible, even if it's only one bite.
- Have timers to help with knowing when you should eat meals to avoid meal skipping.
- Keep ice packs in the freezer to put on your chest when you feel nauseous.

I would even consider things like keeping disposable dishes and utensils on hand for times when having access to clean dishes keeps you from making a meal.

The wonderful part about accommodations is that it can give you the safety and security to know that you're okay, even when things are difficult. And accommodations look different for everyone because we all have different needs.

The key is to not necessarily change your needs immediately, to make them go away, but rather to find ways of working *with* your needs. Whilst on the journey of change, giving yourself the grace to make decisions that make your life more accessible, in the moment, is so important. For example, I used to really beat myself up about using disposable plates occasionally when I was far too depressed to keep up with the dishes. This is until I realized that just by having access to clean dishes I was able to, first, make meals more often and, second, skip fewer meals. Some people may hear that and think, 'That's so wasteful.' But that's ironic, because it's often the same people who'll shame you for using a plastic fork when you're too depressed to wash a dish who wouldn't think twice about getting a plastic fork for themselves with a takeout meal. If something helps you eat, or function better, it's worth doing without shame. You deserve to live comfortably with any accommodations necessary.

The most important thing is: there is hope. Finding the term ARFID and seeking help for it changed my life. This is why I have dedicated myself to spreading awareness: showing people not only what it looks like to be fat and have ARFID, but also that recovery is possible, with compassion. If you or a loved one are struggling, please know you're not alone, and if you feel like no one cares, I do.

When Finding Food Is Like Finding a Needle in a Haystack

Sam Layton

Sam Layton is a mental health advocate and instructor based in North East England. By utilizing public speaking and social media, she shares her experiences of depression and avoidant/restrictive food intake disorder (ARFID) in the hope of reducing the stigma surrounding mental illness. She has a community of more than 30,000 followers across social channels. She is in the process of setting up a charity which aims to improve accessibility to services and provide resources for young people so that they feel they have the knowledge and support that they need. @samlaytonuk

If you tried biting into a block of plastic that had been coated in poison, you would struggle. The texture of the plastic would make it hard to bite through and the worry of the poison would occupy your mind, preventing you from putting any more in your mouth. That is what eating food can feel like to me.

For as long as I can remember, eating has been an issue for me. Whilst I don't personally remember much about the eating difficulties I had as a child, I've had many reminders over the years: family members mentioning how I would refuse to eat as a child, remembering how I would only eat one thing when having lunch at school, or reading through my medical history.

From the day solids were introduced into my diet, I struggled to eat. As a child, I opted to consume large amounts of liquid instead. So much so that I had to be held back a year in school due to frequently going to the toilet. On the occasion that I *did* eat, I didn't eat much.

As a child, I ate tuna sandwiches, custard and a specific brand of cereal. That was pretty much it. And if the cafeteria ran out of the sandwiches I liked, I would happily not eat for the rest of the day. Some say that if a parent doesn't cave in to a child's wants, they'll start eating what they're given. For those like myself, diagnosed with avoidant/restrictive food intake disorder (ARFID), this is far from true. There was a mental block preventing me from eating food that I wouldn't usually eat. Still, today, the list of foods I *do* eat – which I call my safe foods – is much shorter than I would like it to be.

If I had a pound for every time someone gave me unhelpful information, I could buy a mansion:

'Just try new foods.'

'Remove all the foods you normally eat, and you'll be forced to eat a wider variety.'

'Hide the food amongst other foods to make you eat it.'

The list is endless. Whilst many of these may work for picky eating, it doesn't if the issues you're experiencing are a little deeper. If you bribed a fussy eater who refused to eat their bowl of salad with tickets to Disneyland, I'm sure they would cave and eat it. For somebody with ARFID, it's a completely different story. As a child, no bribe would make me eat.

As I got older, to force myself to eat a food I wouldn't normally eat, I would subconsciously try to convince myself that it wasn't food. Some argue that if you do this daily for a prolonged period, the said food will become a safe food. This wasn't the case for me. If I forced myself to eat a food, even if it was one I usually ate but for some reason I'd been slightly put off by it, I would lose my appetite. If this continued for a period of time – where I forced myself to eat a food in the hope of overcoming my barriers surrounding eating it – my barriers would get worse. Rather than getting used to eating the food, I'd convince myself that I had to eat it. So every time I tried to eat the food, I'd lose my appetite, and a simple task of eating would turn into a mammoth mental struggle. This then led to an endless cycle of rarely trying new foods, even though my options were limited.

Over the years, in my travels across the world, finding food has felt like finding a needle in a haystack. In supermarkets the size of a football pitch, I'd find very few foods to eat. When abroad, there would often be nothing I could manage. Despite my family being Palestinian and Pakistani, even when I've been to those countries, it's still a challenge to find food I eat. The same goes for countries like Spain or the Netherlands, where supermarkets are similar to the UK. I'd walk down the sandwich aisle and see tuna and sweetcorn or ham and egg sandwiches. But, argh, why couldn't they have tuna and mayonnaise, or a sandwich with just ham!? I'd walk down the snacks aisle and look at the variety of items on offer: chocolate bars, biscuits, crisps and marshmallows. Nothing. Couldn't eat them. After searching far and wide, I'd finally find something I could eat, but it wouldn't necessarily be the same brand that I was used to. Or maybe the food looked different. All of these were barriers. I often relied on fast food when abroad and then struggled when in a city that didn't have a fast-food restaurant that I was used to eating from.

My inability to have a varied diet was made worse by my inability to taste properly. When I inhale through my nose, all I feel is the air going into my nose and through to my lungs. I can't smell the roses when taking a walk through the park, or the smell of the freshly baked bread when walking past a bakery. That's not because of any virus or allergy; I was born that way. Whilst there's no physical cause for it, it's something many have – congenital anosmia. Whilst not having the sense of smell in and of itself doesn't bother me, the problems it's led to, and continues to lead to, when it comes to eating, do. My lack of smell results in me being unable to taste the cheese on the Margherita pizza I bought for lunch, or the chocolate in the chocolate croissants I snack on throughout the day. Whilst there are some tastes I can taste, these are few and far between. Whether or not I enjoy a food mainly depends on the texture. Sometimes the texture's just right and I'll happily devour a sharer pack of it.

A safe food I frequently eat is croissants with chocolate sauce inside. You know the ones. I really like those. Another product, by the same brand, has chocolate *and* vanilla sauce inside. The difference for most people would be the flavour. For me? The colour. Over the years, I've struggled to get over this block preventing me eating the chocolate and vanilla. I would eat it five times slower than normal, and with every bite I took, my mind would convince me that what I was eating wasn't nice. And if I couldn't find the brand of croissant I liked, I'd either struggle to eat other brands, or flat-out refuse. There may have been little to no difference. Or there may have been a big difference. But the difference was always the texture, as opposed to the taste. I often question how many of those differences were real and how many were psychological.

A commonly misunderstood experience for people with ARFID is the inability to have set meals each day. Whilst this may not affect everybody, I'm one of many who has struggled to have three set meals per day. When I was younger, I remember not being hungry, even for meals. Whilst I don't remember if I skipped meals or not, I remember that if given the choice, I could easily have done so. But when I *did* have meals, I would often snack. When I started expanding my diet to include certain sweets and chocolate, I ended up snacking throughout the day. This, in turn, led to me always being hungry. By the age of 15, if I was in school, I was unable to go even a few hours without having a snack. During multiple lessons throughout the day, I would *have* to have snacks. I got in trouble a fair amount because of it. Now, throughout the day, I can eat around half a dozen sandwiches. Other days, it may look different. I may just buy a large amount of fast food – specifically nuggets and plain burgers – and consume them slowly throughout the day. One burger can take me five minutes to eat if I'm really hungry; normally, it takes about ten minutes, though. Sometimes, I can be eating the same burger for an hour. Whilst this causes problems in my current office-based job, it's thankfully not a major issue. In other jobs, though, I can easily see this being a problem. And it's a fear for when I'm job-hunting in the future.

Are my issues with food something I'd like to continue changing? Definitely. Do I think it's ever going to be easy? Sadly not. Many people in my life think I'm not changing quickly enough because I haven't acknowledged the health issues this has caused – and will continue to cause. Many think it's because I simply like relying on sweets and fast food that I frequently consume. Others think it's because I allow myself to have access to my safe foods and that simply restricting my access to them will force me to eat normally. This is far from the truth. I believe in taking manageable steps. First things first: to cope with my diet. Currently, my diet doesn't cause me any stress throughout the day. It's not something that crosses my mind most days. I'm able to eat in public without worrying what people would think of me if they were to see the difficulties I'd be experiencing otherwise. As a result of not stressing myself out with food, I can focus my attention on other aspects of my life too. This foundation makes it easier to move towards recovery and make those small forward-focused changes.

Accepting that this is not something that will disappear overnight allows me to be able to live my life like anybody else.

You Won't Choke

Shannon Dymond

Shannon Dymond is a Miss Scotland Finalist 2021 and an eating disorders activist. She has collaborated with Beat (the UK's leading eating disorder charity) to raise money for eating disorders. Her words have been featured in the *Daily Record* and *Glasgow Live*. @shannondymondxx

I knew a girl who couldn't eat chips. She said it was her head making her feel this way – not because the chips had any unusual ingredients or anything. She had become so used to the anxiety and fear around chips that she would just avoid them altogether. I used to think she was weird.

Everything is crystal clear in hindsight. At the time, though, it can feel like a murky mess. Now, I can look back knowing that my paralyzing fear of choking – which first reared its head at the age of eight and haunted me for many years – was almost certainly a coping mechanism for anxiety linked to some childhood trauma. But, at the time, it was mighty confusing. I had no idea where this fear was coming from. Every single thing I ate left me dripping in an anxious sweat, questioning when the choking might start. The fear would often fluctuate in intensity; periods of calm followed by deep angst which would return suddenly and intensely, as though with a vengeance. Being so young, not knowing how to cope, with no one around pointing me in the right direction of how to cope, made it all so much worse. I was left undiagnosed for years, totally in the dark with how to manage my ARFID, and the anxiety that came with it.

So the fact that I can now eat, having been fully recovered for five years, I can honestly say feels amazing. I couldn't eat at restaurants as I was terrified that I would have a panic attack. I couldn't enjoy dinner with friends, family or even on my own. I would avoid social events where there was food, and would only eat around certain people at certain times. Oh, and I would absolutely dread Christmas dinner. It was not a fun time for me at all. Which is why I never thought I'd get to this point. To be able to go out for meals, eat in public without thinking I'm going to attract the attention of everyone in the entire restaurant, go on dinner dates with my boyfriend, and eat whatever I want, just feels so nice.

This is probably music to the ears of those who used to say things to me like 'Can you not just eat?' and 'You won't choke, don't be so silly.' I've lost count of the number of times I was called 'fussy' or 'spoiled', or told that I was 'acting out'. To call someone these things without exploring *why* they might not be eating, to me, seems like a pretty lazy thing to do. If someone is *scared* to eat, surely that should make you stop, wonder and question? I mean, think about how many other ways to 'act out' there are instead of starving yourself. For all you know, amongst other things, there may be some form of trauma relating to this that you are completely unaware of – you have no idea. This was the case for me anyway; a reminder that children's mental health is very much real. Now, I love my food, and whenever I eat a good meal, it can put me in such a good mood. I struggle to imagine not eating what I feel like and when I want. I'm totally at one with all those food-induced feel-good endorphins now. My advice to adults is that if you ever come across someone like I once was – irrespective of age, gender or weight – dig deep, and, I beg you, do not dismiss their concerns. I wasn't privileged enough to have someone who fully believed me, or someone who was patient and encouraged me, or took me seriously, or identified that what I was going through was in fact an eating disorder. I didn't have someone with empathy when I needed it most.

Patronizing comments like 'Can you not just eat?' and 'You won't choke, don't be so silly' at the time felt like the very last things I wanted to hear. They really didn't help. The people who said these things included medical professionals, by the way. I was dismissed multiple times by both medical professionals and family members, and was made to feel like I was broken and abnormal. So confusing for someone my age with a petite, developing brain. Imagine telling someone with arachnophobia to go play with a handful of spiders, or throwing a load of almonds at someone with a severe nut allergy, or suggesting someone afraid of heights visits the Glasgow Tower for their birthday. If anyone ever asks me what life with ARFID feels like, I put it like this. It's having your worst fear directly blocking your path to progress. And as I've already suggested, most people completely dismiss ARFID entirely from the eating disorder conversation. But having been through what I went through, I can't even begin to express just how awful it is. ARFID produced in me a fear that was very real and very present in my everyday life.

I had to console myself time and time again: 'It's OK, all these people haven't gone through what you've gone through, so they don't know,' and 'Most people don't understand what ARFID is, and that's OK, one day they'll learn.' I kept telling myself to not be angry at anyone, or at the world, for not being able to relate to my struggles. Somehow, I needed to create channels of ignoring them, and keep tunnel-visioned, trusting the process of recovery.

I remember reading a book, when I was about 11, about a young girl who was heading home from school to have her favourite tea: chicken nuggets, chips and beans. Funnily enough, this was my absolute favourite tea before my eating disorder came on (there was definitely an 'Oh wait, that sounds like me!' moment while I was reading it). I remember reading its pages over and over again. And somehow I seemed to be building up the courage to eat it. I remember salivating, as though the food was already sitting in my mouth. I could virtually taste it. That night, I went home and gave it a go, and was so immensely proud of myself for trying. I wish that I could remember the name of the book because this was at the early stages of me introducing new foods into my 'safe food' family. I knew I had to at some point, but it felt so overwhelming not knowing where to start.

The book was one of a few things, at the start, that helped me regain the confidence to try foods that I had wanted to eat for so many years but couldn't. I tried to control the fear by eating my 'safe foods', which, for me, started out as basically anything mushy. Essentially, what a baby would eat, and a few other bits and bobs. I could only eat liquids and very soft foods. If something was put down in front of me that wasn't one of these 'safe foods', the panic attacks would start instantaneously. First, the hot flushes, followed by the increased heart rate and palpitations, and, lastly, the feeling of my throat closing up (the dreaded choking feeling). This was what I was trying to avoid at all costs. You'd think that, as a child, not being able to eat bread, crisps, meat, chocolate and sweets would be difficult, but for me it wasn't (although I did feel that on some level I was missing out). Kids notice things, and so would always question me at school. But what could I say? I had no clue what the problem was, and why I couldn't eat them! Eventually, I would hide food to avoid disappointing or worrying my family, or anyone else.

I made sure to gradually set goals along the way, trying to not compare my recovery to others. As I got older, I practised a lot more self-care. I love the outdoors, so I started going on regular walks listening to my favourite music or favourite feel-good podcast. Meditation was a huge help to me, as well as visualization. I really tried to understand my mind and take things one step at a time. This wasn't easy, and I had to be patient and give the process time. I aimed to try three different foods a week and would reward myself with something at the end of the month. Aesop must have had ARFID, because slow and steady really did win the race for me. I didn't push it too hard.

* * *

ARFID isn't weird, or any less of an eating disorder than the rest. I've learnt that I'm not just strange, and that there are others who relate to how I felt (like the girl who avoided chips). When you know you're not alone, this can make it easier to step out of your comfort zone. And what I've learned over the years is that leaving your safety net is sometimes what is needed to grow. Not every week will be the same. And I know that now, in hindsight, but wish I could have known this at the beginning. But one thing's for sure, despite it being incredibly difficult at the beginning, it does get easier with time and perseverance. To anyone in recovery, please know that there is hope out there. Keep going. Even though it took ten years, I got there in the end. The recovery journey is not easy at all but is so worth it.

Completely Capable

Laura Mae Ramsey

Laura Mae Ramsey is a content creator. She shares her steps towards recovery from ARFID and obsessive compulsive disorder (OCD) on TikTok to a community of more than 190,000 followers. Through her own recovery, she discovered a passion for helping others feel less alone and has even returned to school to pursue a degree that will allow her to professionally treat ARFID and OCD. In addition to her mental health content, she likes to share aspects of what it is like living with a chronic illness. @lauramaeramsey

It's not about the food. That's what everyone always says when discussing eating disorders, and they're right – it's not about the food, not really. There are always underlying issues, thoughts, conflicts or stressors. But when you're living with ARFID, it becomes extremely difficult to disconnect your anxieties from the food itself. I always had trouble explaining to others that it wasn't food in general! I wanted to eat! I was hungry, sick and exhausted. I didn't want to lose weight, I didn't want to feel so weak and tired. My brain, my survival instincts, had determined that certain foods were dangerous. That if I ate them, I would have an allergic reaction, a heart attack, be poisoned – the list goes on. Sometimes I wasn't even sure exactly what kind of reaction I thought I would have. I just knew, or thought I knew, it would be bad. Starving felt safer.

What makes ARFID particularly difficult to treat is that it can present in so many ways. For some, ARFID is very sensory-based. For others, it is a complete disinterest in food. For me, ARFID is a fear of adverse reactions. And this fear is made worse by obsessive compulsive disorder, another diagnosis of mine which is made worse by posttraumatic stress disorder due to medical trauma.

In 2016, back when I ate with little or no thought and had never even heard of ARFID, I had an adverse reaction to a medication which led to me wearing a Holter heart monitor for 30 days. This incident would spark a five-year-long battle of fighting for answers. My heart rate would spike for seemingly no reason, sometimes reaching 200 beats per minute, on top of countless other mysterious physical symptoms. I was in and out of the emergency room, in the back of ambulances, lying on doctors' tables getting test after test and, all the while, I was so sure I was going to die. Dramatic? Maybe. But when something unknown is happening to your heart, it's hard to not be dramatic. I had no idea why this was happening, what was causing it or how to prevent it. And since I didn't have those answers, I began to fear putting anything into my body. My mind filled in the blanks, trying its best to make sense of a situation that felt entirely out of control. Subconsciously, I had made the decision that if I can't control what is happening within my body, I can at least control what goes in it.

The story my mind spun was: food equals dangerous. Food equals sickness. Food equals bad. Of course, I know now that those conclusions are false. But it helps to be able to look back and see how I ended up where I did – with three safe foods, steadily declining health and a level of panic and anxiety at every meal that made life feel impossible. My brain overcorrected. It took a scary, unknown thing and thought that it could help. When you are able to say, 'Hey, my brain did what it thought was best to protect me,' you take some of the pressure off yourself. You throw away those feelings of shame or guilt or blame. To me, this is the first step to recovery. The first step to healing.

Finding treatment for ARFID is hard. Unfortunately, it is still relatively unheard of, even in professional environments, and this lack of awareness presents a huge barrier when you are seeking help. I went through assessment after assessment, I fought with my insurance company, I begged intensive outpatient programmes to please just help me. I cried to administrative assistants at treatment facilities over and over again when they gave the news that no, they don't treat ARFID or no, they couldn't take my insurance. But recovery – being able to live day to day without as much fear – was worth every bit of it. It is outrageous that we must fight so hard to get the help we need, the help we deserve. But I would do it all again to get to where I am now.

Depending on the type of ARFID you have, your journey with it will look incredibly different. So everything that I say helped me may not help others – and that's okay. It doesn't make anyone wrong, or less than, or not strong enough, or incapable of recovery. It just means a different approach may be needed. I have always called the subtype of ARFID that I deal with 'fear-based ARFID' or 'OCD-based ARFID', so it makes sense that the treatment that helped me the most was exposure therapy – the main form of treatment for OCD. To do this, I needed to find someone who could help me along the way, and since I was having no luck with treatment facilities, I started to think outside of the box.

First, I needed someone who understood nutrition and food. On top of that, I needed someone who had even heard of ARFID. I stayed up all night researching dietitians in my area and compiled a list. I emailed every single one and asked if they had ever heard of ARFID, and I explained what I needed help with. Out of all of my enquiries, only one knew about ARFID and felt confident she could help. One. Anxiety was creeping in at the thought that just one person – a woman about my age working out of a town an hour away from me – was possibly my only chance.

On the morning of my assessment, I was sick to my stomach with nerves. I had experienced so many rejections up to this point and didn't know if I could handle another one. I didn't want to get my hopes up. As soon as our video call began and we started talking, I knew I was finally meeting the person who was going to help me. She knew what ARFID was, she understood everything I was going through and, most importantly, she took away that lingering feeling that I was a lost cause and replaced it with hope.

Initially, the dietitian and I only focused on increasing my intake. She didn't care if I ate the same safe food all day, as long as I was eating. I loved this approach because the idea of eating more in volume and variety right away felt so impossible. But this way, I at least knew I felt comfortable with the food on my plate, even if the amount of times I ate a day felt foreign. The dietitian was with me every step of the way. She gave me her number and let me text her at mealtimes and, believe me, I texted her.

In the first few days, I was experiencing so much anxiety around the changes we were making and was so convinced I was going to become horribly sick that she even gave me a new mantra. *My body is capable*. It is capable of handling this change. It is capable of taking care of me. It is capable of finding a way to feel healthy again. I wrote it on a sticky note and hung it on my mirror. I repeated it to myself at the dining-room table, in the kitchen, sitting on the couch. My body is capable. My body is capable. I am capable. Capable. The word became my anchor, in a way. After years of feeling completely incapable, out of control and inadequate, I was so excited to proclaim to the world that I was wrong! I am capable! I even put it on a t-shirt, dammit.

This was around the time I began making recovery-focused Tik-Toks. As strange as it may sound, making a TikTok when I was overwhelmed or anxious trying to make all of these changes was one of the most helpful tools in my treatment journey. Of course, there were some downfalls. I have received my fair share of mean comments, making fun of the girl who's scared of a Pop-Tart. But for every mean comment, there were hundreds of supportive ones. And besides, it was less about having an audience and more about having an outlet. Something to focus on. I was unemployed at the time, too sick and miserable to maintain a job. And so making these videos made me excited to keep going. To have tangible evidence of how far I've come. To show others struggling with this that they aren't alone.

Whether you want to go on this journey privately, or share it with the Internet, I highly recommend keeping some sort of log for yourself to look back on during the hard moments. There were times I felt like I hadn't got better at all, that I was going to be stuck this way forever. And during those times, I would scroll through my old videos, watching a not-so-far-in-the-past version of myself who would give anything to be where I had got to.

Once the dietitian felt I had got to where I was eating a more acceptable amount each day, we started to work on increasing variety. This was hard, but as terrified as I was, as high as the stakes felt, I was also a little...excited? I used to love food! I loved colourful, vibrant meals with unique flavour combinations. While a part of me felt safer – more in control – with my safe foods, another part of me was just so sick of beige, plain food. I wanted to taste things again.

The approach we took to this is one of my favourite tools for ARFID recovery. It is very accurately called 'food-bridging'. You take a food you feel safe with and find a way to have baby steps that bridge that food to a new food or 'fear food'. So, for example, let's say your fear food is fresh tomato but you feel comfortable with ketchup. You can start with ketchup, move up to tomato sauce, then canned crushed tomatoes and, finally, fresh tomato. The idea is that you move on to the next step when you no longer feel afraid or anxious with the step you're on. It can be a slow process, or you may surprise yourself and realize that you're able to breeze through the steps more easily than you imagined. Either way, it can make the movement from one food to the other less intimidating. While I loved food-bridging and found it incredibly useful, I also realized that sometimes I needed to just jump all in. Without thinking too hard, without obsessing over what might happen, I sometimes wanted to just do it. For those moments, I decided to make it a little game. On small pieces of paper, I wrote down all of the fear foods I had in my pantry or fridge and I put them in a hat. When I was feeling particularly brave and up for a challenge, I would draw one out and do a food exposure. I documented this all on TikTok in what I so creatively titled my 'Fear Food Hat Series' and, I have to admit...it was pretty fun! Don't get me wrong; it was difficult. But putting this spin on it made it feel less like a chore. And I'll let you in on a little secret. If I drew something I didn't feel up to doing, I put it back in and drew again. It's your game! Your recovery! You make the rules.

For the food exposure itself, the goal was always to take at least one bite. But sometimes, if my brain wasn't cooperating, I'd lessen the expectations a little. Not feeling up to taking a bite? Okay, press it to your tongue. Still too much? No problem, just smell it or hold it in your hand. Anything to help make the connection in your mind that this thing is not to be feared. It may not feel like you're making progress but, with each exposure, no matter what the exposure process is, you're telling your mind that you will be okay. And, believe it or not, it works! Your mind will eventually begin to recognize that hey, this thing's not so bad! Avoidance is your worst enemy when it comes to anxiety. It reinforces the fear, sends the message to your mind that it is doing the right thing by reacting so strongly to it. I know, I know – avoidance is literally in the name of this disorder. Facing these fears is truly easier said than done. But each time you do, you are a step closer. It's worth it.

As much as I was growing in confidence with my dietitian, I still needed to get my panic attacks and constant anxiety under control. I had therapists in the past – one of which diagnosed me with ARFID – but none that I felt I truly clicked or progressed, with. I was lucky enough to have a friend recommend someone to me and I was able to get in with her fairly quickly. Thus began my journey with EMDR therapy – something that I truly believe saved my life.

EMDR stands for eye movement desensitization and reprocessing. It is a type of therapy specifically for processing trauma, and since my

ARFID came as a result of some pretty heavy medical trauma, this form of therapy worked wonders for me. It is actually quite common for a traumatic experience to be what jump-starts ARFID in an individual. Severely choking on something, a bad case of food poisoning, a severe allergic reaction or even an experience not tied to food at all can lead to the development of ARFID. Remember what I said about our brains trying to protect us? EMDR helps you process this trauma so you can put it behind you and move forward. It is hard to heal when the traumatic experience lives so fresh in your mind, being triggered with every attempt at recovery. After a few sessions of EMDR, I noticed the exposures were feeling less and less intense. They were still difficult. There were still moments I would sit on the kitchen floor in tears. But it felt doable and that was something I hadn't felt in a long time. Something I didn't realize how badly I needed to feel.

Working in tandem with the dietitian and therapist, things began to fall into place. I have gone from having three safe foods and countless fear foods to having countless safe foods and only a handful of fear foods. I am more present in my life. I sleep better. My mind is clearer. And while I still have my chronic illness (which, if you were wondering, turned out to be postural orthostatic tachycardia syndrome), I feel better physically than I have in years. Through finding a treatment process that worked for me, I was able to learn coping skills to get through the exposure, yes, but more importantly, I felt less alone. And, if you ask me, that's one of the biggest things for someone struggling with an eating disorder of any kind. Eating disorders are isolating. Having an eating disorder no one has ever heard of adds a whole new layer to that loneliness. And if this relates to you, I hope you are comforted knowing that you are not alone. You are not to blame. And you are not stuck. You are capable. Remember?

Black Men
Lee Chambers

Lee Chambers is a Black British psychologist and entrepreneur, and the founder of Essentialise Workplace Wellbeing. He is a Great British Entrepreneur Award winner, has featured in the Startups 100 Index and been inducted into the Black Cultural Archives for services to health and business. He is part of the National Academy of Sciences 2023 'Future Leaders of Science' cohort and has been interviewed by *Vogue*, *Newsweek* and the BBC. @leechambers-1

I've never publicly shared about my disordered eating. Given the fact that I'm a mental health professional, receive regular supervision, and share vulnerably about many other challenges that I've faced, you're probably wondering why.

❊ ❊ ❊

My earliest memories of eating are as a six-year-old child, being forced to sit at a table until I'd eaten more. Certain foods were difficult. The textures were highly unpleasant – from prickly to slimy, rubbery to gritty. Trying to eat these was painful, would reduce me to tears and leave me fighting to avoid putting myself through the misery. Other foods had overpowering tastes that were repellent, repugnant and highly unpleasant, and I had the same fight with these. And the most frustrating thing: most of the challenging foods were vegetables.

I didn't receive my autism diagnosis until I was 36, but I've always been aware of my sensory challenges. Annoyingly, these went the other way too. Foods honed by scientists to be hyper-palatable were highly desirable, leaving me prone to eating to excess for the sheer sensory thrill being activated, again and again. This had minimal impact on my body composition until I hit puberty. It was at this point, as for many young boys, that I started to think about how I appeared to the outside world. Growing up in the 1990s was an interesting time, with boy bands and lad culture all the rage. Naturally, I looked to Black role models and saw a lot of role models in athletics, football, the movies and the music industry. And what I saw was an ideal that I was a long way away from.

Almost all of these role models had physical, muscular and athletic physiques. I was languid, soft and not particularly strong. I'd hear of how strong Black people were, because they had been slaves and grafted. My grandad would talk about lifting massive stones when he worked on the railways. Commentators would refer to them as 'beasts'. And in the wider media, this athletic Black male body standard was exotified, from music videos to films, magazines to television. It felt like such an unobtainable standard; it made me feel like I wasn't Black enough and wasn't attractive. And the knock-on effect of this was not looking after myself, binge drinking, mental health struggles at university, and overall poor body image and self-esteem.

Like many things in life, you get to a point where you take action. At 24, I'd built a video game business that was successful, and I decided to try to replicate such successes for my health. With the scales too high for my liking, and my pants not fitting, this was the tipping point. Being autistic and enjoying routine, I ate pretty much the same thing every day for nine months, and started going to the gym and running. In less than a year, I'd lost so much weight that my colleagues thought I was ill, but I still thought I needed to lose more and wasn't strong enough. My body fat percentage was so low my bottom hurt when I sat on harder chairs.

Instead of seeking help, the comments took me in another direction. I now had to get stronger and bigger. And so began a cycle of overeating and undereating. Over the past 13 years, my weight has cycled continuously, gaining and losing a phenomenal amount of weight, stuck in a place of muscle dysmorphia and fighting against feeling 'too fat'. Only in the past few years have I started to find a level of acceptance in who I am and how I look, alongside exploring my identity as an autistic individual and what it means to be a Black man.

I have explored within my own community why Black men don't reach out for support. There is distrust in the medical field from the Black community, with cultural sensitivity often lacking and accessibility limited. Many of the tools used to bring Black men towards mental wellbeing, such as football and music, give little space to talk about eating disorders. The hypermasculine culture that many Black boys grow up in punishes any show of vulnerability, and sharing your struggles is frowned upon. In a world where you can turn social media on in the morning and see someone who looks like you being the subject of violence – sometimes from the very institutions that are meant to be protecting you – your disordered eating can feel like the smallest problem.

This is compounded by the lack of research and the eating disorder stereotypes that exist. There are complex links between food, culture, race and body image. There are links between trauma and eating disorders, and the impact of racial discrimination can amplify this.

The reality is, as it stands, eating disorders are invisible in the Black community. There is next to no mainstream representation, very few culturally sensitive services in the UK, and a range of barriers to identification through to treatment.

I didn't receive any type of therapy until 2016, after over ten years of struggling mentally. Despite being a professional, I delayed the process because I felt like I had to deal with it myself, it didn't feel as big of a problem as it was, and I didn't want to appear weak or out of control. The help wasn't for my eating, though. And if *I* didn't go on that journey, how many other Black men are struggling today with an eating disorder who have never spoken a word about it?

❋ ❋ ❋

It's time to open a much-needed conversation. And *that's* why I'm sharing my story.

Other Specified Feeding and Eating Disorder (OSFED)

Diagnostic Criteria

1. Feeding or eating behaviours that cause clinically significant distress and impairment, but do not meet the full criteria for any of the other disorders

Examples include atypical anorexia nervosa, binge eating disorder (of low frequency and/or limited duration), bulimia nervosa (of low frequency and/or limited duration), purging disorder and night eating syndrome. OSFED is not limited to these five examples.

If unable to determine, the label 'unspecified feeding and eating disorder' (UFED) is given.

(Based on DSM-5)

❝ In my mind I never really liked atypical anorexia because it was basically the same as anorexia but there's one box you're not ticking – extremely low weight. Everything about the behaviours and relationship with food are exactly the same. The whole thing is quite challenging. We were in a lucky position with how treatment went. It's an intense, almost impossible process, really. I was on some courses that they do locally, with loved ones and carers. I found it really weird being a husband there, rather than a parent, like everyone else. There were all the emotions at some point. I started off confused because I didn't really understand it, then frustrated because I was always trying to do something to help. I wanted to make it better. I wanted to wave a magic wand. I now know I wouldn't have been able to do that because it's a process that she had to go through. Anything I did never felt like it actually helped at any point. It's a tedious time and can make you quite upset. It's soul-destroying when it's at that stage where you feel like you don't seem to be getting anywhere. You're there every day with them, and you kind of don't know what to do. Do I be more forceful? Do I leave her to it a bit? I started off by doing things that were probably enabling her to begin with. There's no right answer, right thing to do or right solution, because it almost always changes all the time. What I say and do may or may not help. It's just a case of trying your best and muddling through. You can't rush them through it.

Simon Bartlett, a husband

Introduction

Sam Clark-Stone

Sam Clark-Stone is a mental health nurse. He has led and developed the Gloucestershire NHS all-age Eating Disorders Service since 1996. He was a trainer for the Eating Disorders Association for eight years and has presented at numerous conferences. He has worked with local universities to establish primary prevention utilizing the Body Project. He has contributed to several research publications and was actively involved in setting up the British Eating Disorders Society (BREDS), being the Chair of Trustees since it became a charity in 2018. He is a member of the Beat Clinical Advisory Group and recently became co-chair of the Child and Adolescent Mental Health Services (CAMHS) Eating Disorders Research Consortium. @sam-clark-stone

My career in eating disorders started in 1986 with Professor Gethin Morgan and colleagues in the eating disorders clinic at the Bristol Royal Infirmary psychiatric outpatient department. I had applied for a community psychiatric nurse post and part of the job was to work with the clinic one and a half days per week. My role was to assess and support parents or partners of adults who attended the clinic. The literature at the time was far more limited than now and was divided into descriptions of anorexia nervosa and bulimia nervosa as very separate illnesses. I quickly learned that, in routine clinical practice, patients came in all sizes and often moved from one diagnosis to another over time. By the 1990s, most patients being referred did not easily fit into the diagnostic criteria for anorexia nervosa or bulimia nervosa, and the *Diagnostic and Statistical*

Manual, Fifth Edition (DSM-5), published in 1994, recognized this with the introduction of the category eating disorders not otherwise specified (EDNOS). This was later split, in 2013, to form other specified feeding and eating disorders (OSFED) and unspecified feeding or eating disorder (UFED).

After two years working solely with relatives, I started to see patients myself. I looked for guidance on treatment strategies but found only untested guidance in chapters in handbooks which focused on anorexia nervosa and bulimia nervosa separately. The 1990s saw the beginnings of randomized controlled trials to test treatment approaches, but it was the work of Professor Christopher Fairburn and his team in Oxford that began to really inspire me, around the turn of the century. Professor Fairburn and colleagues developed a transdiagnostic theory of the maintenance of eating disorders that acknowledged what he called diagnostic temporal migration (moving from one eating disorder diagnosis to another over time) and the core psychopathology and behaviours that keep people locked into an eating disorder, but not a particular diagnosis. This work led to the development and testing of enhanced cognitive behaviour therapy (CBT-E), which can be used to treat any eating disorder regardless of diagnosis. Randomized controlled trials included people with EDNOS for the first time ever and CBT-E demonstrated its effectiveness with this group.

I was very excited by Professor Fairburn's work and arranged for my small team to be the first clinical team in the world to train and be supervised in CBT-E. We went to Oxford fortnightly for over a year for four hours of group supervision. This led to me facilitating CBT-E training courses all over the UK in an attempt to improve the quality of and access to evidence-based treatment for all people with an eating disorder, regardless of diagnosis.

I have been lucky enough to be able to develop a specialist all-age eating disorders service and have seen time and time again how people with OSFED (and UFED) can be helped to overcome their difficulties.

Sometimes patients have a history of anorexia nervosa or bulimia nervosa, but often they have never been significantly underweight or binge eaten. Having a treatment that addresses the core maintaining factors and puts diagnosis to one side has liberated therapists and enabled many more people with eating disorders to embark on and accomplish full recovery.

There's a Monster in My Head

Amanda Taylor

Amanda Taylor is a creative director and photographer from Kingston, Jamaica. Founder and CEO of the digital storytelling platform The Unplug Collective, they are on a mission to transform the world to become a safe space for people in marginalized bodies, including queer people, people in larger bodies and people with disabilities. They have built a digital community of over 67,000 people alongside Unplug COO Zara Harding, and interviewed with several acclaimed publications such as *British Vogue*, *Forbes* and *VICE*. They have worked on partnerships with Nike, among other industry leaders. Their long-term career goal is to create a world without body standards. @theunplugcollective

Having an eating disorder is like living with a monster in your head. A monster so horrific that it makes you enjoy the sensation of emptiness and vacancy in your stomach as it growls because you haven't eaten in days. A monster so gruesome it makes even the most delicious food item on a restaurant menu seem repulsive and unpalatable. A monster so deceitful that it makes you believe *yourself* to be a monster when you look in the mirror.

I have a hard time remembering myself without an eating disorder. By the time I was six, I learned it would be okay to grow up to be anything – anything except fat. As I transitioned from what society deemed 'normal' size to a chubby kid, I entered a world where, suddenly, everyone had input on my body and how to shrink it. I remember so vividly the first time I heard the doctor tell my mum, 'She's overweight. If she keeps going down this path, she'll have a hard life ahead of her.' I learned early to be at war with my body. There is a common phrase that says if you 'eat less and move more' you will remain thin. There is a common ideology that weight gain results only from 'overindulgence'.

I became obsessed with strenuous exercise and eating very little, only to remain in my chubby childhood body.

The older I got, the more fixated and determined I became to achieve thinness. The doctor said I would have a 'hard life ahead of me' and society made me feel doomed. I would hear explicitly on repeat, 'You are disgusting, you are ugly, you are unlovable,' both in my mind and, in subtle and not so subtle messaging, from adults. There was no escaping it, not even when I was asleep. The monster in my head found its way to my dreams. Other times, the voice crept in insidiously – in the form of a new lose-20-pounds-in-a-week diet on the Internet, or fitness influencers dangling a new body if you bought their new workout. I checked my weight every morning, pinched my body fat in the mirror, dressed in clothing that made me very, very uncomfortable but (I hoped) made others find me attractive, and stayed in harmful, one-sided relationships because they mirrored how I spoke to myself. This obsession did not lead to the 'health' I was promised; it became illness.

Body shame – and more specifically, the fear and hatred of fatness – is so deeply ingrained into every last corner of society that no matter how sick years of starvation and dieting can make a person, there was always someone applauding me for losing weight. Fainting from not eating, severely injuring myself in the gym from overexercising, experiencing heart palpitations from high levels of stress and anxiety at every meal, or living with severe exhaustion from malnutrition felt like a small price to pay for society's grand prize of being thin. Whether this was a friend who would commend my 'summer glow-up', a dance teacher who would congratulate me on my 'new body' and place me at the front of the formation, or a doctor who would tell me I was 'on the right track', there always seemed to be so many benefits to making myself sick that it never occurred to me to stop.

The irony is that, over time, the more I starved myself, the more I gained weight. No matter what I accomplished, my life felt ill-fated as I struggled to control the number I saw on the scale. There has been, and continues to be, a misconception that a calorie deficit or food restriction always leads to long-term weight loss or thinness. When I founded *The Unplug Collective* – a platform for people to share their own stories with mental health and body image – I learned just how often people in larger bodies experience an obsession, a fixation and, ultimately, a deadly illness that usually not only goes undiagnosed but is celebrated.

I was lucky enough to begin eating disorder treatment five years ago. My therapist was the first person, ever, who helped me realize how deeply cruel, mean and destructive the voices in my head were. I can now articulate this miserable existence by saying it feels like living with a monster; before, 'You are disgusting, you are ugly, you are unlovable' just felt like the truth.

My treatment was about creating a safe space in my body for myself. A space so safe that no messaging or treatment from anyone on the outside could take that away from me. A space where I spoke to myself lovingly, where I learned to listen to my body's deepest cravings, where I stopped feeding the monster.

Very slowly, but surely, instead of fuelling the voices with eating disorder behaviours, I pushed back. I pushed back explicitly on repeat: 'You are enough, you are deserving, you are lovable.' I got to know the many sensations that I had forced myself to ignore. As I learned to silence the hateful and controlling voices in my head, an entirely new world appeared.

For the first time, I began to hear so much more than what others wanted me to be; I heard who I actually was. Now, instead of being consumed by the stress of eating the meal in front of me, I let myself discover new flavours and foods as they sat on my tongue for the first time. It was in these moments that I learned to nourish a previously malnourished body, gained increasingly better and more reciprocal relationships with friends and family, filled my expanding skin with my own curation of tattoos and, most importantly, developed a deeply loving relationship with myself. One where no matter what is said about my body, or the bodies of others, making myself sick is no longer an option.

We say we want to create a safe world for kids, but we often create a lifetime of psychological unsafety for kids who are not thin. We teach these kids to live in fear of body changes, to obsess over others' opinions of their appearance and, ultimately, to shrink themselves. Often, kids with this experience end up with life-long eating disorders of all kinds, and it is our responsibility to change the way we speak about our bodies, our kids' bodies and bodies all around us.

I stopped feeding the monster and started feeding myself. This is when the beauty of life unfolds.

Girl, You Sure? Ain't No Way!

Bayadir Mohamed-Osman

Bayadir Mohamed-Osman is a Sudanese American public health professional, activist and author based in Maryland. Her life is dedicated to researching, preventing and addressing health disparities. She graduated from American University, Washington DC, with a bachelor's in Public Health and is pursuing her Master of Public Health at Johns Hopkins Bloomberg School. Professionally, she has trained young adults with disabilities on professional development and worked in international development. Her poetry examines the intersectionality of her identities and experiences with mental illness. She has performed poetry from her debut book, *Secondhand Smoke*, in dozens of cities in the United States. She leverages her platform, poetry and research to advocate for marginalized communities and her home country, Sudan. @yourbaya

Imagine being the daughter of a family who fled poverty and war in a third-world country and managed to build a new life in America. One filled with educational and economic opportunities and even a fridge filled with food. Now she has to muster the courage to tell them that her mind is too ill to eat any of it. In Sudan, my aunts stand hours in line to buy an expensive batch of bread while I throw away that bag of rotten vegetables I couldn't eat fast enough because my eating disorder flared up. We send monthly payments to cousins overseas for meals, while I have trouble swallowing mine. Eating disorders don't discriminate and no one is immune.

Having immigrated to the United States, I do not feel fully American. I live in limbo – my different identities appear in different moments. Too Sudanese on some days, too American on others. I hopscotch between the hyphens in my identities. My eating disorder is just as ambiguous. Initially, I was diagnosed with avoidant/restrictive food intake disorder (ARFID) and eventually felt relief, clarity and belonging. Now, my diagnosis is with what my therapist terms 'eating disorder, unspecified'. That means I do not meet the criteria for just one of the traditional eating disorder options in the *Diagnostic and Statistical Manual of Mental Disorders* (DSM) because I fall into various categories.

My eating disorder diagnosis came after years of therapy and an initial diagnosis of generalized anxiety disorder (GAD). When I began therapy, my anxiety was at its worst. Panic attacks, irrational fears and repetitive thoughts led to spiralling. I grew up as a straight-A student, the one who went above and beyond and stayed away from trouble. Simply put, I was too anxious to fail. I felt as though making mistakes and taking risks were synonymous with failure and, consequently, rendered me unlovable. So, when I received the GAD diagnosis, it was not a shock to me or to anyone in my life. In therapy, I learned about grounding skills, mindfulness and the benefits of journalling, and I began employing these strategies. Throughout the sessions, I began briefly mentioning my issues with eating and my unstable relationship with food. I was expecting a tip or two about how to improve this relationship. Instead, I received an unexpected response. One that still replays endlessly in my head to this day.

'Baya, you have an eating disorder.'

I felt confusion, uncertainty and disbelief.

Girl, you sure? Ain't no way! Me? Just look at me: I am a Black immigrant hijabi refugee. My community does not experience this. We experience mental illness, definitely, but eating disorders? No way. I do not look like the kind of girl who compares her physique to models in magazines. How could I fall into that category? Those magazines weren't exactly the kind of reading material lying around my traditional Sudanese household. Where could this have come from?

I tried to convince my therapist that since I did not have body dysmorphia I could not possibly have an eating disorder. She replied simply that eating disorders are not just about body image – there is a spectrum of experiences. At that moment, I was forced to unpack my own misconceptions and biases. I was so miseducated on the topic that I didn't realize I was *a part* of the topic.

Through my eating disorder, specifically with my restrictive and avoidant tendencies, I was aiming to find control in my life. I felt suffocated by the world around me and helpless at times. So I began to subconsciously find comfort in controlling my food intake. For instance, on some days I try to see how long I can go without eating. Or I confuse serious hunger with an adrenaline rush and feel accomplished when I can work through the hunger. I've even left plates of food in front of me to see how long I can go without indulging. The general theme of my actions is a yearning for accomplishment and control.

Ain't accomplishments what make me lovable?

One of the heights of my eating disorder was in 2019, the year the Sudanese people revolted against a 30-year dictatorship. Omar El-Bashir's oppressive, corrupt and inhumane regime is the sole reason my family and millions of Sudanese people had to flee our home. Specifically, my father was a freedom fighter, human rights activist and political figure in Eastern Sudan who unequivocally opposed the injustices of the regime. So, to no one's surprise, the oppressive regime sent out a warrant for his execution. We found political asylum and refuge in the United States in 2000. In 2019 and 2020 I witnessed the downfall of Omar El-Bashir and stood in solidarity with the people. I spent my days – hours at a time – reading the news, following the protests and finding ways to support the protesters. My community and I hosted protests around the states, lobbied elected officials, fundraised money and used every platform to advocate for our home. In between the sleepless nights and watching videos of peaceful protesters bleeding, I began to lose my appetite and control. The survivors' guilt swallows me to this day.

How can I eat when my home country is bleeding?

Will I ever be able to return home?

Will my cousin who is protesting today be shot?

How can I have an eating disorder when those at home cannot even afford to eat?

The privilege I have is a fridge full of food, yet I do not 'want' to eat it.

Internalized shame and guilt are my childhood friends that continue to pick on me. My parents sacrificed so much to grant me opportunities. My inner child that is afraid of failure reminds me that my father revolted against a dictator and my mother endured 70-hour work weeks all for me to have trouble chewing and swallowing a chicken breast. I work through my shame and internalized stigma in therapy. Because I'm a poet, my therapist encourages me to write and journal my thoughts and habits. One of the first tasks I was given was to maintain a food log. This isn't a log to track my calories, but rather to track the feelings that surround my eating habits. After weeks of logging, with my therapist's help, I homed in on the triggers that cause me to avoid eating or restrict myself. I began picking up on the time of day, the locations and the stressors that caused my body to shift into fight or flight mode. Once I began to understand myself, the healing process transitioned into a new phase – the pursuit of recovery. My therapist asked me to write a break-up letter to my eating disorder, so I did.

Break-Up

My therapist asked me to write a breakup letter to
My eating disorder.

I don't know how to write about us
without romanticization

We've only just met.
I don't know her aspirations
What keeps her up?

I'm afraid of separation 'cause
I don't know what parts of me will
leave with her.

What is there left to take?

She keeps me up.
obsessive. competitive.
*   persuasive.*
We hold hands sometimes.
Other times a long-distance lover.

You think by the time this book is published –
I will have unclenched my jaw &
Mastered self-love?

My relapses have turned into a relay

How many meals do I need to eat to reach
recovery?
As soon as I touch the finish line,
It leaves again.

It's a journey, a process

Translation:
You can't separate the illness from the mind
But only add obstacles in between.

Translation:
Two people not together
can still be in love.

I'd love to write a poem about us without it
sounding like a honeymoon
I might accidentally convince you to fall for her

I want to tell you how light she makes me feel
No literally – how light I feel
Like I'm on cloud 9
More water, less substance

Isn't this what love feels like?
A rush of adrenaline
I feel accomplished, worthy
Ooops there I go again – glorifying us

The most effective way to write this,
Is to invite her.

Should I continue writing this
and risk triggering myself?

Ain't that what poets do –
Binge on pain
Purge it into poetry?
All for some snaps, likes, and book sales?

How can I write a breakup
Before even writing
a love letter?

During recovery, I had to examine my habits' root causes. I feel my accomplishments determine my value even though I know that isn't true. Growing up as an honour roll student, I was involved in my community and even held leadership positions. I am dependable to my loved ones, my supervisors and my community. Folks crown me as generous when, in reality, I am just afraid to not be loved. While maintaining my commitments to everyone, I overlook my commitments to myself. I think I went so long without a diagnosis because my eating disorder was only harming me. No one noticed because I did not want them to. I was okay with harming myself but not the people around me. So in some sort of twisted poetic way, *even in my illness*, I chose others over myself.

Another reason I think my illness was overlooked for so long is that I am a hijabi. I wear a head covering as well as long-sleeve clothes, so any changes in my body are hard to tell. There is this misconception that only thin people can have eating disorders, but any body type can. There was a time I dropped to a concerning body weight which provided my loved ones visible proof of my illness. But before that, I was praised for my weight and, unintentionally, my eating disorder. I remember in college, a friend complimented me on my body and asked me what I was doing to maintain it. In my head, I thought, 'Sadness', but out loud I just uttered, 'Oh, I've just been drinking more water.'

Culturally competent care from my therapists at Positive Changes Counseling Center has been critical to my healing. They are not experts on Sudan or Islam, but my therapists have not tried to sweep my identity under the rug. They incorporate my Sudanese traditions and Islamic beliefs into my recovery. Consequently, when Ramadan of 2019 rolled around, my therapist was delicate with this new challenge. In my adult life, I have always fasted during the holy month of Ramadan, unless I was sick or menstruating. This year was unique because I was attending therapy weekly and maintained food logs. After months of gaining the courage and endurance to eat at least two nutrient-dense meals a day, Ramadan knocked on the door. After conversations with my therapist and psychiatrist, I decided I was not well enough to fast. I felt immense guilt and shame for not being able to participate in a holy tradition. However, I also knew that not eating or drinking anything for over 12 hours a day would send me backward in recovery.

What will my family think of me?

Am I a bad Muslim?

How will I participate in the blessings of the month?

When I told my father about my decision, he afforded me grace and compassion. He reminded me Allah (the term meaning 'God' in Islam) does not require those who are ill to fast. Just as pregnant women or those with chronic illnesses are not required to fast, my mental illness also exempts me from fasting. When I shared with my mother I wasn't going to fast, she asked, 'Why? Do you think you can't do it?' I responded with 'I can do it. The problem is I am too good at it.' I explained to her and to myself that if I did fast during Ramadan, I would not know if I was doing it for the sake of Allah or for the sake of my eating disorder. Ramadan is a month to better yourself. I wanted to be closer to Him and not my illness.

I tried to incorporate my religion even more during Ramadan. I was not successfully eating two meals a day regularly then. Therefore,

I challenged myself, 'While others fast this month for the sake of God, you will eat more for the sake of God.' My form of worship was not traditional, but I tried my best to practise my religion and pursue recovery.

Some days I wish I fell neatly into one box. I wish my eating disorder was 'specified'. I wish I had clear answers and an absolute home. However, since my experience and identity don't fall neatly into a box or category, my diagnosis fell through the cracks in my early life. Even I, a student majoring in public health, never noticed the red flags within myself. My parents did not know and my friends were not able to tell either. This is no one's fault. Now that we know better, we all have the responsibility to do better. I implore all of us to look at who and/or what has fallen in between the cracks. We have all created 'boxes' in our minds and we constantly sort people into those boxes. How accurate are our sortings? Who does not fit into just one box? Why are we not comfortable with ambiguity? We need to acknowledge those who are collateral damage when we practise bias. The more I try to control and categorize, the more I lose my power. As I am learning to love food again, I am also learning to love the ambiguity that exists within myself and the world around us.

Finding a conclusion for this piece has been challenging. There is no fairy-tale ending or miracle cure. I still live with my eating disorder and I do not think I will ever write *the breakup letter*. She is a part of me and my journey. She tries to protect me and help me cope in a collapsing world, though, unfortunately, her methods are troubling and dangerous. I acknowledge her sadness and anger, but I do not need to follow her lead any more. I am no longer focused on breaking up with her but rather on falling in love with myself unconditionally, regardless of accolades or accomplishments. My recovery is the pursuit of surrendering my innate desire for clarity and control.

I choose me.

I choose ambiguity.

Atypical

Raffela Mancuso

Raffela Mancuso is a mental illness and fat liberation activist. She uses social media to destigmatize mental health and centre marginalized bodies, while also sharing about her own personal journey. She has been diagnosed with atypical anorexia and works hard to break the stigma surrounding it. @raffela_mancuso

Whenever I talk about my experience with eating disorders, and anorexia specifically, I always make sure to put the 'atypical' in front of it to try to avoid the blank stares and looks of confusion. 'Atypical' is the shield I put out to try to protect myself from any potential judgement that might come my way. 'Atypical' is the whisper in my ear reminding me that I'm not normal; that my experience isn't valid.

What's so 'atypical' about me anyways? Is it how my thighs touch when I walk, or that my belly moves when I laugh? Is it the fact that fashion brands have decided that I'm not worthy of clothing, and that doctors tell me that all medical issues are my own fault?

It seems to me that the only 'typical' thing around here is how normalized anti-fatness is in our societies. It's so normal for us to view larger bodies as bad or wrong. We don't even question when fat people are made fun of and discriminated against, because we've all been taught our whole lives that the very worst thing you could ever be is fat.

Isn't that one of the main factors of eating disorders? The fear of fatness? The belief that it would be better to self-harm through various methods of disordered eating rather than being seen as fat?

My first memory of being called fat was in kindergarten when I was five years old. And I've lived every day of the past 21 years with the deep shame of knowing that I'm fat. Sometimes, when I'm scrolling through social media, I'll see a post that talks about how much diet culture has harmed us and that life was so much better when we were children and didn't care about our bodies – and I can't relate. Reading those posts makes me realize that I've never had a day of peace with my body, not even as a young child. A peaceful childhood was ripped away from me, not because of my body size, but because of how the people around me treated me because of it.

It feels really uncomfortable for me to talk about eating disorders, and my own personal experience with it, because I truly don't feel like I belong. It feels like my 'atypical' label is a stamp on my forehead that tells everyone else that I'm just an imposter in this space. I've always engaged in classic anorexia nervosa behaviours such as restriction, excessive exercise and deep fear of fatness, but it was never seen as a problem – instead, an accomplishment.

Could you imagine speaking to someone living with anorexia who is engaging in dangerous behaviours and telling them that they're doing a great job? That they should keep up the good work? So why are we saying that to fat people who are doing the same things? Just because I'm living in a larger body, that doesn't mean that my behaviours are any less dangerous and harmful. But that's not how we're treated.

Growing up, I was praised every time I restricted my food intake or made any attempt to shrink my body, and I was scolded or shamed every time I did the opposite. I learned pretty quickly that my body was bad and that I was bad because of it.

I wasn't diagnosed with atypical anorexia until two years ago, which seems unbelievable when I think about it. That means that for the past 24 years I've been actively trying to shrink myself in order to feel loved and accepted. I don't know whether to be sad or furious, honestly. When I was diagnosed, the psychiatrist explained it to me as 'It's the same thing as normal anorexia, just without the requirement of being at a low weight.' And that's exactly how I explain it to the people around me who get confused when I speak up about my experiences and diagnoses: 'It's literally the same thing as normal anorexia, I'm just not underweight. That's it.'

It's been really scary to try to recover from anorexia while living in a larger body, as sometimes that means that your body may change as you learn how to nourish yourself properly – which is terrifying. Even underweight people are terrified of the potential weight gain that may come from anorexia recovery, so imagine how it must feel as someone who is already fat knowing that you might become fatter! The world is telling me to eat less and work out more, but my dietitian is telling me that I'm not eating enough; how can we possibly navigate that? I regularly receive messages on social media that I'm 'promoting obesity' by simply existing and that I should lose weight to be healthier, but the reality is that eating more and potentially gaining weight is actually the healthiest thing I could do for myself. People with 'normal' anorexia are battling a monster in their minds, but people with 'atypical' anorexia are battling not only a monster in their minds, but also the entire world around them actively echoing their greatest fears back to them. By recovering, we have to fight ourselves and also the whole world.

How can I find comfort in a community that has the common fear of looking like me? How can I recover when people automatically assume that I have a binge eating disorder just by looking at me?

I know that I want to recover and be fully nourished so that I can do all of the things that I want to do in life, but how can I do that when recovery is also my fear? Right now, I can mentally protect myself from fatphobic comments about my weight, or my food intake, because I know that I have atypical anorexia so I know that they're wrong. But what happens if I recover? If I recover and eat more, then does that mean I'm just like all of the other fat people? Does that mean that I did this to myself, and that my body size is my fault?

I want to be very honest about this experience, because people can tell you every day that you deserve to be fully nourished, and then five seconds later you'll hear your friend make a fat joke, and all of your resilience and hard work will come crashing down around you. I want to be honest so that others labelled as 'atypical' can know that they're not alone, and that their wellbeing is more important than what anyone thinks of them.

Your body is not bad.

You are not bad.

Your body isn't your fault, and it's not your job to 'fix' it.

You do not need to earn food; nourishment is a human right.

Eating while fat is a form of resistance!

The Underacknowledged

Muscle dysmorphia and autism can both be linked to eating disorders. This link is, however, often underacknowledged.

Muscle Dysmorphia

George Mycock

George Mycock is a mental health speaker, writer and researcher. He is the Founder of MyoMinds and board member for the Applied Psychologists in Physical Activity Network. He has collaborated on projects with Mind, First Steps ED and the Body Dysmorphic Disorder Foundation. His work has been featured on the BBC, Talk TV and Sky News. He uses his lived experience of muscularity-oriented disordered eating, exercise addiction and body image issues to improve awareness. @myominds

Muscle dysmorphia, sometimes referred to as bigorexia, is a form of body dysmorphic disorder that is characterized by a pathological obsession with muscle growth, which often results in muscularity-oriented disordered eating. It has seen explosive growth in recent years, with up to 1 in 200 men predicted to be suffering with it (Pope et al. 2005). Here, George briefly discusses the pressure on men, and the challenging nature of this phenomenon which has 'ripped' through society pretty insidiously.

Much like many others' experiences, muscle dysmorphia and muscularity-oriented disordered eating were severely debilitating to my life. The behaviours and fears caused me to miss important occasions, lose friends and spiral into suicidal ideations.

I grew up believing I wasn't what I was supposed to be. I was a boy in a world that idealized everything about men that I felt I wasn't. As an 11-year-old, I didn't believe I was tough, emotionless or hard-working, and I felt a lot of shame about that. It was that shame that drove me to adopt the 'health and fitness' world as a way of renegotiating my masculinity. The fitness community is one that values hard work, endurance through pain and discomfort, and the pursuit of a large, lean and, most importantly, muscular body. To my 15-year-old self, this community promised the honour and respect that I thought I would never attain.

I delved deeper and began following the guidance delivered by my online, self-appointed, moral superiors. I was fed a string of beliefs and ideologies that revolved around the idea that those who could handle more extreme behaviours were those that demanded the most respect, and that those who said otherwise, demanded none. They would explain how those looking in would try to stop me, how they wouldn't understand what I was doing but that it was my responsibility – as a member of this group (and as a man) – to ignore those who attempted to 'get in my way'. This world of masculine-enthused pressures became the perfect echo chamber for me (and, I believe, many other people) to push further and further with my exercise and diet, and take pride in comments from friends, family and health professionals who felt my obsession with being muscular was a bad thing. Every comment was the manifestation of everything the fitness gurus warned me of – and I was prepared to ignore them. I pushed away and placed down barriers that I felt were necessary, despite the growing symptoms rising from my muscularity-oriented prison.

The goals of muscularity are contrasting. On the one hand, you want to gain weight to build muscle. But on the other hand, you want to lose weight to remain lean. This leads to constantly feeling like you're undoing the progress you've already made whilst, simultaneously, making progress towards what you're desperate to reach. You can't win.

I existed in a world that fed me constant negative self-assessment whilst promising me that the only way out was by digging deeper and pushing through the pain. I fear that there are many people who exist in this world, viewed by society as 'dedicated' or even 'healthy'. I fear for men, like me, who feel that seeking help will result in the loss of respect that they so desperately crave without realizing that even if they were to get it, it would never be enough.

Autism

Sophie Baverstock

Sophie Baverstock is a professional makeup and hair artist for television, film and multimedia. She obtained degrees in Art, Design and Makeup from University of Arts London and Arts University Bournemouth with first-class honours and is best known on social media for winning BBC/Netflix's *Glow Up* in 2021. On the show, she shared her experience as a late-diagnosed woman with autism and advocates for autism awareness in the UK and worldwide. She has not spoken publicly about her struggles with disordered eating within her adolescence but hopes to contribute to shining a light on the subject within this book. @sophiebaverstock

There is a strong link between autism and disordered eating. It used to be believed that autism impacted males at a higher rate; however, emerging research states that this may be due to the fact it is more easily missed in females. A recent study suggested that 80 per cent of women with autism remain undiagnosed at the age of 18. Sophie was never diagnosed with an eating disorder but speaks of her experience with autism, and how her autism related to her eating habits.

As a child, I was described as a 'picky eater', 'fussy' and 'difficult' when it came to food. I found it difficult to eat full meals, eat at other people's houses and, especially, try new foods. It would give me a strong sense of discomfort. Parents of '90s children are from a generation where being a picky eater isn't an option, and although I agree to an extent that parents should determine a child's diet, it was a battle for my mother – a single parent at the time – to constantly accommodate my 'behaviour' just so I wouldn't starve. As I got older, and more able to voice my discomfort, I progressively argued that this wasn't 'bad behaviour'. I just didn't like certain foods. With an older sister who would eat anything, my fussy eating was compared to this, thus solidifying my label as 'difficult around the dinner table'.

My mum is highly educated in child development, yet growing up, even she was unable to perceive I had autism because I was so good at masking, even with family. Autism is often underdiagnosed in females. In my case, I was social, so most of my issues surrounding autism hadn't been outwardly affecting me beyond being described as having an 'odd' personality. My mum just saw me as 'gifted' and 'funny'. So, whilst she made efforts to rectify my problematic eating – eventually accommodating by giving me options and buying my 'comfort' meals – this was purely to make sure I ate more freely with my family, causing fewer issues. As a family, we were always sitting together at the table, and this is something I think was vital in making sure I ate what was in front of me. It was just the three of us; I have really fond memories of these dinnertimes. My sister and I learnt how to cook from a very young age, and eventually cooked our own dinners. We would cook for our mum too. I think this is what led to my obsession with food, baking and nutrition – a sort of 'hyper-focus'.

✳ ✳ ✳

Into my teenage years, I had more control over what I ate, and what I didn't eat. This is when I started eating alone, avoiding the dinner table at home, or making sure I was out of the house at dinnertime pretending I 'ate elsewhere'. To me, eating was a chore. First finding something I liked, then having to cook it; I would often cook then not feel hungry by the end of it. I loved the process of the *cooking* more than the eating. So I started to love only cooking for others. I wanted to make sure everyone else was eating around me. Baking for my friends, cooking dinner for my family, learning new dishes. It was to control what was around me. If I cooked dinner, I could control it to be something I was comfortable with. I would only eat if someone would eat with me because I was becoming scared of food.

* * *

My allergies to food, and my anaphylactic reactions to nuts in primary school, caused a dramatic shift in my attitude towards food. I became obsessed with learning recipes and controlling food to help me fear it less. Checking the packaging of everything I ate for nuts, and not eating in restaurants, became routine. I was terrified to experience something like that again as I was genuinely traumatized. In my opinion, severe food allergies and disordered eating often come hand in hand. But it didn't feel like my fault. The control aspect around food clearly developed in my teenage years into disordered eating. Something I think added to my fears, and discomfort, was the communities I would stumble across on the Internet.

When I was younger, we didn't have Instagram or TikTok; we had Tumblr. An uncensored cesspit of 'pro-ana' (pro-anorexia) pages showing black-and-white images of emaciated women, promoted under the guise of aesthetics when really they were devastating in their effects. I leaned into it. As someone who was already skinny, it was almost 'easy' to fall into. But I never felt a sense of belonging like so many other girls, because it wasn't a self-confidence issue to begin with; it was an honest fear of food itself. Hormonal changes, difficult times as I was diagnosed with autism at 17, moving from my childhood home and falling behind in my A-levels – all of these meant my self-esteem took a knock too. It soon *did* become not only about food, but now my body.

* * *

It got out of hand. I would take photos of my body constantly ('body checking'), weigh myself every day, go on runs without eating – not eat breakfast or lunch, then just have a little bit of dinner. Again, as my sister and I are 'naturally slim', it didn't become obvious to anyone. Especially as I only wore baggy clothes, as I still do. Eventually, I would get dizzy and cold in lessons, and my teachers would regularly ask me if I was okay. I remember my good friend, Helen, having strong words with me about it, having noticed how skinny I had become – although I never saw it like she did. It was a hyperfixation, not a disorder.

My time at the end of sixth form, during which I was diagnosed with autism, was a low point in my life. Having always been 'smart', I felt lost and unintelligent with the lack of support I received. It was only when I found what I really wanted to do outside of school – a foundation art degree, then makeup – that I had enough of feeling like air. I felt empty and rotten. I decided in between leaving sixth form and starting this foundation year of art, before university, that I needed food to focus. I started to eat more, feel better, work hard and succeed. When I could adapt my learning to focus on something I was good at, allow myself to be autistic and pursue the arts, my mental and physical health improved.

At university, it was even better as I had a studio flat with my own kitchen due to my disability. I started to cook again, and eat what I made. In second year, I was known to my housemates as the 'mum of the house'. Always cooking homemade meals, baking bread and cakes, and eating them, I prided myself in being healthier and happier. Although I was still only comfortable eating when others were eating and still never ate other people's cooking.

✻ ✻ ✻

Relapsing into old behaviours of disordered eating is common, and something I still find hard. It never goes away in my mind. At stressful times, I stop eating. I still avoid eating other people's cooking. But it's the knowledge and self-awareness – educating myself on this topic and experiencing the benefits of recovery – that allow me to think, 'This is a temporary lapse, I'll eat properly again when I'm less stressed...' Then, I go food shopping, cook up my favourite dishes and get back on track. I guess that's progress. I'm aware that some of my behaviours are still unusual. I had cognitive behavioural therapy (CBT) for my fears of food poisoning, extreme emetophobia and obsessive-compulsive routines around food. A lot of this probably relates to my autism, so I can control it by understanding that it no longer affects my long-term physical health. I still hope to one day have a better relationship with food, but until then I'm proud to be alive, well and a good cook.

Epilogue

Dr Chuks

In 1857, in Central Paris, at Académie des Beaux-Arts, French artist Jean-Francois Millet unveiled his latest work at arguably the greatest art event in the Western world at the time – The Salon. *The Gleaners*, which depicted three peasant women gleaning a field of stray stalks of wheat after the harvest, was greeted with disgust by the upper classes because it was deemed to be sympathetic to poor people (Kimmelman 1999). The oil painting would later become one of Millet's best-known works.

Gleaning is the process of gathering leftover grain after the reapers' harvest. And today, we can draw parallels with this 2000-year-old form of social welfare when looking to the future of eating disorders care delivery. By *gleaning*, we can gather leftover knowledge and wisdom from those who have been through the fiery trials of an eating disorder (much like we hope this book will do) and learn from it. This can help inform future practice – building upon previous work – to provide much-needed sustenance for those suffering and in greatest need.

California-based clinical psychologist Dr Kelli Rugless described eating disorders as a 'social justice issue'. She said:

> [eating disorders] are at the intersection of racism, patriarchy and diet culture...if we can start to discuss the context in which eating disorders develop, food deserts, food swamps, blind spots in

healthcare, lack of access to private treatment facilities and exposure to trauma, we can remove the stigma, which [will invite] more open discussion and hopefully an increased willingness to seek treatment. (Kupemba 2021)

A way of removing the stigma around eating disorders – which Rugless so rightly called for – is to understand the context in which they develop. Apart from gleaning, one of the ways this can be done is through research. Whether it's learning more about neurodiversity and eating disorders to inform better treatment options; about the emerging link between premenstrual dysphoric disorder (PMDD) and eating disorders; or about the intersectionality of attributes such as race, gender, wealth, and so on. For example, are Black men with eating disorders viewed differently from White men with eating disorders? There are countless paths of understanding yet to be fully explored.

Dr Agnes Ayton, Chair of the Royal College of Psychiatrists Eating Disorders Faculty, said that 'we need to reintroduce therapeutic optimism in the field [of eating disorders]'. She went on to say that 'Yes, NHS services and research are underfunded, but there are important breakthroughs in the field that can lead to better treatment in the future' (Ayton 2023). Indeed there are. The Eating Disorders Genetics Initiative (EDGI), the largest ever research project on eating disorders, is under way globally and set to help us better understand the role both genes and the environment play in eating disorder development; the evolutionary aspects of eating disorders are beginning to be better understood – a field gaining traction within this specialty; and a promising future for the therapeutic use of psychedelics in eating disorders is within sight. There are countless other research projects.

Another way of removing the stigma around eating disorders is through education. It is this proactivity in creating learning platforms – enabling more open discussion and dialogue – that will help quell the need for the reactive healthcare which we see all too much of today.

From children to the elderly, a basic level of understanding about eating disorders is needed across society so prompt observations can be made for earlier interventions to occur. For example, school teachers should be better educated to identify potential issues with students. Knowing the fundamentals, such as early warning signs, could further help in signposting to the right services. Further information for what people should then do if confronted by services that are overwhelmed will be important too. This will avoid many feeling stranded and in despair.

As part of this education, literature may need to improve. Children's books may need to convey a more balanced approach to nutrition, highlight the inappropriateness of certain language, and portray characters being unapologetically proud of their bodies. Medical textbooks may need to emphasize the importance of ethnocultural knowledge in the delivery of eating disorders care.

In the words of Mary Pipher, author and clinical psychologist, 'to treat eating disorders is to treat our culture' (Pipher 1995). The issues are systemic and will take time to fix. But, there is hope. First, though, let's glean.

References

Foreword

Smink, F. R., van Hoeken, D., and Hoek, H. W. (2012). Epidemiology of eating disorders: Incidence, prevalence and mortality rates. *Current Psychiatry Reports*, *14*, 4, 406–414.

Preface

Michel, A. (2015). *Slim Truth: A Textual and Autoethnographic Analysis of Celebrity Eating Disorder Coverage in People Magazine*. Master's Theses (2009–), paper 309. Milwaukee, WI: Marquette University. Available at: http://epublications.marquette.edu/theses_open/309 (Accessed 30 October 2022).

Introduction

All-Party Parliamentary Group on Eating Disorders (APPG). (2021). *Breaking the Cycle: An Inquiry into Eating Disorder Research Funding in the UK*. Norwich: Beat. Available at: https://beat.contentfiles.net/media/documents/APPG_Research_Funding_inquiry_report.pdf (accessed on 9 August 2022).

Baird, A. (2022). Giving up on a perfect recovery actually helped me heal from my eating disorder. *Buzzfeed.News*. Available at: www.buzzfeednews.com/article/addybaird/eating-disorder-recovery-definition (accessed on 22 November 2022).

Balodis, I. M., Molina, N. D., Kober, H., Worhunsky, P. D., *et al.* (2013). Divergent neural substrates of inhibitory control in binge eating disorder relative to other manifestations of obesity. *Obesity (Silver Spring)*, *21*, 2, 367–377.

Barrett, M. (2022a). 23 April. Available at: https://twitter.com/_madi_faith/status/1517952489697464323?s=20 (accessed on 25 June 2022).

Barrett, M. (2022b). 23 April. Available at: https://twitter.com/_madi_faith/status/1517838250861379586?s=20 (accessed on 25 June 2022).

Beat. (2023). Statistics for Journalists. Norwich: Beat. Available at: www.beateatingdisorders.org.uk/media-centre/eating-disorder-statistics (accessed on 22 April 2022).

Biederman, J., Ball, S. W., Monuteaux, M. C., Surman, C. B., Johnson, J. L., and Zeitlin, S. (2007). Are girls with ADHD at risk for eating disorders? Results from a controlled, five-year prospective study. *Journal of Developmental and Behavioral Pediatrics*, *28*, 4, 302–307.

Butler, S. (2022). Rising cost of basic food items leaving poorest people worst off, UK study finds. *The Guardian*. Available at: www.theguardian.com/business/2022/dec/22/rising-cost-of-basic-food-items-leaves-poorest-people-worst-off-ons-finds (accessed on 8 September 2022).

Cardona Cano, S., Tiemeier, H., Van Hoeken, D., Tharner, A., *et al.* (2015). Trajectories of picky eating during childhood: A general population study. *International Journal of Eating Disorders*, *48*, 6, 570–579.

CPD Online College. (2023). What is anorexia and bulimia? Huddersfield: CPD Online College. Available at: https://cpdonline.co.uk/knowledge-base/mental-health/what-is-anorexia-bulimia (accessed on 31 October 2022).

Deloitte Access Economics. (2020). *Social and Economic Cost of Eating Disorders in the United States of America: A Report for the Strategic Training Initiative for the Prevention of Eating Disorders and the Academy for Eating Disorders*. Cambridge, MA: Deloitte Access Economics/STRIPED. Available at: www.hsph.harvard.edu/striped/report-economic-costs-of-eating-disorders (accessed on 7 November 2022).

Dinkler, L., Yasumitsu-Lovell, K., Eitoku, M., Fujieda, M., *et al.* (2022). Development of a parent-reported screening tool for avoidant/restrictive food intake disorder (ARFID): Initial validation and prevalence in 4–7-year-old Japanese children. *Appetite*, *168*, 105735.

Dinkler, L., Wronski, M. L., Lichtenstein, P., Lundström, S., *et al.* (2023). Etiology of the broad avoidant restrictive food intake disorder phenotype in Swedish twins aged 6 to 12 Years. *JAMA Psychiatry*, *80*, 3, 260–269.

Downs, J., Ayton, A., Collins, L., Baker, S., Missen, H., and Ibrahim, A. (2023). Untreatable or unable to treat? Creating more effective and accessible treatment for long-standing and severe eating disorders. *Lancet Psychiatry*, *10*, 2, 146–154.

Eating Recovery Center. (2023). Other Specified Feeding and Eating Disorder.

Denver, CO: Eating Recovery Center. Available at: www.eatingrecoverycenter.com/conditions/osfed (accessed on 27 July 2022).

ESPN. (2021). 27 February. Available at: https://twitter.com/SportsCenter/status/1365549208795758594 (accessed on 1 November 2022).

First Episode and Rapid Early intervention for Eating Disorders (FREED). (2023). What is FREED? London: FREED. Available at: https://freedfromed.co.uk/what-is-freed-for-professionals (accessed on 11 December 2022).

Gaudiani, J. L., Bogetz, A., and Yager, J. (2022). Terminal anorexia nervosa: Three cases and proposed clinical characteristics. *Journal of Eating Disorders*, *10*, 23.

Goh, A. Q. Y., Lo, N. Y. W., Davis, C., and Chew, E. C. S. (2022). #EatingDisorderRecovery: A qualitative content analysis of eating disorder recovery-related posts on Instagram. *Eating and Weight Disorders*, *27*, 4, 1535–1545.

GOV.UK. (2020). Policy Paper: Tackling Obesity: Government Strategy. London: GOV.UK. Available at: www.gov.uk/government/publications/tackling-obesity-government-strategy (accessed on 11 August 2022).

Gregory, A. (2022). NHS unable to treat every child with eating disorder as cases soar. *The Guardian*. Available at: www.theguardian.com/society/2022/jan/04/nhs-unable-to-treat-every-child-with-eating-disorder-as-cases-soar (accessed on 4 July 2022).

Guinhut, M., Godart, N., Benadjaoud, M. A., Melchior, J. C., and Hanachi, M. (2021). Five-year mortality of severely malnourished patients with chronic anorexia nervosa admitted to a medical unit. *Acta Psychiatrica Scandinavica*, *143*, 2, 130–140.

Harney, M. B., Fitzsimmons-Craft, E. E., Maldonado, C. R., and Bardone-Cone, A. M. (2014). Negative affective experiences in relation to stages of eating disorder recovery. *Eating Behaviors*, *15*, 1, 24–30.

Hilbert, A. (2019). Binge-eating disorder. *Psychiatric Clinics of North America*, *42*, 1, 33–43.

Hudson, J. I., Hiripi, E., Pope, H. G., Jr, and Kessler, R. C. (2007). The prevalence and correlates of eating disorders in the National Comorbidity Survey Replication. *Biological Psychiatry*, *61*, 3, 348–358.

Hunnicutt, C. (2018). New study reveals perception about eating disorders. Wickenburg, AZ: Rosewood Centers for Eating Disorders. Available at: www.rosewoodranch.com/new-study-reveals-perception-about-eating-disorders (accessed on 1 July 2022).

Jáuregui-Garrido, B., and Jáuregui-Lobera, I. (2012). Sudden death in eating disorders. *Vascular Health and Risk Management, 8*, 91–98.

Jenkins, Z. M., Mancuso, S. G., Phillipou, A., and Castle, D. J. (2021). What is OSFED? The predicament of classifying 'other' eating disorders. *BJPsych Open, 7*, 5, e147.

Kenny, T. E., Trottier, K., and Lewis, S. P. (2022). Lived experience perspectives on a definition of eating disorder recovery in a sample of predominantly white women: A mixed method study. *Journal of Eating Disorders, 10*, 1, 149.

Keski-Rahkonen, A., and Mustelin, L. (2016). Epidemiology of eating disorders in Europe: Prevalence, incidence, comorbidity, course, consequences, and risk factors. *Current Opinion in Psychiatry, 29*, 6, 340–345.

Kornstein, S. G., Kunovac, J. L., Herman, B. K., and Culpepper, L. (2016). Recognizing binge-eating disorder in the clinical setting: A review of the literature. *The Primary Care Companion for CNS Disorders, 18*, 3, 10.4088. Available at: https://doi.org/10.4088/PCC.15r01905 (accessed on 15 December 2022).

Michel, A. (2015). *Slim Truth: A Textual and Autoethnographic Analysis of Celebrity Eating Disorder Coverage in People Magazine*. Master's Theses (2009–), paper 309. Milwaukee, WI: Marquette University. Available at: http://epublications.marquette.edu/theses_open/309 (Accessed 30 October 2022).

Mitchison, D., Mond, J., Bussey, K., Griffiths, S., *et al.* (2020). DSM-5 full syndrome, other specified, and unspecified eating disorders in Australian adolescents: Prevalence and clinical significance. *Psychological Medicine, 50*, 6, 981–990.

Morris, J., and Twaddle, S. (2007). Anorexia nervosa. *BMJ, 334*, 7599, 894–898.

National Institute for Health and Care Excellence (NICE). (2021). Eating Disorders Statistics. London: NICE. Available at: https://cpdonline.co.uk/knowledge-base/mental-health/what-is-anorexia-bulimia (accessed on 31 October 2022).

National Institute of Mental Health (NIMH). (2021). Eating Disorders. Bethesda, MD: NIMH. Available at: www.nimh.nih.gov/health/statistics/eating-disorders (accessed on 12 July 2022).

NHS Digital. (2021). Hospital Admissions for Eating Disorders. Leeds: NHS Digital. Available at: https://digital.nhs.uk/supplementary-information/2021/hospital-admissions-for-eating-disorders-2015-2021 (accessed on 20 August 2022).

Nicely, T. A., Lane-Loney, S., Masciulli, E., Hollenbeak, C. S., and Ornstein, R. M. (2014). Prevalence and characteristics of avoidant/restrictive food intake disorder in a cohort of young patients in day treatment for eating disorders. *Journal of Eating Disorders*, *2*, 1, 21.

Our World in Data. (2022). Eating Disorders Prevalence, by Age, United States, 2019. Oxford: Our World in Data. Available at: https://ourworldindata.org/grapher/prevalence-of-eating-disorders-by-age?country=~USA (accessed on 16 November 2022).

Pathway for Eating Disorders and Autism Developed from Clinical Experience (PEACE) (2023). Why Eating Disorders and Autism? London: PEACE. Available at: www.peacepathway.org/about-comorbidity (accessed on 17 August 2022).

Prentice, A. M., and Jebb, S. A. (2001). Beyond body mass index. *Obesity Reviews*, *2*, 3, 141–147.

Puhl, R. M., Lessard, L. M., Himmelstein, M. S., and Foster, G. D. (2021). The roles of experienced and internalized weight stigma in healthcare experiences: Perspectives of adults engaged in weight management across six countries. *PloS One*, *16*, 6. Available at: https://doi.org/10.1371/journal.pone.0251566 (accessed on 10 August 2022).

Royal College of Psychiatry Eating Disorder Faculty. (2023). 18 February. Available at: https://twitter.com/rcpsychEDFac/status/1626880357202112512?t=foDtpQ01g84mAtyHcAqaxw&s=19 (accessed on 27 February).

Santomauro, D. F., Melen, S., Mitchison, D., Vos, T., Whiteford, H., and Ferrari, A. J. (2021). The hidden burden of eating disorders: An extension of estimates from the Global Burden of Disease Study 2019. *Lancet Psychiatry*, *8*, 4, 320–328.

Saukko, P. (2006). Rereading media and eating disorders: Karen Carpenter, Princess Diana, and the healthy female self. *Critical Studies in Media Communication*, *23*, 2, 152–169.

Sbaragli, C., Morgante, G., Goracci, A., Hofkens, T., De Leo, V., and Castrogiovanni, P. (2008). Infertility and psychiatric morbidity. *Fertility and Sterility*, *90*, 6, 2107–2111.

Scharner, S., and Stengel, A. (2019). Alterations of brain structure and functions in anorexia nervosa. *Clinical Nutrition Experimental*, *28*, 22–32.

Schleider, J. (2021a). 4 October. Available at: https://twitter.com/JSchleiderPhD/status/1445159283893710848?s=20 (accessed on 10 October 2022).

Schleider, J. (2021b). 5 October. Available at: https://twitter.com/JSchleider PhD/status/1445366689621807110?s=20 (accessed on 10 October 2022).

Schleider, J. (2022). 23 April. Available at: https://twitter.com/JSchleiderPhD/status/1517947257118728192?s=20 (accessed on 11 October 2022).

Schmidt, R., Vogel, M., Hiemisch, A., Kiess, W., and Hilbert, A. (2018). Pathological and non-pathological variants of restrictive eating behaviors in middle childhood: A latent class analysis. *Appetite, 127*, 257–265.

Sebastiani, G., Andreu-Fernández, V., Herranz Barbero, A., Aldecoa-Bilbao, V., *et al.* (2020). Eating disorders during gestation: Implications for mother's health, fetal outcomes, and epigenetic changes. *Frontiers in Pediatrics, 8*, 587.

Siber, K. (2022). You don't look anorexic. *New York Times*. Available at: www.nytimes.com/2022/10/18/magazine/anorexia-obesity-eating-disorder.html (accessed on 1 December 2022).

Sole-Smith, V. (2023). Why the new obesity guidelines for kids terrify me. *New York Times*. Available at: www.nytimes.com/2023/01/26/opinion/aap-obesity-guidelines-bmi-wegovy-ozempic.html (accessed on 11 August 2022).

Statista. (2022). Most Popular Sports in the United States. Hamburg: Statista. Available at: https://statisticsanddata.org/data/most-popular-sports-in-the-united-states (accessed on 31 October 2022).

Stice, E., Marti, C. N., and Rohde, P. (2013). Prevalence, incidence, impairment, and course of the proposed DSM-5 eating disorder diagnoses in an 8-year prospective community study of young women. *Journal of Abnormal Psychology, 122*, 2, 445–457.

Swinbourne, J. M., and Touyz, S. W. (2007). The co-morbidity of eating disorders and anxiety disorders: A review. *European Eating Disorders Review, 15*, 4, 253–274.

Thomas, J. J., Lawson, E. A., Micali, N., Misra, M., Deckersbach, T., and Eddy, K. T. (2017). Avoidant/restrictive food intake disorder: A three-dimensional model of neurobiology with implications for etiology and treatment. *Current Psychiatry Reports, 19*, 8, 54.

Tomiyama, A. J., Hunger, J. M., Nguyen-Cuu, J., and Wells, C. (2016). Misclassification of cardiometabolic health when using body mass index categories in NHANES 2005–2012. *International Journal of Obesity, 40*, 5, 883–886.

Treasure, J., Duarte, T. A., and Schmidt, U. (2020). Eating disorders. *The Lancet, 395*, 10227, 899–911.

Udo, T., Bitley, S., and Grilo, C. M. (2019). Suicide attempts in US adults with lifetime DSM-5 eating disorders. *BMC Medicine, 17*, 120.

Ulfvebrand, S., Birgegård, A., Norring, C., Högdahl, L., and von Hausswolff-Juhlin, Y. (2015). Psychiatric comorbidity in women and men with eating disorders results from a large clinical database. *Psychiatry Research, 230*, 2, 294–299.

Wang, G. J., Geliebter, A., Volkow, N. D., Telang, F. W., *et al.* (2011). Enhanced striatal dopamine release during food stimulation in binge eating disorder. *Obesity (Silver Spring), 19*, 8, 1601–1608.

World Health Organization (WHO). (2023a). ICD-11 for Mortality and Morbidity Statistics: 6B82 Binge eating disorder. Geneva: WHO. Available at: https://icd.who.int/browse11/l-m/en#/http%3a%2f%2fid.who.int%2ficd%2fentity%2f1673294767 (accessed on 10 June 2022).

World Health Organization (WHO). (2023b). ICD-11 for Mortality and Morbidity Statistics: 6B81 Bulimia nervosa. Geneva: WHO. Available at: https://icd.who.int/browse11/l-m/en#/http%3a%2f%2fid.who.int%2ficd%2fentity%2f509381842 (accessed on 12 June 2022).

World Health Organization (WHO). (2023c). ICD-11 for Mortality and Morbidity Statistics: 6B80 Anorexia nervosa. Geneva: WHO. Available at: https://icd.who.int/browse11/l-m/en#/http%3a%2f%2fid.who.int%2ficd%2fentity%2f263852475 (accessed on 12 June 2022).

World Health Organization (WHO). (2023d). ICD-11 for Mortality and Morbidity Statistics: 6B83 Avoidant/restrictive food intake disorder. Geneva: WHO. Available at: https://icd.who.int/browse11/l-m/en#/http%3a%2f%2fid.who.int%2ficd%2fentity%2f1242188600 (accessed on 12 June 2022).

World Health Organization (WHO). (2023e). ICD-11 for Mortality and Morbidity Statistics: 6B85 Rumination-regurgitation disorder. Geneva: WHO. Available at: https://icd.who.int/browse11/l-m/en#/http%3a%2f%2fid.who.int%2ficd%2fentity%2f1205760590 (accessed on 10 June 2022).

Wright, E. K. J. (2021). 2 October. Available at: https://twitter.com/EKJWright1/status/1444435272142311445?t=6dAibo-BK69vwD34yGOwgg&s=19 (accessed on 11 September 2022).

Zimmerman, J., and Fisher, M. (2017). Avoidant/restrictive food intake disorder (ARFID). *Current Problems in Pediatric and Adolescent Health Care, 47*, 4, 95–103.

Reflections

American Psychological Association. (2019). Demographics of the U.S. Psychology Workforce. Washington, D.C.: American Psychological Association. Available at: https://www.apa.org/workforce/data-tools/demographics (accessed on 12 March 2023).

Dismantling Stereotypes

Andersen, A. (1999). Eating Disorders in Males: Critical Questions. In R. Lemberg and L. Cohn (eds), *Eating Disorders: A Reference Sourcebook*. Phoenix, AZ: Oryx Press.

ARFID Awareness UK. (2023). What Is ARFID? London: ARFID Awareness UK. Available at: www.arfidawarenessuk.org/copy-of-what-is-arfid-1 (accessed on 1 June 2022).

Barakat, S., McLean, S. A., Bryant, E., Le, A., *et al.* (2023). Risk factors for eating disorders: Findings from a rapid review. *Journal of Eating Disorders*, *11*, 1, 8.

Bierce, A. (1911). *The Enlarged Devil's Dictionary*. London: Dover Publications.

Blouin, A., and Goldfield, G. (1994). Body image and steroid use in male bodybuilders. *International Journal of Eating Disorders*, *18*, 159–165.

Cassidy, S. (2008). Pressure to grow old beautifully drives over-50s to anorexia. *The Independ*ent. Available at: www.independent.co.uk/life-style/health-and-families/health-news/pressure-to-grow-old-beautifully-drives-over50s-to-anorexia-788563.html?amp (accessed on 29 October 2022).

Costin, C. (2007). *The Eating Disorder Sourcebook: A Comprehensive Guide to the Causes, Treatments, and Prevention of Eating Disorders*. New York, NY: McGraw-Hill.

Darling, K. E., Fahrenkamp, A. J., Wilson, S. M., D'Auria, A. L., and Sato, A. F. (2017). Physical and mental health outcomes associated with prior food insecurity among young adults. *Journal of Health Psychology*, *22*, 5, 572–581.

Deloitte Access Economics. (2020). *Social and Economic Cost of Eating Disorders in the United States of America: A Report for the Strategic Training Initiative for the Prevention of Eating Disorders and the Academy for Eating Disorders*. Cambridge, MA: Deloitte Access Economics/STRIPED. Available at: www.hsph.harvard.edu/striped/report-economic-costs-of-eating-disorders (accessed on 7 November 2022).

Duffy, M. E., Henkel, K. E., and Earnshaw, V. A. (2016). Transgender clients' experiences of eating disorder treatment. *Journal of LGBT Issues in Counseling*, *10*, 3, 136–149.

Flament, M. F., Henderson, K., Buchholz, A., Obeid, N., *et al.* (2015). Weight status and DSM-5 diagnoses of eating disorders in adolescents from the community. *Journal of the American Academy of Child and Adolescent Psychiatry*, *54*, 5, 403–411.

Gadalla, T. M. (2008). Eating disorders and associated psychiatric comorbidity in elderly Canadian women. *Archives of Women's Mental Health*, *1*, 5–6, 357–362.

London Review Bookshop. (2018). Hunger: Roxane Gay [Review]. London: London Review Bookshop. Available at: www.londonreviewbookshop.co.uk/ stock/hunger-a-memoir-of-my-body-roxane-gay (accessed on 12 September 2022).

Goeree, M. S., Sovinsky, M., Ham, J. C., and Iorio, D. (2011). *Race, Social Class, and Bulimia Nervosa*. IZA Discussion Paper No. 5823. Available at: https://ftp. iza.org/dp5823.pdf (accessed on 12 December 2022).

Gordon, K. H., Perez, M., and Joiner, T. E., Jr. (2002). The impact of racial stereotypes on eating disorder recognition. *International Journal of Eating Disorders*, *32*, 2, 219–224.

Huryk, K. M., Drury, C. R., and Loeb, K. L. (2021). Diseases of affluence? A systematic review of the literature on socioeconomic diversity in eating disorders. *Eating Behaviors*, *43*, 101548.

Johns Hopkins Medicine. (2023). Frequently Asked Questions about Eating Disorders. Baltimore, MD: Johns Hopkins Medicine. Available at: www. hopkinsmedicine.org/psychiatry/specialty_areas/eating_disorders/faq.html (accessed on 1 June 2022).

Johnston, A. (2013). *Eating in the Light of the Moon: How Women Can Transform Their Relationship with Food through Myths, Metaphors, and Storytelling*. Carlsbad, CA: Gurze Books.

Kupemba, D. N. (2021). Black women are failed when it comes to eating disorders. New York, NY: Refinery29. Available at: www.refinery29.com/en-gb/ eating-disorders-black-women-uk (accessed on 18 October 2022).

Lawley, R. (2018). Victoria's Secret Enough Is Enough – It's Time to Stand Up for Ourselves! San Francisco, CA: Change.org. Available at: www.change. org/p/women-everywhere-victoria-s-secret-enough-is-enough-it-s-time-to-stand-up-for-ourselves (accessed on 11 September 2022).

Mangweth-Matzek, B., Rupp, C. I., Hausmann, A., Assmayr, K., *et al.* (2006). Never too old for eating disorders or body dissatisfaction: A community study of elderly women. *International Journal of Eating Disorders*, *39*, 7, 583–586.

Nagata, J. M., Garber, A. K., Tabler, J. L., Murray, S. B., and Bibbins-Domingo, K. (2018). Prevalence and correlates of disordered eating behaviors among young adults with overweight or obesity. *Journal of General Internal Medicine*, *33*, 8, 1337–1343.

Nassoori, J. (2022). Football and mental health: Defying the game's 'hypermasculine' culture of silence. Manchester: BBC Sport. Available at: www.bbc.co.uk/sport/football/63476095 (accessed on 18 November 2022).

National Eating Disorders Association (NEDA). (2018). Eating Disorders in LGBTQ+ Populations. White Plains, NY: NEDA. Available at: www.nationaleatingdisorders.org/learn/general-information/lgbtq (accessed on 27 May 2022).

Nwuba, C. (2021). 11 August. Available at: https://twitter.com/doctor_chuks/status/1425535245269483528?s=20 (accessed on 1 December 2022).

Salmon, L. (2023). Half of men with eating disorders don't get any help: 8 warning signs somebody needs support. *The Independent*. Available at: www.independent.co.uk/life-style/health-and-families/eating-disorders-people-friends-b2290272.html (accessed on 17 November 2022).

Sparrow, A. (2019). Eating disorder stereotypes prevent people finding help. Surrey: Happiful. Available at: https://happiful.com/eating-disorder-stereotypes-prevent-people-finding-help (accessed on 20 October 2022).

Stanford, S. C., and Lemberg, R. (2012). A clinical comparison of men and women on the eating disorder inventory-3 (EDI-3) and the eating disorder assessment for men (EDAM). *Eating Disorders*, *20*, 5, 379–394.

Strother, E., Lemberg, R., Stanford, S. C., and Turberville, D. (2012). Eating disorders in men: Underdiagnosed, undertreated, and misunderstood. *Eating Disorders*, *20*, 5, 346–355.

Swanson, S. A., Crow, S. J., Le Grange, D., Swendsen, J., and Merikangas, K. R. (2011). Prevalence and correlates of eating disorders in adolescents: Results from the national comorbidity survey replication adolescent supplement. *Archives of General Psychiatry*, *68*, 7, 714–723.

Sweeting, H., Walker, L., MacLean, A., Patterson, C., Räisänen, U., and Hunt, K. (2015). Prevalence of eating disorders in males: A review of rates reported in academic research and UK mass media. *International Journal of Men's Health*, *14*, 2, 86–112.

Talbot, D., Smith, E., and Cass, J. (2019). Male body dissatisfaction, eating disorder symptoms, body composition, and attentional bias to body stimuli evaluated using visual search. *Journal of Experimental Psychopathology*. Available at: https://doi.org/10.1177/2043808719848292 (accessed on 10 July 2022).

Taylor, J. Y., Caldwell, C. H., Baser, R. E., Faison, N., and Jackson, J. S. (2007). Prevalence of eating disorders among Blacks in the National Survey of American Life. *International Journal of Eating Disorders*, *40*, S10–S14. Available at: https://doi.org/10.1002/eat.20451 (accessed on 2 August 2022).

Tester, J. M., Lang, T. C., and Laraia, B. A. (2016). Disordered eating behaviors and food insecurity: A qualitative study about children with obesity in low-income households. *Obesity Research and Clinical Practice*, *10*, 544–552.

Thomas, T. (2020). NHS hospital admissions for eating disorders rise among ethnic minorities. *The Guardian*. Available at: www.theguardian.com/society/2020/oct/18/nhs-hospital-admissions-eating-disorders-rise-among-ethnic-minorities (accessed on 25 August 2022).

Uri, R. C., Wu, Y. K., Baker, J. H., and Munn-Chernoff, M. A. (2021). Eating disorder symptoms in Asian American college students. *Eating Behaviors*, *40*, 101458.

US Department of Agriculture: Economic Research Service (USDA ERS) (2022). Definitions of Food Security. Washington, DC: US Department of Agriculture. Available at: www.ers.usda.gov/topics/food-nutrition-assistance/food-security-in-the-u-s/definitions-of-food-security (accessed on 10 December 2022).

Bulimia Nervosa: Introduction

Russell, G. (1979) Bulimia nervosa: An ominous variant of anorexia nervosa? *Psychological Medicine*, *9*, 3, 429–448.

When It Comes to Eating Disorders, Brown Girls Don't Measure Up

National Eating Disorders Association (NEDA). (2012). *Eating Disorders in Women of Color: Explanations and Implications*. White Plains, NY: NEDA. Available at: www.nationaleatingdisorders.org/sites/default/files/ResourceHandouts/EatingDisordersinWomenofColor.pdf (accessed on 1 August 2022).

Food

Achamrah, N., Coëffier, M., Rimbert, A., Charles, J., *et al.* (2017). Micronutrient status in 153 patients with anorexia nervosa. *Nutrients*, *9*, 3, 225.

Barakat, S., McLean, S. A., Bryant, E., Le, A., *et al.* (2023). Risk factors for eating disorders: Findings from a rapid review. *Journal of Eating Disorders*, *11*, 1, 8.

Boston Medical Center. (2023). Fatphobia. Boston, MA: Boston Medical Center. Available at: www.bmc.org/glossary-culture-transformation/fatphobia (accessed on 10 February 2023).

Beat. (2021a). *Why the Government Must Drop Its Plan to Make Calorie Labels Mandatory*. Norwich: Beat. Available at: https://committees.parliament.uk/publications/6182/documents/68918/default (accessed on 22 April 2022).

Beat. (2021b). Beat's Response to Government Plan For Calorie Counts on Menus. Norwich: Beat. Available at: www.beateatingdisorders.org.uk/news/beats-response-government-plan-calorie-count (accessed on 4 May 2022).

Be Real. (2017). Somebody Like Me: A Report Investigating the Impact of Body Image Anxiety on Young People in the UK. London: Be Real. Available at: www.berealcampaign.co.uk/research/somebody-like-me (accessed on 2 February 2023).

Bovingdon, M. (2023). Anger as Edinburgh council signs 'Plant Based Treaty'. *Farmers Weekly*. Available at: www.fwi.co.uk/news/environment/anger-as-edinburgh-council-signs-plant-based-treaty (accessed on 15 December 2022).

Brumberg, J. J. (1997). *The Body Project: An Intimate History of American Girls*. New York, NY: Vintage.

Byrne, C. (2022). 'Diet culture' isn't just about smoothies and food-tracking apps. New York, NY: SELF. Available at: www.self.com/story/what-is-diet-culture (accessed on 2 November 2022).

Cannon, E. (2022). 20 December. Available at: https://twitter.com/Dr_Ellie/status/1605143764762492928?s=20 (accessed on 30 December 2022).

CBS Mornings. (2021). Chef Bryant Terry on new book Black Food: Stories, Art & Recipes from Across the African Diaspora [online video]. Available at: https://youtu.be/tQKNuRODKtw (accessed on 19 September 2022).

Degener, M. (2021). Is it okay to eat vegan or vegetarian during eating disorder recovery? San Diego: Equip. Available at: https://equip.health/articles/recovery/vegetarian-vegan (accessed on 1 November 2022).

Farrar, T. (2015). Veganism and Eating Disorders: Let's Be Frank. Tabitha Farrar [blog post], December. Available at: https://tabithafarrar.com/2015/12/veganism-and-eating-disorders-lets-be-frank (accessed on 1 November 2022).

Gaesser, G. (2002). *Big Fat Lies: The Truth about Your Weight and Your Health.* Carlsbad, CA: Gurze Books.

Ge, L., Sadeghirad, B., Ball, G. D. C., da Costa, B. R., *et al.* (2020). Comparison of dietary macronutrient patterns of 14 popular named dietary programmes for weight and cardiovascular risk factor reduction in adults: Systematic review and network meta-analysis of randomised trials. *BMJ, 369,* m696. Available at: https://doi.org/10.1136/bmj.m696 (accessed on 10 August 2022).

GOV.UK. (2021). Calorie labelling on menus to be introduced in cafes, restaurants and takeaways. GOV.UK. Available at: www.gov.uk/government/news/calorie-labelling-on-menus-to-be-introduced-in-cafes-restaurants-and-takeaways (accessed on 15 March 2021).

Graham, G. (2023). An updated approach to eating disorder-related content. San Bruno, CA: YouTube. Available at: https://blog.youtube/news-and-events/an-updated-approach-to-eating-disorder-related-content (accessed on 30 April 2023).

Hampl, S. E., Hassink, S.G., Skinner, A.C., Armstrong, S. C., *et al.* (2023). Clinical practice guideline for the evaluation and treatment of children and adolescents with obesity. *Pediatrics, 151,* 2. Available at: https://publications.aap.org/pediatrics/article/151/2/e2022060640/190443/Clinical-Practice-Guideline-for-the-Evaluation-and (accessed on 25 February 2023).

Hearts Minds and Genes Coalition for Eating Disorders (HMGCED). *The Cost of Eating Disorders in the UK 2019 and 2020.* London: HMGCED. Available at: www.yumpu.com/en/document/read/65877873/the-cost-of-eating-disorders-in-the-uk-2019-and-2020-with-annex (accessed on 2 October 2022).

Herranz Valera, J., Acuña Ruiz, P., Romero Valdespino, B., and Visioli, F. (2014). Prevalence of orthorexia nervosa among ashtanga yoga practitioners: A pilot study. *Eating and Weight Disorders 19,* 4, 469–472.

Hesse-Biber, S. (2006). *The Cult of Thinness.* New York, NY: Oxford University Press.

Kessel, S. (2021). 11 December. Available at: https://twitter.com/Summer Dietitian/status/1469619216949129217?t=-ntmKaSHh2C8VSGsO8AIAA&s=19 (accessed on 7 August 2022).

Kids Know Best (KKB). (2021). Gen Alpha and the Rise of Vegetarianism. London: Kids Know Best. Available at: https://kidsknowbest.co.uk/thinking/gen-alpha-and-the-rise-of-vegetarianism (accessed on 11 December 2022).

Kupemba, D. N. (2021). Black women are failed when it comes to eating disorders. New York, NY: Refinery29. Available at: www.refinery29.com/en-gb/eating-disorders-black-women-uk (accessed on 18 October 2022).

Liu, A. G., Ford, N. A., Hu, F. B., Zelman, K. M., Mozaffarian, D., and Kris-Etherton, P. M. (2017). A healthy approach to dietary fats: Understanding the science and taking action to reduce consumer confusion. *Nutrition Journal 16*, 1, 53.

Luck-Sikorski, C., Jung, F., Schlosser, K., and Riedel-Heller, S. G. (2019). Is orthorexic behavior common in the general public? A large representative study in Germany. *Eating and Weight Disorders 24*, 2, 267–273.

Malmborg, J., Bremander, A., Olsson, M. C., and Bergman, S. (2017). Health status, physical activity, and orthorexia nervosa: A comparison between exercise science students and business students. *Appetite, 109*, 137–143.

Micali, N., Ploubidis, G., De Stavola, B., Simonoff, E., and Treasure, J. (2014). Frequency and patterns of eating disorder symptoms in early adolescence. *Journal of Adolescent Health, 54*, 5, 574–581.

National Eating Disorders Association (NEDA). (2014). Get the facts on eating disorders. White Plains, NY: NEDA. Available at: www.nationaleatingdisorders.org/get-facts-eating-disorders (accessed on 20 December 2022).

National Health and Nutrition Examination Survey (NHNES). (2018). Attempts to Lose Weight among Adults in the United States, 2013–2016. Atlanta, GA: CDC. Available at: www.cdc.gov/nchs/products/databriefs/db313.htm (accessed on 30 July 2022).

Niedzielski, A., and Kaźmierczak-Wojtaś, N. (2021). Prevalence of orthorexia nervosa and its diagnostic tools – a literature review. *International Journal of Environmental Research and Public Health, 18*, 10, 5488.

Petimar, J., Zhang, F., Cleveland, L. P., Simon, D., *et al.* (2019). Estimating the effect of calorie menu labeling on calories purchased in a large restaurant franchise in the southern United States: Quasi-experimental study. *BMJ, 367*, l5837. Available at: https://doi.org/10.1136/bmj.l5837 (accessed on 12 August 2022).

Public Health England (PHE). (2018). *Calorie Reduction: The Scope and Ambition for Action*. London: PHE. Available at: https://assets.publishing.service.gov.uk/government/uploads/system/uploads/attachment_data/file/800675/Calories_Evidence_Document.pdf (accessed on 1 October 2022).

Ramanathan, L. (2015). Why everyone should stop calling immigrant food 'ethnic'. *Washington Post.* Available at: www.washingtonpost.com/lifestyle/food/why-everyone-should-stop-calling-immigrant-food-ethnic/2015/07/20/07927100-266f-11e5-b77f-eb13a215f593_story.html (accessed on 21 September 2022).

Royal College of Psychiatrists (RCPsych). (2019). *Consensus Statement on Considerations for Treating Vegan Patients with Eating Disorders.* London: RCPsych. Available at: www.rcpsych.ac.uk/docs/default-source/members/faculties/eating-disorders/vegan-patients-eating-disorders-mar19.pdf?sfvrsn=be96d428_2 (accessed on 1 October 2022).

Russell, T. (2021). Who gets to be healthy? San Francisco, CA: Healthline. Available at: www.healthline.com/health/nutrition/who-gets-to-be-healthy#1 (accessed on 19 October 2022).

Smolak, L. (2011). Body Image Development in Childhood. In T. Cash and L. Smolak (eds.), *Body Image: A Handbook of Science, Practice, and Prevention* (2nd ed.). New York, NY: Guilford.

Strings, S. (2019). *Fearing the Black Body: The Racial Origins of Fat Phobia.* New York, NY: New York University Press.

Taylor, R. A. (2018). Diversity in Dietetics: Why Does It Matter? [Masters thesis]. Chapel Hill, NC: University of North Carolina at Chapel Hill. Available at: https://doi.org/10.17615/zd96-et82 (accessed on 20 September 2022).

Turner, P. G., and Lefevre, C. E. (2017). Instagram use is linked to increased symptoms of orthorexia nervosa. *Eating and Weight Disorders, 22,* 2, 277–284.

University of North Carolina at Chapel Hill (UNC). (2008). Three out of four American women have disordered eating. Rockville, MD: ScienceDaily. Available at: www.sciencedaily.com/releases/2008/04/080422202514.htm (accessed on 1 August 2022).

Urban, L. E., Weber, J. L., Heyman, M. B., Schichtl, R. L., *et al.* (2016). Energy contents of frequently ordered restaurant meals and comparison with human energy requirements and US Department of Agriculture Database Information: A multisite randomized study. *Journal of the Academy of Nutrition and Dietetics, 116,* 4, 590–598.

USA Today. (2021). TikTokers are sick of seeing ethnic foods get a bad rap: 'We need to redefine healthy'. McLean, VA: USA Today. Available at: https://eu.usatoday.com/story/life/health-wellness/2021/06/15/tiktok-food-videos-aim-combat-unhealthy-myth-ethnic-cuisine/7634627002 (accessed on 19 September 2022).

Wolf, N. (1991). *The Beauty Myth: How Images of Beauty Are Used against Women*. New York, NY: Anchor Books.

Family-Based Treatment

Blackwell, D., Becker, C., Bermudez, O., Berrett, M. E., *et al.* (2021). The Legacy of Hope Summit: A consensus-based initiative and report on eating disorders in the US and recommendations for the path forward. *Journal of Eating Disorders*, *9*, 1, 145.

Hart, L. M., Granillo, M. T., Jorm, A. F., and Paxton, S. J. (2011). Unmet need for treatment in the eating disorders: A systematic review of eating disorder specific treatment seeking among community cases. *Clinical Psychology Review*, *31*, 5, 727–735.

An Unconventional Recovery

Academy of Nutrition and Dietetics (ACEND). (2023). Accreditation Council for Education in Nutrition and Dietetics. Chicago, IL: ACEND. Available at: www.eatrightpro.org/acend (accessed on 3 July 2023).

Duignan, B. (2013). Speciesism. Chicago, IL: Encyclopedia Britannica. Available at: www.britannica.com/topic/speciesism (accessed on 30 December 2022).

Melina, V., Craig, W., and Levin, S. (2016). Position of the Academy of Nutrition and Dietetics: Vegetarian diets. *Journal of the Academy of Nutrition and Dietetics*, *116*, 12, 1970–1980.

Tribole, E., and Resch, E. (2012). 10 Principles of Intuitive Eating. Newport Beach, CA: Intuitive Eating. Available at: www.intuitiveeating.org/10-principles-of-intuitive-eating (accessed on 30 December 2022).

The Underacknowledged

Pope, C. G., Pope, H. G., Menard, W., Fay, C., Olivardia, R., and Phillips, K. A. (2005). Clinical features of muscle dysmorphia among males with body dysmorphic disorder. *Body Image*, *2*, 4, 395–400.

Epilogue

Ayton, A. (2023). 24 January. Available at: https://twitter.com/AgnesAyton/status/1617824312630865924?t=zYLGwe9SDwOclb7S4w4nqQ&s=19 (accessed on 22 February 2023).

Kimmelman, M. (1999). Art Review: Plucking warmth from millet's light. *New*

York Times. Available at: www.nytimes.com/1999/08/27/arts/art-review-plucking-warmth-from-millet-s-light.html (accessed on 13 January 2023).

Kupemba, D. N. (2021). Black women are failed when it comes to eating disorders. New York, NY: Refinery29. Available at: www.refinery29.com/en-gb/eating-disorders-black-women-uk (accessed on 18 October 2022).

Pipher, M. (1995). *Reviving Ophelia: Saving the Selves of Adolescent Girls*. New York, NY: Ballentine.

Recommended Resources

There are so many organizations, books, podcasts and blogs that we could recommend, but these are just a few of the ones that, over the years, patients, friends, families and those who work in the eating disorder field have recommended.

Organizations

Beat

UK's leading charity supporting and campaigning for those affected by eating disorders.
beateatingdisorders.org.uk

Been There

A charity offering free one-to-one support for those experiencing body image issues.
beenthereapp.com

Body Dysmorphic Disorder Foundation

A charity that aims to increase awareness and knowledge of body dysmorphic disorder.
bddfoundation.org

Centre for Clinical Interventions

A clinical psychology service in Australia, specializing in treating eating disorders amongst other comorbidities.
cci.health.wa.gov.au

Diabulimia Helpline

A non-profit organization providing education and support for people with diabetes and eating disorders.
diabulimiahelpline.org

ED Families Australia

Organization providing education and support for carers and families impacted by an eating disorder.
edfa.org.au

ED Neurodiversity Australia

Not-for-profit, neurodivergent-led organization advocating for better eating disorder prevention efforts.
edneuroaus.com

Equip Health

Virtual, evidence-based care that empowers families to help their loved ones in eating disorder recovery.
equip.health

F.E.A.S.T.

A global community of parents of those with eating disorders.
feast-ed.org

FEDUP Collective

A collective of gender-diverse people passionate about eating disorder care in marginalized communities.
fedupcollective.org

First Steps ED
UK-based eating disorder charity.
firststepsed.co.uk

FREED
Early intervention service giving young people rapid access to treatment for eating disorders.
freedfromed.co.uk

Inside Out Institute
Australia's national institute for eating disorders research and clinical excellence.
insideoutinstitute.org.au

Nalgona Positivity Pride
Xicana-brown body positivity and eating disorder support for people of colour.
nalgonapositivitypride.com

NEDC
National Eating Disorders Collaboration (NEDC) is an Australian initiative to develop evidence-based prevention and treatment of eating disorders.
nedc.com.au

PEACE
A community supporting people with comorbid autism and an eating disorder, and their carers.
peacepathway.org

Project HEAL
A non-profit organization in the US focused on equitable treatment access for those with eating disorders.
theprojectheal.org

Royal College of Psychiatrists Eating Disorder Faculty

Brings together psychiatrists working with eating disorders, aiming to exchange information and improve services.
www.rcpsych.ac.uk/members/your-faculties/eating-disorders-psychiatry

Seed

A charity offering support from those who have first-hand experience of eating disorders.
seed.charity

SupportED Scotland

Charity that works across Scotland to support people with an eating disorder, their families and carers.
supportedscotland.org

SWEDA

The Somerset and Wessex Eating Disorders Association (SWEDA) is a regional charity supporting people with eating disorders.
swedauk.org

TalkED

National, peer-led charity offering eating disorder support.
talk-ed.org.uk

The Body Positive

Non-profit organization helping people end the harmful effects of negative body image, such as eating disorders.
thebodypositive.org

Wednesday's Child

A social enterprise that supports those experiencing an eating disorder.
wednesdayschild.co.uk

Books

A Cognitive-Interpersonal Therapy Workbook for Treating Anorexia Nervosa by Ulrike Schmidt, Helen Startup and Janet Treasure

Aid to recovery for those with anorexia nervosa, their families and mental health professionals.

Anorexia and Other Eating Disorders by Eva Musby

Guides through each stage of eating disorder recovery.

Anti-Diet by Christy Harrison

A radical alternative to diet culture, helping readers reclaim their bodies, minds and lives.

Body Positive Power by Megan Jayne Crabbe

Inspirational and practical book on how to stop dieting, make peace with your body, and live.

Brave Girl Eating by Harriet Brown

A family's journey into the world of anorexia nervosa, where starvation threatens body and mind.

Caring for a Loved One with an Eating Disorder by Jenny Langley, Gill Todd and Janet Treasure

A training manual providing a framework for carer skills workshops.

Decoding Anorexia by Carrie Arnold

Explains anorexia nervosa from a biological point of view.

Eating in the Light of the Moon by Anita Johnston

Helps those preoccupied with their weight address the issues behind their negative attitudes towards food.

Eating While Black by Psyche Williams-Forson

How anti-Black racism operates in the practice and culture of eating.

Eat Up by Ruby Tandoh

Ruby, who has lived experience of disordered eating, offers advice on mental health and recipe ideas.

Fat Talk by Virginia Sole-Smith

Stirring, deeply researched book about parenting in the age of diet culture.

Fearing the Black Body by Sabrina Strings

Highlights that the contemporary ideal of slenderness is racialized and racist.

Food Chaining by Cheryl Fraker, Mark Fishbein, Sibyl Cox and Laura Walbert

Approach for dealing with picky eating and feeding problems at any age.

Healing Your Hungry Heart by Joanna Poppink

A step-by-step programme that identifies challenges to early eating disorder recovery.

Help Your Teenager Beat an Eating Disorder by James Lock and Daniel Le Grange

Provides tools to build a united family against an eating disorder.

Hunger by Roxane Gay

A memoir exploring compulsive eating, gaining weight and emotional and psychological struggles.

Inside My ED by Zoe Burnett

Personal story about the battle to get treatment and recognition for atypical anorexia nervosa.

Intuitive Eating by Evelyn Tribole and Elyse Resch

A book on rebuilding a healthy body image and making peace with food.

It's Always Been Ours by Jessica Wilson

Urges a rejection of diet culture that disproportionately harms Black women.

Just Eat It by Laura Thomas

Anti-diet guide to help with attitude to food and ditching punishing exercise routines.

Lighter than My Shadow by Katie Green

Memoir about anorexia, eating disorders and the journey to recovery.

Living with Your Body and Other Things You Hate by Emily Sandoz

Learning to live with the reality that painful thoughts and beliefs about oneself will arise from time to time.

Not All Black Girls Know How to Eat by Stephanie Covington Armstrong

Describes the author's struggle as a Black woman with bulimia nervosa.

Rehabilitate, Rewire, Recover! by Tabitha Farrar

A 'toolkit' to help with the neural rewiring process in anorexia nervosa recovery.

Sick Enough by Dr Jennifer Gaudiani
A comprehensive, accessible review of the medical issues that arise from eating disorders.

Suffering Succotash by Stephanie Lucianovic
The author explores her own food phobias and what it means to be a picky eater.

The Eating Disorder Recovery Journal by Cara Lisette
Brings together creative activities and approaches to challenge an eating disorder.

The Practical Handbook of Eating Difficulties: A Comprehensive Guide from Personal and Professional Perspectives by James Downs, Mark Hopfenbeck, Hannah Lewis, Isla Parker and Nicole Schnackenberg
Practical guide to understanding and helping people with eating difficulties.

The Reading Cure by Laura Freeman
An account of hunger and happiness, addiction, obsession and anorexia nervosa recovery.

Treating Black Women with Eating Disorders by Charlynn Small and Mazella Fuller
Culturally sensitive material intended for addressing the concerns of Black women with eating disorders.

When Your Teen Has an Eating Disorder by Lauren Muhlheim
Resource for parents and people who work with those with an eating disorder.

You Are Not a Before Picture **by Alex Light**

An empowering guide to disavowing diet culture and learning to make peace with our bodies.

Podcasts

Appearance Matters **(University of the West of England)**

A podcast all about appearance, featuring exclusive interviews with experts in the field.

Body Justice

Hosted by licensed therapist Allyson Ford, promoting messages of body justice and mental health advice.

Eating Disorders in Discussion **(Wednesday's Child)**

Captures discussions, insights and inspiration from those who have battled eating disorders, those who support others, and those with views about body image, food and exercise.

Food Psych

Registered dietitian Christy Harrison hosts discussions about intuitive eating, body image and diet culture.

Full of Beans

Hosted by Han, this podcast seeks to reduce eating disorder stigma and increase eating disorder awareness.

Let's Talk **(Butterfly Foundation)**

This podcast speaks with experts, people with eating disorder lived experience, and their families and carers.

Maintenance Phase

Michael Hobbes and Aubrey Gordon debunk the 'science' behind health and wellness fads.

Real Pod

Conversations about mental health and body image, and relatable conversations about everyday struggles.

Recovery Warriors

For those seeking eating disorder recovery; also discussions about society's unrealistic beauty standards and systems of oppression.

The Weigh Up: Eating Disorder Diaries (BBC Sounds)

Molly, who has eating disorder lived experience, discusses eating disorders and hears others' stories.

Blogs

A Hunger Artist by Emily Troscianko

Blog on the experience and the science of eating disorders.
psychologytoday.com/us/blog/hunger-artist

Anorexia Myths

Dedicated to dispelling myths around anorexia nervosa.
anorexiamyths.com

Cara's Corner by Cara Lisette

An eating disorder recovery and mental health blog.
caras-corner.com

Equip Health

Explores the complex and ever-changing realities of eating disorders, food and bodies.
equip.health/blog

ORRI

Blog about important issues relating to eating disorders.
orri-uk.com/blog

The BED Post

Seeks to raise the awareness of binge eating disorder.
thebedpost.blog

The Butterfly Foundation

A blog for sharing body image and eating disorders content.
butterfly.org.au/blog

The No-Nonsense Guide

A guide for people with exercise addiction or food restriction.
nononsenseguide.net